The
Arthur Young
Guide To
Raising
Venture Capital

The
Arthur Young
Guide To
Raising
Venture Capital

G. Steven Burrill and
Craig T. Norback

LIBERTY HOUSE ®

LIBERTY HOUSE books are published by LIBERTY HOUSE, a division of TAB BOOKS Inc. Its trademark, consisting of the words "LIBERTY HOUSE" and the portrayal of Benjamin Franklin, is registered in the United States Patent and Copyright Office.

FIRST EDITION
FIRST PRINTING

Copyright © 1988 by TAB BOOKS Inc.
Printed in the United States of America

Library of Congress Cataloging in Publication Data

Burrill, G. Steven
The Arthur Young guide to raising venture capital / by
G. Steven Burrill, and Craig T. Norback.
p.   cm.
Bibliography: p.
Includes index.
ISBN 0-8306-3014-7
1. Venture capital. I. Norback, Craig T. II. Title.
HG4751.N67 1988   88-1897
658.1'5224—dc19   CIP

Questions regarding the content of this book
should be addressed to:

Reader Inquiry Branch
TAB BOOKS Inc.
Blue Ridge Summit, PA 17294-0214

DEDICATION

This book is dedicated to my friends and colleagues at Arthur Young and to those in the venture capital and legal communities, without whom, none of this would have been possible. I am especially grateful to Brook Byers and Christopher Kaufman, who have shared their expertise and knowledge, and I am grateful to the entrepreneurs who have shared their dreams with me. My thanks also go to Allison Smith for her contributions as a writer and editor, and my special thanks to my wife Kelli, whose patience with me was wonderful.

G. Steven Burrill

Contents

Preface

What is venture capital? From whom does it come? And how does the entrepreneur obtain it? *The Arthur Young Guide to Raising Venture Capital* was written to provide answers to those questions, but the answers are not as clear-cut or simple as you might think. It seems every time we got ready to make a rule about the industry, we remembered an important exception.

Probably what makes venture capital an intriguing—or even glamourous—pursuit for the entrepreneur is that it's a very individualized phenomenon. Instead of hard and fast rules, the industry is known by the anecdotes it has generated, almost a mythology that entrepreneurs who have looked for and found, or failed to find, venture capital have created, much in the same way travelers tell each other stories of unique places they have visited.

The traditional view of venture capital is that of a private partnership with a million to ten million dollars to invest in an aggressive high technology start-up that promises a ten-to-one return on investment in three years when the company makes a splashy debut in the public markets. Even when the dream comes true, this image is an oversimplification of the industry and its goals.

In truth, venture capital is as diverse as both the people who invest in it and as the people who seek it. Financing can be obtained from individual investors with a spare million dollars or so to invest; it can be found at multinational financial institutions backed by corporate billions, or anything in between. Not all companies looking for venture capital are high tech. Some of them are in specialty retail, others are service companies, fast food chains, or old-line manufacturers. Some venture capitalists specialize in a particular high tech market, while other venture firms are diversifying their portfolios to incorporate more, so-called "low tech" or "non-tech" industries. Not all companies are in the start-up stage: some of them need money for acquisition, others for turnaround situations, or leveraged buyouts. Nor do venture capitalists expect all companies to generate astronomical rates of return in a short period of time: some investors are in for the long haul, others hope to pull out their money in under five years.

Actually, this diversity is also one of the real values of venture capital money. It can meet the needs of a lot of different companies in different situations and conditions. That is also why it is so important for the individual entrepreneur to be very clear about why he wants venture capital money, as opposed to another kind of financing, and what exactly he intends to do with it.

Because the industry is made up of individuals, venture capital is a very fluid thing. It can respond immediately to changes in marketplaces as they develop, mature, and overcrowd. Venture capital responds to the availability of cash, to economic climates of confidence and crises, and to government legislation, such as the Tax Reform Act of 1986. In fact, one of the challenges to writing about venture capital is that it is easy to date yourself—so quickly does the industry change. So perhaps the only blanket statement we feel safe in making about venture capital is that you can find it in a variety of settings for a variety of needs, and that the industry keeps changing.

That would be taking the easy way out. Of course, *The Arthur Young Guide to Raising Venture Capital* will tell you more than that. For instance, one of the great truisms of the industry is that venture capitalists back people first, markets second, and technologies last. Venture capitalists go on their gut instincts when considering the merits of a new management team. That means a certain *x factor* takes effect in the process of sealing a venture capital deal. Although we cannot tell you whether or not a management team is going to click with prospective investors, we can give you some rules of thumb that have been gleaned from years of experience in matching entrepreneurs with venture investors.

The Arthur Young Guide to Raising Venture Capital explains, in detail, everything you need to know about how venture capitalists work, how to find the right venture capitalist for your needs, how to write a

good business plan, how to conduct a winning interview, how to survive
the due diligence process, and ultimately how to secure venture capital.
In an appendix to the book, we offer some ideas about alternatives to
venture capital. And for convenience, we've included a directory of names,
addresses, and telephone numbers of several venture capital firms across
the country. Arthur Young also has a toll-free number, 800-3HI-TECH
(800-344-8324), for anyone who might have questions about this book
or any aspect of venture capital.

Chapter 1

The
Venture Capital World

Venture capital is a private source of financing for high-risk business endeavors. It is one financing alternative among many sources of capital that are available to growing companies. Venture capital is generally invested in equity ownership of a company or new venture, (or ownership that is expected to be converted into equity). The investment is usually in the form of stock, or sometimes in the form of a convertible debt, which is a loan that becomes a stock holding at some point. Offsetting the high risk the investor takes is the promise of a very high return on investment. Venturing is a "no guts-no glory" proposition.

Venture capitalists seek out companies and opportunities in which to invest with the hope of getting the highest possible return on their investment. Sometimes, this is achieved in as short a period of time as possible—frequently, in three to seven years. At that point, the business has matured to the level at which it can make an initial public offering, be sold or merged, or can find other capital sources to buy out the venture capitalist. Whatever happens, the company must sufficiently compensate the venture capitalist for the risk. Sometimes the rewards do not come until several more years pass, and sometimes the rewards do not come at all.

A key to understanding the venture capitalist is to understand his objectives and to determine how those objectives are attainable through an investment in the entrepreneur's venture. Another important key is to recognize that all venture capitalists are different. They have different investment skills, areas of interest, geographic or industry preferences, and different requirements placed on them by their capital sources. So talking about venture capitalists as a generic phenomenon is simplistic.

Successful venture capitalists have a lot of experience screening investment alternatives, negotiating investments, then watching over their portfolios, managing companies through phases of significant growth, and nurturing them through the growing pains that herald the next stage of development. Consequently, successful venture capitalists know what to look for in companies that seek their financing, and they are highly selective. An arduous *due diligence* process of reviewing investment opportunities is one way the venture capitalist can offset the high risk factor. Due diligence benefits not only the venture capitalist but also the entrepreneur, because the entrepreneur runs a high risk of losing everything in a deal that goes sour. Talking with venture capitalists can actually help the entrepreneur to develop the best business possible, to select the fittest management team, to clarify his market goals, and so increase his chances for success.

PEOPLE VERSUS TECHNOLOGY

In 1973, Albert J. Kelley, then Dean of the Boston College School of Management, was quoted in *Business Week* as saying that less than one percent of all new ventures would receive venture capital, although many more venture capital firms existed at that time than ever before. Today, many more venture capital firms exist. There are over 600 private independent venture capital firms existing in the United States, but many more venture capitalists. Only about two percent to three percent of all new ventures applying for venture capital receive funding. (Source: Venture Economics, Inc., Wellesley Hills, MA, reprinted with permission.)

One reason for this extremely low investment rate lies in a popular misconception about venture financing. Many entrepreneurs believe that if they develop spreadsheets featuring attractive growth rates and write a business plan describing an innovative technology, they are shoo-ins for venture financing. In fact, venture capital is not a numbers business; it is a business about people.

Venture capitalists are more concerned about who will run the company than about the type of company in which they are investing. The process by which venture capital firms screen new ventures depends so heavily on the strength of the company's management team that there is virtually no chance of a new venture receiving capital on the basis of a business plan alone. If a company experiences difficult times, the investor may have to step in and take over. He may have to manage the company himself, or finding someone more capable than the original management to do the job. For obvious reasons, this is a messy business. It creates severe difficulties for the venture capitalist who has a whole portfolio of companies to watch over. If every one of them had management problems, the venture capitalist could not be expected to take over for all of them. Clearly, the new venture must have merit; however, venture capitalists ultimately look for proven entrepreneurs and managers in which to invest. Without the right people, a good idea or an excellent product will fail.

A BRIEF HISTORY

Although many ventures were financed by various means throughout history, venture capital as a separate and distinct business began only right after World War II. J. H. Whitney established the first privately held venture firm in 1946 with an initial capitalization of about $10 million. Whitney coined the term "venture capital," and he was the first person to structure the venture capital business as a partnership, the most common arrangement today (Wilson, 1985).

Soon, Boston city leaders pulled together enough capital to form the American Research & Development Corp., which was organized to nurture and develop the work of local entrepreneurs. General George Doriot was appointed president of ARD, which is best known for backing Digital Equipment Corporation. Doriot, himself, is famous for instituting the ethos of the venture capital industry—the venture capitalist as one who guides and manages a growing company through times thick and thin. The result of such effort, according to Doriot, was not only profit, but also the long-term development of successful companies (Wilson, 1985).

The Small Business Investment Act of 1958 gave entrepreneurism a boost. Through the Small Business Administration, Small Business Investment Companies (SBICs) and Minority Enterprise Small Business Investment Companies (MESBICs) could leverage government funds four-four-to-one against privately raised capital. In turn, SBICs and MESBICs, which are privately managed, could make capital available to small The program grew quickly—by 1964 there were 649 SBICs; but the but the misuse of funds caused reforms, and today there are about 360 SBICs (Wilson, 1985).

TAX REFORMS
THEIR EFFECT ON VENTURE CAPITAL

Through changing tax structures, government also plays a role in the historical development of venture capital. The effects of changing capital gains tax rates on the availability of risk capital are shown in Fig. 1-1.

The pendulum continues to swing back and forth. Effective in 1987, the Tax Reform Act of 1986 repealed the favorable tax rate on individual capital gains, set at a maximum of 20 percent and was raised to 28 percent by the 1986 reform. Some industry analysts suggest that the capital gains tax increase could put a damper on seed and start-up financings, which are often backed by private individual investors. Other analysts aver that an 8 percent increase, although undesirable, is not significant enough to derail the industry, and they note that successful venture-backed companies with high returns on investment will more than compensate for funds lost to taxes.

FINANCING INFLUENCES BUSINESS STRATEGY

Business theory asserts that a relationship exists between financing strategy and business strategy. We might also add here that the dynamic between the two strategies frequently affects both the venture capitalist and the entrepreneur. Broadly, this dynamic delineates why venture capitalists make the decisions they do, and what the entrepreneur should consider before he seeks venture capital.

The key to understanding business strategy is to realize that financing strategies dictate the business strategy, especially in younger enterprises. For example, if a young company decides to go public, it must meet public stockholder expectations. That means the company probably will have to generate quarter-to-quarter results that consistently improve, and so bolster investor confidence. This need for consistent short-term growth may challenge the company's ability to afford long-term product development projects, which could eventually hinder long-term company growth opportunities. So a strategy results to meet the shorter-term quarter-to-quarter expectations, and long-term development activities frequently become too expensive. On the other hand, if a young company

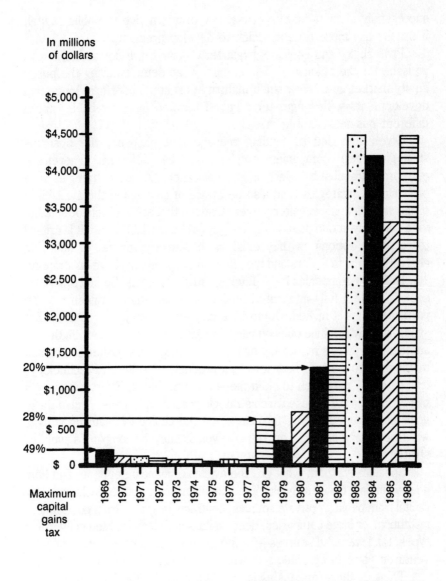

Fig. 1-1. Effect of capital gains tax reductions on venture capital funds.

Source:
Figures provided by Venture
Economics, Inc.

successfully attracts private capital, as an alternative to public capital, it usually has more time in which to develop products.

Profitability and consistent quarterly growth are not as immediate an issue for the financiers. The company can defer entering the public equity market until later, when maturity permits. Therefore, long-term developments with longer-term payoff become more probable, and a different business strategy results.

Given the kind of funding management chooses, the business strategies two companies employ will be different. Therefore, entrepreneurs must be aware of the ramifications financing strategies have on business strategies, and also be aware of changes in the availability of the various financing alternatives. Options that are available or suitable for a company at one point in time might not be available later. It is critical to research options as they exist in the current market of financing alternatives and to understand the effect such options will have on strategy.

Different companies have different strategic goals. Some companies seek to build a fully-integrated business, while others concentrate on particular market niches. Companies may enter into joint ventures that synergistically combine one company's product development strength with another company's marketing or manufacturing skills. Other companies might wish to become licensors of a product, or sellers of technology, or a company may wish to be in the service business. Every company's management must choose which strategic goals it will pursue. Any of these goals could require some financing, and the choice of financing vehicle will have a major influence on, or may even dictate, the company's eventual strategy.

Specifically, then, what are the available financing options, and how do they impact business goals? Traditional financing choices include equity capital from public or private sources, contracts or grants from government institutions or large companies, debt capital—both standard and convertible types, tax leveraged sources—frequently through partnerships, and joint ventures—or strategic linkages, which can come in a multitude of forms.

Think of these options as layers of a triangle, the base of which is formed by equity capital. Most companies use equity capital as the foundation for future financings, no matter how small that original equity may be. Frequently *sweat equity* is the largest initial source of capital; equity capital, other than sweat equity, usually comes from private sources initially—the entrepreneur's savings, from relatives, friends, private investors, and venture capitalists. Later on, a company might sign research contracts or get grants, and still later, it may establish joint venture relationships. Usually, debt financing comes at a much later stage, when products are in the marketplace producing cash flows to service the debt. And throughout the venture's growth, the company frequently taps the same sources of capital again. Financing is not a sequential exercise. Equity capital is added throughout the growth process, often from private sources first, then frequently through the public, and later sometimes through a combination of both. See Fig. 1-2.

Aside from strategic goals, a company must also consider its stage of development. How much financing is necessary and when? How much risk is there, both to the company and to the investors? If, with the benefit of hindsight, one could look back on a perfectly executed financing strategy, one would see there has been perfect job if each of the financings happened at a major "risk step-down" point. That is, a company's risk profile decreases every time it meets the next milestone. Additional financings at each of these milestones permit the company to develop to the next risk step-down point. Over time, the company maximizes the valuation at each investment point and minimizes dilution. In the end, the company would have always had the ideal financing, appropriately valued

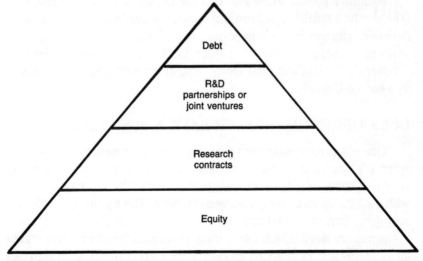

Fig. 1-2.

and perfectly timed. The result is minimum financing at the maximum price—a perfect strategy.

Actually, it is difficult to plan a financing strategy so closely. Most things cost more and take longer than planned. The key is to choose the right financing mix and balance valuation against dilution, to ensure that both the entrepreneur and the investor maximize their return with acceptable risk.

Management must consider the market conditions, and therefore, the availability of particular kinds of financing. Also, management must balance the alternatives of getting too much or too little capital in exchange for too much or too little equity. Company founders may not want to surrender the 40 percent to 60 percent of equity to venture capitalists that is frequently required on the initial round of financing. (However, control may not be the real issue, because according to the "golden rule" of venture capital, "he who has the gold, rules.")

Management may decide that going public is the best financing strategy, but if it is too early in the company's development, or if the window to public equity markets is closed, the company could anticipate a low offering price and a low valuation, as well as the significant strategic cost of going public. So, going public may not be the optimal strategy, after all.

By now it should be obvious that the choice of financing strategy is critical—the availability of financing options, valuation, timing, strategic direction, and synergy are important to understand. Venture capital is only one of these choices. All of these factors are discussed in detail in Chapter 5, "Negotiating the Deal," and in Appendix A, "Alternatives to Venture Capital."

DOES THE ENTREPRENEUR HAVE A BUSINESS?

One of the most common stumbling blocks entrepreneurs encounter when seeking venture capital is their misconception about what really creates a business. Using an analogy from horticulture, imagine a plant with a strong stem bearing a gorgeous flower. The flower buds, blooms into great brilliance, and then shrivels and dies. Many single-product companies are like this. After producing one fantastic product, experiencing an astonishing growth spurt, and achieving market dominance, they decline and disappear.

Alternatively, imagine a plant with many branches, new shoots, and flowers—one that continually produces new growth. As one flower starts to wilt, others begin to blossom. So it is in business. If the company has a single product that does well in the marketplace, but which disappears after some time, that is not a business, per se, and is probably not a candidate for venture capital. Only ventures with several "branches" are viable candidates.

Through painful experience, venture capitalists have learned to invest in solid businesses that promise more than one market opportunity. The business must have, not only a product, but also a marketplace and other product offerings for that marketplace. The business must be able to support enough research and development to continue the flow of products into markets as those markets mature and change. Before seeking venture capital, the entrepreneur must satisfy himself that his venture can become a real business and support all the necessary functions that a company needs. It must be more than an interesting market "play" that lasts for only a few years. Venture capitalists are financing businesses, not products.

WHERE THE VENTURE
CAPITALISTS GET THEIR MONEY

Entrepreneurs should remember that the venture capitalist is also in business and seeks financing from investors. This means that the venture capitalist's objectives and operating philosophies will be shaped by the way in which he himself is financed. For instance, private independent firms are often funded, in part, by the partners of the firm, but they also receive additional financing from large corporations, insurance companies, pension funds, banks, private individuals, endowments, and foreign investors. Table 1-1 reviews the sources of venture capital funds for the years 1984-1986.

So why do these pension funds, corporations, individuals and others invest in venture capital? The reason is simple. They can get higher returns than are available from other forms of investment. A study of investment returns shows that during the last few years, investors saw returns of about 7 percent from money market funds and 8 percent from Certificates of Deposit. Investors were able to get about 11 percent returns from residential real estate, and up to 30 percent returns or more from mutual

Table 1-1. Capital Commitments
(Independent Private Firms Only)

	Total Capital Committed (millions)			Percent of Total Capital Committed		
	1984	**1985**	**1986**	**1984**	**1985**	**1986**
Pension Funds	$1,085	$ 767	$1,672	34%	33%	50%
Corporations	463	274	350	14	12	11
Individuals and Families	467	303	392	15	13	12
Foreign Investors	573	548	361	18	23	11
Insurance Companies	419	254	348	13	11	10
Endowments and Foundations	178	181	209	6	8	6
Total	$3,185	$2,327	$3,332	100%	100%	100%

(Source: Venture Economics, Inc., Wellesley Hills, MA, reprinted with permission.)

funds and from other equity investments (common and preferred stocks). (*Wall Street Journal*, January 2, 1987.)

In order to attract capital and to adequately compensate the investors for their risk taking, the venture capital firm usually needs to provide at least a 30 percent return on investment. To make good on that promise, venture capitalists invest in many deals, thereby creating a portfolio that will mitigate the potential losses of a company that fails. Let's consider a portfolio of ten investments: if three out of ten investments have a 100 percent annual return on investment, and if the others have a zero return, and all investments were equally made, the portfolio would yield a 30 percent ROI—barely enough to compensate for the greater risk. Although figures vary, the number of new businesses that fail in the first five years is high. Therefore, for the venture capitalist to perform well, he must expect exceptionally high returns on investment—frequently in the 50 percent to 100 percent per year range, from the companies that do succeed.

Without good portfolio performance, the venture capitalist's own sources of money dry up and the proceedings come to a screeching halt. Venture capitalists invest in those businesses that they believe will obtain very high returns in a reasonable period of time, to compensate them for the risk, and to reward them adequately for their efforts. Of the total amount of capital raised by the private venture funds in the U.S. in 1986, most of the funds—74 percent—to went to the venture capital firms that have been in existence for 10 years or more. A significantly large amount of the venture capital today is in the hands of very experienced venture capitalists. The entrepreneur may wish to keep this in mind when he

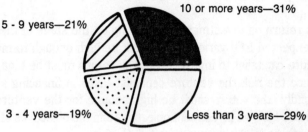

Number of firms
by experience level

5 - 9 years—21%

10 or more years—31%

3 - 4 years—19%

Less than 3 years—29%

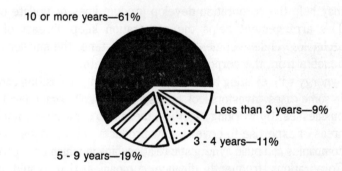

Capital resources
by experience level

10 or more years—61%

Less than 3 years—9%

3 - 4 years—11%

5 - 9 years—19%

Fig. 1-3. (Source: Venture Economics, Inc., Wellesley Hills, MA, reprinted with permission.)

more capital available for funding, but also much more experience. Consequently, older firms may have more value to add to the deal. They may also be more critical in their evaluation of new deals. See Fig. 1-3.

WHY VENTURE CAPITALISTS INVEST—INVESTOR OBJECTIVES

Knowing where venture capitalist's get their money should help the entrepreneur realize that a key to attracting venture capital financing— or any other kind of financing—is to understand the investor's objectives. Entrepreneurs should remember that the venture capitalist will review a deal to learn whether or not participating in it will help him achieve his researches which funds to approach. The older firms not only may have own objectives as an investor. Venture capitalists have different goals, but usually they include:

- High return on investment. Depending on the stage of the company, the expected ROI varies, but it must be high enough to motivate the venture capitalist to invest. First, the return must be high enough to balance the risk the venture capitalist takes in financing a new deal. Secondly, the return must be high enough for the venture capitalist to realize his own investment objectives and the objectives of the people who invest in the venture capitalist's firm.
- Establishing a window on technology. Through venture capital financings, corporations often seek alliances with smaller companies. These alliances give the corporation access to new technologies that may help the corporation develop product lines or update old ones. This arrangement helps the corporation keep abreast of current technological developments. At the same time, the smaller company benefits from the corporation's deep pockets.
- Synergy with existing businesses, or nurturing acquisition candidates. In some cases, investors look for a synergistic collaboration with existing businesses. By working together, these two companies combine their areas of expertise to develop new products. Through joint ventures, companies can build synergistic relationships in which both parties win. Corporations frequently finance companies that would be good candidates for acquisition. Typically, the larger entity provides, not only cash, but also a marketing and manufacturing infrastructure, and access to its own technology.
- Building their own business along with the entrepreneurs. Investment bankers and banks usually hold this objective. These organizations can actually build their own clientele by financing companies in early and mezzanine stages. For instance, investment bankers frequently have venture capital funds to finance and build companies that will later need their services when the companies go public or have complex financing requirements.

Just a brief word here about another factor that shapes the venture capitalist's investment objectives—the exit. The venture capitalist's choice to finance a company is governed as much by the way he expects to be able to leave a deal as by the way he got into it. This is because the venture capitalist's return on investment is really only measured at the exit. The timing of the exit is critical. At what point in the company's growth has the venture capitalist given the optimum value-added for potential return on investment? What will the market conditions be at the time he wants to exit? Will the public equity markets give the company a high valuation? If the company is not growing, or "ramping up" fast enough to meet the projected ROI, should it be sold to investors with different objectives, or merged? Only if the venture capitalist can anticipate a satisfactory means of leaving the deal, will he want to get into it. For more information, see Chapter 5, Negotiating the Deal.

SOURCES OF VENTURE CAPITAL FUNDING FOR THE ENTREPRENEUR

The venture capital industry is made up of:

- Individual and family investors
- Private venture capital partnerships
- Public venture capital funds. Large corporate venture capital funds
- Investment banking and other financial institutions with venture capital operations
- Government funded sources of venture capital, including Small Business Investment Companies (SBICs), Minority Enterprise Small Business Investment Companies (MESBICs), and economic development commissions.

A few words about each:

Individual Investors

Individual investors can be friends, family members, or financially successful people who have only a few thousand dollars or as much as several million dollars to invest in new ventures. An individual may be involved in only one deal, or he may finance several different ventures at the same time. These ventures may relate in some way to the investor's own background and expertise, or they may be helpful to the investor's community or local economy.

Although there is no formal network or organized body of individual investors at present, these people can be identified through business and social contacts and networks in certain areas. Attempts are being made in a limited way and in localized areas to develop a means of making contact and communication between investor and entrepreneur easier. This is being accomplished through investment clubs, President's Clubs, and general business meetings. Private equity groups managed by investors interested only in young companies also exist and frequently can be contacted through brokers at small investment banking firms or through other professionals in the financial community.

Quite often, individual investors provide *seed capital* to a fledgling entrepreneur who has only the germ of an idea for a company. At this stage, it is the individual investor who is willing to stake capital on a business deal that a venture capitalist might consider too risky, according to the firm's investment guidelines. Although these "early-stage deals" carry a lot of risk, they also have the potential to bring equally high rewards if the business is successful.

Individual investors are a large source of capital—albeit often difficult to find—with varied investment interests and objectives. Particularly in the early stages of a company's development, this is the most frequently used source of capital.

Private Venture Capital Funds

The majority of venture capital sources are private venture capital firms. As noted earlier, there were about 600 private firms in the United States in 1986. In the preceding ten years, their number grew dramatically in response to the favorable tax treatment of capital gains and in part to the burgeoning high technology industries.

Private venture capital firms are usually partnerships with limited partners investing from $25,000 or $100,000 to tens of millions of dollars or more each. Some partnerships have very limited capitalization and do small deals. Others are capitalized in excess of $1 billion and can do very large deals concurrently. In each case, the limited partners share in the profits based upon the percentage of their participation, with appropriate compensation to the general partner and management group. Partnerships are most frequently formed for a limited duration, the most common period is from seven to 10 years, but it depends upon the firm's investment life cycles and the general partners' prerogative. The general partner, who is usually a professional manager of the venture capital firm or financial institution, will oversee the management of the investment portfolio. For this the general partner receives an annual fee, usually in the 1 percent to 5 percent range, and an interest in the net capital gains, usually in the 10 percent to 30 percent range. This high incentive is another reason for the rapid growth of such partnerships: substantial money can be made over the life of a fund through prudent investments in solid new ventures. This is especially true if a majority of these new ventures are successful businesses and the venture capitalist exits appropriately.

Public Venture Capital Companies

A few public venture capital companies exist today. These venture capital companies obtain their equity through the public equity markets and invest in new ventures, like the private venture capitalists. Because public companies are required to disclose details about their operations to the public, as required by the Securities and Exchange Commission (SEC), it is easier to get information about them than about the private venture firms. Generally, however, the public and private firms operate in a similar fashion, the only difference stems from their investor pool.

Corporate Venture Capital Funds

Many major corporations have established true venture capital groups as separate entities, subsidiaries, or divisions. These groups operate in much the same way as private venture firms except that historically they have different goals. The difference in these goals reflects the different sources of capital. Private venture funds generally invest to achieve a high return on investment and to grow companies, while corporate venture groups are backed by corporate dollars seeking access to new technologies. While corporations invest in young companies hoping to create a "window on technology," they may also fund companies that they hope to acquire later on. An entrepreneur seeking venture capital from such a firm should consider the pluses and minuses of the corporate venturer's philosophy and objectives.

Advantages:

1. While the entrepreneur makes new technologies available to the Corporation, the corporation contributes, not only cash, but also the

benefits of being associated with a profitable business. These benefits include credibility with vendors and future lenders, contact with an established base of customers, and a ready-made corporate infrastructure that can frequently help in administrative areas. The corporation can also provide access to manufacturing facilities, as well as management, marketing services, and distribution channels.

2. Corporations that have a strong bottom-line can provide deep pockets to help early-stage companies, and funds may be readily available for subsequent stages of development, expansion, and growth. Although most corporate investors want to see profit early in the venture's life, they are often willing to continue a business relationship for more than seven to ten years.

3. The corporation may be an excellent candidate for a future merger or acquisition.

Disadvantages

1. The parent corporation may experience changes in its top management or of its agenda. These changes can have repercussions for the venture capitalist working under the corporate aegis. The corporation may be unable, or may decide not to allocate as much money to its venture activity as originally planned. Or the corporation may direct some of its resources away from the entrepreneur's venture and focus them in another area. To protect his company from this eventuality, the entrepreneur should make certain when the deal is in its initial stages that the corporation is truly committed to financing a long-term relationship.

2. The entrepreneur and the corporation must clarify their reasons and their objectives for entering into an agreement. If the venture is to be successful, both parties must share a vision and reach a consensus concerning product development and the direction of the venture. Corporate funding can sometimes mean less control for the entrepreneur than if he had chosen a private venture route.

3. The corporate culture generally is not compatible with the entrepreneurial process. The new venture may not show signs of profitability or success for several years, and the corporation must remain patient and supportive. Those in charge of the new venture should not need to spend a lot of time on reporting procedures. The corporation

should also grant the corporate venture capitalists enough autonomy to make decisions quickly as the new venture reaches inevitable crisis points.

Investment Bankers and Other Financial Institutions

In the past, investment banking firms have helped later-stage companies find financing by taking the company public, by making private equity placements, or by providing debt capital. Many investment bankers also invest capital in early stage companies and now reap the rewards of traditional venture investing—a high return on investment and the satisfaction of nurturing a growing company. In addition to which, they generate a tremendous source of clients for their "mainstream" investment banking or financing business. These venture financing activities therefore give an investment firm the opportunity to get in with companies on the ground floor and slowly build them to the point where the investment bankers can help provide later stage financings.

Government Financing Sources

SBICs and MESBICs—Small
Business Investment Companies

SBICs were created by the Small Business Investment Act of 1958 as a vehicle for providing long-term funding for small businesses. SBICs are privately owned and managed, but they are licensed, regulated, and financed directly by the Small Business Administration through long-term loans that leverage one dollar of private capital against four dollars in government-guaranteed loans.

In 1969, the Office of Minority Business Entrepreneurs of the Department of Commerce formed the MESBICs or Minority Enterprise Small Business Investment Companies. Similar to the SBICs, their purpose is to provide long-term funding and management assistance to new ventures started by minorities and the disadvantaged, specifically the handicapped. In 1986, they accounted for 140 of all SBIC licenses.

At the end of 1986, over 400 SBICs and MESBICs existed, with about $6 billion under management disbursed through approximately 70,000 loan and investment transactions. SBICs and MESBICs are capitalized by corporations, individuals, financial institutions or a combination of these, and some have raised capital through IPOs and are publicly traded.

SBICs may buy stock (common or preferred) in the new venture, or provide capital through loans or convertible debentures. However, since SBICs must service the debt on the funds they borrow from the SBA, investments in the form of loans with favored interest rates coupled with the right to buy stock is the "standard" type of financing. This structure gives the SBIC immediate returns with which to service their debt. This means that SBICs are not a good source for funding start-up ventures likely to lose money in their initial years.

Deals may be financed for as little as $100,000, or for over $ 1 million, depending on the individual SBIC's preferences. SBICs finance a wide variety of industries, everything from restaurants and retail ventures to construction, communications and research companies. The investment objectives are similar to the private venture capital pools, except for the restrictions placed on their investments by the SBA. SBICs offer funding to small businesses only; that is, by definition:

1. A business with a net worth of $6 million and less.
2. A business with an average net after-tax profit for the two prior fiscal years of $2 million or less. In addition, SBICs cannot invest in:

1. Investment companies.
2. Lending institutions.
3. Manufacturing companies that employ over 500 people, unless the manufacturing company meets the criteria for net worth and after-tax profit listed above.

Business Development Companies

Business Development Companies (BDCs) are public corporations owned by private investors, licensed by the state, and regulated by the Security Exchange Commission (SEC). They are chartered to invest in geographically defined areas that are economically deprived. Economic development and job creation are their goals.

Business Development Companies' policies vary as much as the geographic and economic areas they serve vary. Some operate like SBICs, offering venture capital investments, backed by the SBA; others make direct loans like a bank or other financial institution; still others engage in lease buy-backs, the financing and building of a new plant which the entrepreneur will lease/purchase from the BDC until he owns it, usually within 20 years.

The private venture capitalists who own the BDCs generally offer management assistance. In fact, BDCs are required by the Small Business Investment Incentive Act of 1980 to actively participate in the management of the new venture as well as secure 25 percent or more equity interest in the firm.

There are BDCs in over 20 states including: Arkansas, California, Florida, Georgia, Iowa, Kansas, Kentucky, Maine, Maryland, Massachusetts, Mississippi, Missouri, Montana, Nebraska, New Hampshire, New York, North Carolina, North Dakota, Oklahoma, Pennsylvania—Pittsburgh and Philadelphia, Rhode Island, South Carolina, Virginia, Washington, West Virginia, and Wyoming.

WHAT KIND OF VENTURE CAPITAL FINANCING DOES THE ENTREPRENEUR NEED?

One of the keys to understanding venture financing is to understand the venture's stage of development and the types of capital that are most appropriate for each stage. Although it is not consistently used, a terminology has emerged to describe the different types of capital.

Seed Financing

Seed financing is usually between $50,000 or less and up to $250,000. It is given to an entrepreneur for researching his concept, writing a business plan, assembling a management team, and conducting market research. Venture capital is available at this stage, with about 5 percent to 10 percent of all venture capital financing in 1986 falling into this category.

At this early stage in the company's development, seed capital may be the most expensive capital the entrepreneur will ever get, and obtaining financing at this level brings with it the disadvantage of significantly less ownership should the business succeed. This is because the high risk the venture capitalist takes by investing in the business must be offset by the promise of greater returns through holding a larger percentage of the company. If the company grows, the equity the entrepreneur trades now for financing could represent enormous value years down the road.

Therefore, it is advisable for the entrepreneur to try to move the company along as far as possible before seeking venture capital, if only to maintain a greater degree of control and ownership. The entrepreneur often benefits if he is willing to seek financing from his own resources, relatives, other founding members of his team, and from government grants, or by *bootstrapping* his venture through the operations of the business.

Having said that, we hasten to add that some companies should seek venture capital funding at the seed stage. This is especially true for company's whose founders lack business experience and/or do not have a strong, well-rounded management team. Typically, the person seeking venture financing is a scientist or researcher who has developed a technology or product idea that, with the right backing, could become a company. Venture capitalists who specialize in seed companies bring more than money to a deal. They also bring expertise in the particular needs of young companies. Such venture capitalists can anticipate the various problems young companies will experience at each phase of growth, and they take satisfaction from helping entrepreneurs develop embryonic companies into strong publicly owned entities.

Start-Up Financing

Most start-up capital is given to companies who are about one-year old and have written a business plan and gathered a management team. In the start-up stage, the company puts the finishing touches on the product and poises to launch into its marketing plan. A capital infusion is critical if the company is to take the product out of the laboratory and into the hands of customers. At this stage in the company's growth, the entrepreneur may also find financing through private individual investors, government grants, or through corporate venture capital groups.

First and Second-Stage Financing

If the product sells successfully in its initial marketing phase, the entrepreneur will need first stage financing to develop manufacturing and sales capabilities. As the company grows, it requires capital to expand operations. Second-stage financing is used to build or lease property and equipment, and to increase inventory for a growing customer base. Generally, venture capital is readily available for companies at these stages of growth. Other sources of capital at these stages include private equity investors, and R & D arrangements.

Mezzanine or Expansion Financing

Mezzanine financing is commonly referred to as "bridge" or "expansion" financing, or pre-public expansion capital. Mezzanine generally means "in between." In this case, mezzanine means the company is between the venture financing stages and the public equity markets. At this stage, a company frequently manufactures and ships a product or sells its services with a reliable degree of success. The company may want to hire its own sales force, expand its product line, expand its research and development efforts, increase its marketing efforts, and broaden its manufacturing capabilities or service capabilities.

Venture capitalists want to invest in this stage of development for two reasons: 1) reduced risk based upon previous performance. The company's management and its operations are in place. They have established a successful track record, so the risk factor has declined significantly; 2) fast expansion and growth over the next year or two. This growth stage is appealing for venture capitalists because the company should be ramping up and could be close to making its first public offering. If it is the company's intention, an infusion of venture capital at this stage will prepare the company for its big leap into the public markets, where the investor may *exit* the deal. Mezzanine investments are a "quick in and out" for the venture capitalist and tend to be more liquid than investments in other stages.

However, at this stage returns may be more limited if circumstances change quickly. For instance, the window for initial public offerings may narrow or close, making liquidity more difficult, or public valuations may not be as high as expected; therefore, not all venture capitalists believe these investments meet their investment objectives. Other sources of capital for companies at the mezzanine stage include institutional investors, large private investors, large corporations, and sometimes debt capital from banks or other lenders.

Public and Post-IPO Financing

One of the most successful ways for a company to raise money is through an initial public offering. By registering its stock with the Securities and Exchange Commission, a company can sell equity to the American public and establish an on-going source for capital. Funds from a successful offering increase the company's growth potential and operating scope, making it possible to finance everything from R & D to acquisitions.

For the venture capitalist, a public offering means his private equity holdings achieve new status in the public marketplace. The stock's valuation may increase dramatically at the time of the offering, since publicly traded stock usually has a higher valuation than private equity. Also, because the marketplace determines the value of the stock, the stock is easier to sell.

Traditionally, we think of venture capitalists exiting a deal through a public offering. While that is often true, the venture capitalist does not become liquid as a result of a public offering. In fact, the company is merely switching investor bases—away from the venture capitalist and to the public. Venture capitalists like their companies to go public, not because they can liquidate their holdings, but because they will hold publicly tradeable securities, with all the prestige and value public status confers. Following a public offering, the venture capital partnership may choose to distribute shares of public stocks to their initial investors, so they can honor their commitments to those investors. The venture capitalists then turn around and raise more money for the next partnership. This is why there is sometimes pressure on a company to go public as quickly as possible. The sooner it goes public, the sooner the venture capital firm meets the obligations to its investors and can begin its second partnership. By raising more funds in successive partnerships and doing more deals, the venture capitalist slowly builds his holdings. (For more information about going public, see Appendix A, "Alternatives to Venture Capital.")

Although popular, going public is not an inevitable step. At this stage in a company's maturity, capital is available from many different sources: public equity markets, debt instruments, bank financings, joint ventures, institutional investors, and large corporations.

Leveraged Buyout

Recently, many venture capitalists have invested funds in leveraged buyouts. This is entirely different financing for venture capitalists, and their success will depend on their knowledge of the industries, companies, and managements involved in buyout deals.

A leveraged buyout is the purchase of an existing business or product line, usually by an entrepreneur, present management, or an outside firm using the company's own assets to secure loans. When present company assets are not sufficient, the prospective buyer might seek venture capital to help finance the buyout.

The key factor in leveraged buyouts is the management team. If the buyout includes present management, the risk factor is greatly reduced since present management will have an operational understanding of the business. If the transaction involves an entirely new team, the risk factor increases significantly. An element of uncertainty and the potential for unanticipated problems are introduced, both through the new players and their lack of knowledge about the business. On the other hand, a change in management can also bring high energy, innovation, and a fresh commitment to succeed.

Other factors affecting a venture capitalist's decisions regarding a leveraged buyout include the company's contracts, its reputation with suppliers and customers, the strength of its competition, and the current state of the industry in which the company operates. For many venture capitalists, leveraged buyouts are a new field of investment. They are a risky undertaking because they carry a high debt load. However, as returns in certain businesses decline, other businesses become more attractive, so leveraged buyouts do fit into some venture capital portfolios.

Turnaround Financing

Venture capitalists also occasionally provide funds for turnaround situations, for companies in bankruptcy or with extremely poor equity and cash positions. Turnarounds are risky to finance, and in fact, few venture capitalists will even entertain such proposals. The key to a successful turnaround is the ability and track record of the new management team. Customer relations will probably be fair to poor, investors are difficult, and creditors are usually not much more cooperative. Some venture capitalists show interest in a turnaround situation only if the new management team has directly related experience, a good track record, and a plan that allows for adequate reaction time to the many things that can go wrong in an ailing or bankrupt company.

Table 1-2 shows how venture funds were allocated by stage in 1985,

Table 1-2.
Disbursements by Financing Stage.

	Percent of Number of Financings		Percent of Dollar Amount Invested	
	1986	**1985**	**1986**	**1985**
Seed	6	6	2	2
Startup	15	14	16	10
Other Early Stage	18	17	17	12
Total Early Stage	39%	37%	35%	24%
Second Stage	25	30	25	33
Later Stage	21	21	19	27
Total Expansion	46%	51%	44%	60%
LBO/Acquisition	9	6	17	11
Other	6	6	4	5
Total Other	15%	12%	21%	16%
Total	100%	100%	100%	100%

(Source Venture Economics, Inc., Wellesley Hills, MA, reprinted with permission.)

based on 1,522 venture capital financings, and in 1986, based on 1,324 financings.

WHAT ARE VENTURE CAPITALISTS LOOKING FOR?

Traditionally, venture capital is associated with high-technology products, such as micro or macro computers, electronic peripherals, telecommunications, materials technology such as galium arsenide and conductive polymers, biotechnology, software, and artificial intelligence. High technology companies were a popular investment choice for venture capitalists in the mid-1970s and into the early 1980s. Historically, these enterprises grew rapidly, created new and unexploited marketplaces, attained high market values, and so gave the venture investors extremely rewarding return on investment. For instance, when personal computers first came out, they offered venture capitalists an almost unlimited growth potential and a proportionately high rate of return on investment. It is clear that venture firms like products that deliver a high-technology solution to an industrial problem for a substantial price. However, because of recent fluctuations in high-tech markets and exciting investment opportunities elsewhere, venture investors have broadened their portfolios to include

Table 1-3. Disbursements by Industry Category.

	Percent of Number of Companies Financed			Percent of Dollar Amount Invested		
	1986	1985	1984	1986	1985	1984
Commercial Communications	4	4	3	5	7	4
Telephone and Data Communications	11	11	10	11	14	11
Computer Hardware and Systems	16	19	22	19	22	29
Software and Services	14	14	14	10	9	11
Other Electronics	11	12	13	13	12	13
Genetic Engineering	4	3	3	4	4	2
Medical/Health Care Related	13	12	11	12	9	8
Energy Related	1	2	2	2	1	2
Industrial Automation	3	3	3	2	4	3
Industrial Products and Machinery	4	4	4	2	3	3
Consumer Related	9	9	7	9	7	7
Other Products and Services	10	7	8	11	8	7
	100%	100%	100%	100%	100%	100%

(Source: Venture Economics, Inc., Wellesley Hills, MA, reprinted with permission.)

so-called "low" or non-technology companies. For instance, many venture capitalists are now entering the retail markets.

Table 1-3 shows how venture capitalists deployed their funds in 1984, 1985, and 1986. Figure 1-4 illustrates investments in non-technology companies from 1981 through 1986.

WHAT ROLE DO VENTURE CAPITALISTS PLAY IN A NEW VENTURE?

Most venture capitalists serve as advisors. They are usually involved in several ventures at once and lack the time to play any other role. As advisors, they serve on the Board of Directors, suggest changes in the business to make it more profitable, help find new managers, and meet with the entrepreneur regularly to track the progress the business is making. Because venture capitalists invest in the businesses they know best, their advice is valuable. It is a good idea to tap their knowledge on a regular basis, especially in the initial stages of the business.

Occasionally, the venture capitalist becomes directly involved in the day-to-day operations of the business, functioning as a manager. This is not the usual role of a venture capitalist, but there are some venture capitalists who want involvement, especially in the start-up or developmental stages of the venture. Frequently, the management team may have key executives for every position, but lack a chief executive officer (CEO). In this situation, the venture capitalist often will step in to serve in that capacity until he has recruited the right person for the job.

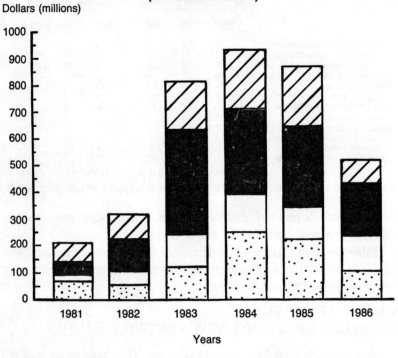

**Investments in Non-Technology Companies
1981-1986
(in millions of dollars)**

Dollars (millions)

Other   Consumer   Medical   Communications

Investments in non technology companies by industry
1981-1986*

	Number of Companies	Number of Financings	Total Amount Invested (millions)
Communications	160	246	$ 850
Medical	113	214	590
Consumer	348	527	1380
Other	303	420	900
Total	924	1407	$3720

* Data for 1986 is approximately 50% complete.

Fig. 1-4. (Source: Venture Economics, Inc., Wellesley Hills, MA, reprinted with permission.)

Control is in the hands of the person or company with more than 50 percent of the voting interest. In any financing, the percentage of ownership changes, resulting in a shift in the control of the company. Depending on how an equity financing is structured, the entrepreneur may lose control of the company to the venture capitalist, especially if the financing occurs in an early stage of the company's development, where the majority of equity goes to the venture capitalist to compensate him for his financial risk.

This has both benefits and drawbacks. A *controlling* venture capitalist may be good for the business if it is difficult to launch and if the investor has direct experience managing such businesses. In this case, an entrepreneur can learn a great deal from the venture capitalist, and the chances for success increase. On the other hand, a controlling venture capitalist may be perceived as intrusive, unless all parties understand from the outset that the venture capitalist is the captain of the ship. Sometimes, entrepreneurs reject venture funding because they are concerned about losing control of their company. However, for two important reasons, the entrepreneur should be careful not to turn down a winning deal over the issue of control. First, after a number of different financings, through the gradual process of dilution, management will normally have a minority percentage of the company anyway. This is discussed in greater detail in Chapter 5, "Negotiating the Deal." Secondly, most venture capitalists do not have time to supervise closely a company's growth, nor do they want to. They prefer to back winning management teams who already know the ins and outs of running a business. Venture investors know from experience that if a company requires a lot of outside management, it is probably in trouble. Finally, it is important to remember the "golden rule" . . . "he who has the gold . . . rules." While this may be an overstatement in fact, the theory is pretty good. If you're dependent on someone else's money, that investor has "practical" control, without regard to stock ownership percentages.

Negotiations regarding control should begin in a spirit of fairness and cooperation. Historically, working with a venture capitalist is like being involved in a good marriage: there is a lot of give and take. The two parties should have common objectives and a common goal—the success of the company. This should serve as a guide in striking any deal with a venture capitalist.

HOW VENTURE CAPITALISTS OPERATE

Although every venture capital firm establishes its own procedures for reviewing investment opportunities, the following is a general guideline of the venture financing process.

The First Review

Some venture capital firms receive literally hundreds of executive summaries and business plans in a week. A few of those plans are reviewed—and even fewer financed. There is a simple reason—venture capitalists are busy people. Among other things, they must raise capital, manage that capital, find the best investments, negotiate and make the investments, and then manage those investments to meet their objectives and keep their own investors happy. In fact, finding new investments is only a small part of a venture capitalist's day. Venture investors once spent up to 60 percent of their time in pursuit of investment opportunities; now many spend about 40 percent, with the larger percentage helping to manage and oversee investments already made.

How does the entrepreneur get the venture capitalist to look at his executive summary? One way is to send it to the venture capitalist with the recommendation of other venture capitalists or entrepreneurs he knows and likes. The entrepreneur should also use his network of accountants, lawyers, or financial advisors. At this point, the business plan or executive summary is the entrepreneur's sales tool. The entrepreneur should refer to his professional network for their advice on improving the quality of his executive summary or business plan. Their suggestions will contribute to a more cohesive plan and a better presentation.

When a venture capitalist receives an executive summary or a business plan, he may scan it for only several minutes, to determine whether or not the proposed business is worth his time. Something must catch his fancy to make him read on and begin investing his time in the deal. Often, the entrepreneur's first attempt at writing a proposal involves more sizzle than steak. The first look by the venture capitalist is critical, though, because it is on this basis—and frequently this basis alone—that the venture capitalist decides if he will spend more time reading the plan.

In some firms, a staff member keeps a log to record all pertinent data about a new venture. Other firms may be less formal, depending on the size of the venture firm and the number of employees and the amount of deal flow. Usually the individual who first reads the executive summary or the business plan notes the company's stage of development and makes a judgment on the originality of the product or service, the size of the market, and the merit of the management team.

The Venture Capitalists Confer

In larger venture capital firms—those with more than just one or two individuals—a deal log or memo regarding the entrepreneur's business might be circulated to all appropriate parties in the firms. The investors study the proposal and frequently meet to discuss its potential and to determine whether an interview will be set and, on to the next step, or a rejection letter sent.

The Presentation

Assuming the venture capitalist is interested in the entrepreneur's proposed business, he will then meet with the entrepreneur to gain a better understanding of the entrepreneur's background, his management team, and the business. This is one of the most important meetings in the entire process. If the meeting doesn't go well, the deal is dead. If the meeting is successful, the venture capitalist will want to learn more about the business, the market, and perhaps to talk with other venture investors who might also be interested in the deal. The entrepreneur should be ready to discuss everything in his plan. If the entrepreneur feels he needs assistance in discussing his plan or his business in general, he should request that his management team be present.

If the venture firm rejects the proposal, the entrepreneur might want to know why he was turned down. The entrepreneur should call the firm and ask to speak with the venture capitalist about his proposal and its rejection. The entrepreneur may have major errors in his business plan, he may not know his market as well as he should, or possibly he has overestimated his sales and underestimated his competition. Sometimes a deal is turned down simply because it is not in the venture capitalist's field of expertise or an area of interest to him. The proposed venture may not meet the venture capitalist's investment criteria. The most important thing for the entrepreneur to do is to learn from a rejection. He should not continue to submit his plan without first finding out if it needs altering or improving. Also, sometimes the venture capitalist will recommend another venture capitalist for whom the deal may be more appropriate.

Due Diligence

If the first meeting is successful, and the venture capitalist and the entrepreneur are still interested in structuring a deal, the next step is for the venture capitalist to investigate the entrepreneur's business and to learn as much as possible about the deal. This investigation process is called *due diligence*. It usually includes visiting the entrepreneur's company, meeting with his key people, and evaluating the facilities and delivery systems. It may also involve talking with the entrepreneur's creditors, his customers, his references, and his former employers— people who can help the venture capitalist come to a decision about the entrepreneur's venture. The best posture for the entrepreneur to take is to have an open door policy for any and all aspects of his or her business, and to be scrupulously honest. If the venture capitalist finds errors or misstatements in the plan, the entrepreneur will most likely not receive funding. A complete discussion of the due diligence process can be found in Chapter 4.

The Term Sheet

After the due diligence process has been completed, and if the venture capitalist is convinced that the proposed venture is exciting and one in which his firm should invest, the negotiations regarding the form of the investment and the valuation begin. To some extent, the negotiations began at the very beginning, since what the entrepreneur expects to get and what he gives up are generally indicated early; however, now it begins for real. At some point, the entrepreneur frequently will be given a term sheet, which outlines the terms of the deal. It is essential for the entrepreneur to request this in writing. The due diligence process can take months, and while the entrepreneur is waiting, he does not receive financing. Entrepreneurs may be tempted to accept a handshake deal so that the money will flow and they can get on with business. However, this is not recommended, since the entrepreneur may not know the actual terms of the agreement: how much he will have to give up, how much ownership the venture capitalist wants, who else will be part of the deal, and what happens to him and the present management team. The entrepreneur should take the time to discuss the terms and have them reduced to a term sheet, so he and the venture capitalist are clear about the proposal.

Contracts

After substantial negotiating and haggling about valuation, control, and other matters, the process should move to a definitive agreement. The final step is the signing of a contract that represents the expectations and commitments of both the entrepreneur and the venture capitalist. The protocol concerning contracts frequently differs between the East and West Coasts of the country, and internationally, as well. Quite often, a term sheet is sufficient documentation for closing a deal on the West Coast, while a more formal process of signing contractual agreements is required on the East Coast. Once final agreements are signed, the entrepreneur is funded and can continue carrying out the goals of the business plan. In most venture capital agreements, there is an exit plan that outlines how the venture capitalist will liquidate his investment, and what happens when budgets, milestones, and other goals are not met.

WHAT ARE THE ENTREPRENEUR'S CHANCES OF RECEIVING VENTURE CAPITAL FINANCING?

Venture capitalists' livelihoods depend upon their judgment of prospective new ventures. They must be right more often than business mortality statistics project, or their winners so big that they cover the big losses. One of the drains on venture capital investing is "the walking wounded." We hear a lot about the great successes—and they are far and few between—and we even hear about some great disasters, but what about everything in between? The famous "walking wounded" continue to take the venture capitalists cash and management time, but provide little opportunity for exit. Too many of these companies can really kill a venture capitalist's portfolio, his return on investment, and his opportunity for additional funds to invest.

A recent survey of private independent venture capital firms that Venture Economics conducted with the National Venture Capital Association showed that in 1985 the survey's 183 respondents made 2,810 investments in 1,089 companies, 31 percent of which received financings for the first time. (Source: Venture Economics, Inc., Wellesley Hills, MA, reprinted with permission.) Nationally, about two percent to three percent of all proposals applying for venture capital receive venture financing. In short, these figures indicate that the entrepreneur's chance of receiving venture capital is slim, indeed, but not impossible. It is a chance worth pursuing, because along with venture funding, an entrepreneur also gets a vote of confidence that says his company could be a winner. It has crossed the first hurdle on the road to success.

Chapter 2

How To Find
Venture Capital

Entrepreneurs sometimes believe that any venture capitalist with money to invest is the right venture capitalist for them; however, an industry standard notes that how much money you raise is less important than whose money you raise. Like many of the companies they finance, venture capitalists use a niche strategy. Some venture capitalists favor a geographic area, or a certain size of investment, or a specific list of technologies or service sectors.

Whether or not the venture capitalist is appropriate for the entrepreneur's venture will depend on the venture capitalist's appetite for investments and the size of his current portfolio, his competitive investments, and the availability of capital. One must also consider finding a good match between the business objectives of the entrepreneur and that of the venture capitalist. What kind of value-added expertise does the venture capitalist bring to the deal, what are the venture capitalist's financial goals and do they mesh well with the entrepreneur's professional expectations, and do both parties agree on which direction the company should take?

HOW MUCH IS THE VENTURE
CAPITALIST WILLING TO INVEST?

It is important for the entrepreneur to determine how much capital each firm is willing to invest in new ventures. Determining the amount of capital the firm currently has available for investment is also important because the entrepreneur's needs may be too great or even too modest for the venture capitalists in his area. For the most current information on venture capitalists, the entrepreneur should call the firms in which he is interested and ask them what type of companies they invest in and how much capital they have to invest per deal or in total. Venture firms are usually quick to share this information because it helps them screen out new ventures that don't meet their investment criteria.

Pratt's Guide to Venture Capital Sources lists this information, as does *Venture Magazine* in its "Guide to International Venture Capital." Also, the Small Business Administration (SBA) publishes two directories that include everything the entrepreneur needs to know about Small Business Investment Companies (SBICs) and Minority Enterprise Small Business Investment Companies (MESBICs), including the amount of capital each company is willing to invest.

PRODUCT/INDUSTRY EXPERTISE

Venture firms generally specialize in areas in which the venture capitalists are experienced. Whether it is semiconductors or biotechnology, the venture capitalist is most interested in financing businesses he understands, so that he can add value and avoid making critical errors. For example, it may be difficult to persuade a venture capital firm specializing in mainframe computers to finance a new method for analyzing blood samples . . . it's too far-removed from their area of expertise.

It will help an entrepreneur to work with a venture capitalist that understands his business, his competitors, and his critical success factors. This is the value added benefit of venture capital. The venture capitalist's network of contacts may be useful for hiring key managers, for getting consultants involved when appropriate, and for avoiding "the learning curve" everytime a decision needs to be made.

WHERE TO FIND VENTURE CAPITALISTS

Venture capitalists are located in most of our major cities, but there is a concentration of venture capital money on either coast, especially in New York, Massachusetts, California and Connecticut, and particularly in San Francisco, New York City, and Boston. Table 2-1 illustrates venture capital activity by region.

The proximity of the entrepreneur's business to the venture capital firms in which he is interested may be a factor to consider. Some investors will make deals wherever they believe the opportunities are the best;

Table 2-1.
Distribution of Industry Resources by Geographic Region.
(Source: Venture Economics, Inc., Wellesley Hills, MA, reprinted with permission.)

	Capital (billions)				Offices			
	1986	Percent of Total	1985	Percent of Total	1986	Percent of Total	1985	Percent of Total
Northeast (CT, MA, ME, NH, NJ, NY, RI):	$10.82	45	$8.05	41	236	32	215	32
West Coast (CA, OR, WA):	7.74	32	6.79	35	221	30	204	30
Midwest/Plains (IL, IN, IA, KS, MI, MN, MO, OH, WI):	2.42	10	2.25	12	98	13	88	13
Southwest/Rockies (AZ, CO, LA, MT,NM, NV, OK, TX):	1.47	6	1.27	6	94	13	91	14
Mid-Atlantic (DC, DE, MD, PA, VA):	1.16	5	.84	4	47	7	39	6
Southeast (AL, FL, GA, KY, MS, NC, SC, TN):	.53	2	.37	2	37	5	31	5
Total	$24.14	100%	$19.57	100%	733	100%	668	100%

however, in some cases, venture capitalists won't invest in companies further than an hour's travel time by car, plane, or further than they can travel to and from again in the same day. The venture capitalist needs easy access to the entrepreneur and his company for board meetings, to stay current with company developments, and to be available for hands-on management should it be required.

To help the entrepreneur get started in his search for funding, we have included at the back of this book a directory of venture capital firms. Although it is not our objective to provide a detailed or exhaustive listing of firms, the directory is organized by state or province and gives the name, address, and phone number of many of the biggest and best known venture capital firms in the United States and Canada. Because a firm's investment objectives, geographic and industry preferences, and funding capabilities change constantly, current details should be obtained directly from the venture capitalists themselves. Other sources of information on venture capital may be useful:

National Association of Investment Companies
915 Fifteenth St. NW, Suite 700
Washington, DC 20005
(202) 347-8600
To order a directory, send a check or money order for $3.39.

National Association of Small Business Investment Companies
1156 15th St. NW
Washington, DC 20005
(202) 833-8230
To order a directory, send $1.00 and include a self-addressed stamped envelope.

National Venture Capital Association
1655 North Fort Meyer Drive, Suite 700
Arlington, VA 22209
(703) 528-4370
To order a directory, call 202-956-5522, or for further information call, 703-528-4370.

Pratt's Guide to Venture Capital Sources
Venture Economics, Inc.
16 Laurel Avenue
Wellesley Hills, MA 02181
(617) 431-8100
Pratt's Guide is very comprehensive and can be purchased by sending a check for $95.00, plus $5.00 for shipping and handling (plus $4.75 sales tax for Massachusetts residents). The guide can also be found in libraries, especially of colleges and universities with good business schools.

HOW TO INVESTIGATE A VENTURE CAPITAL FIRM

To determine if he has found the right venture capital firm, the entrepreneur should talk with companies and professionals doing business with the venture capitalist; talk to the managers of companies the venture firm has funded; and in general collect as much information as possible. The entrepreneur should ask the venture capitalist for references and follow up on them. He should also consult with his own lawyers and accountants concerning the venture capitalist's reputation, experience, and skill.

When talking with companies the venture capitalist has funded, the entrepreneur will learn how long it took to receive funding; what problems arose; whether the company received the funding management wanted; whether management was happy with the venture capitalist; and to what extent the venture capitalist participated in running the business. Also the entrepreneur should ask about the issues that came up in the due diligence process. In general, the entrepreneur should look for any information that might help him decide if he can get along with the venture capitalist, or if there might be major differences that would block the funding or success of his company.

The entrepreneur may run into "sour grapes" stories from the companies who did not pass the due diligence test, or for some other reason did not receive funding from the venture capitalist. The entrepreneur should try to discover what the difference is between these companies and the ones that did receive funding. He should find out what went wrong, how the two parties reacted, and, what they could have done, if anything, to put the deal back on track. Again, he should look for information that will help him decide if he wants to work with this particular venture capitalist, and if the venture capitalist is reputable, well-financed, and organized enough to serve his company's needs.

So, it's a two-way street. The venture capitalist is evaluating the entrepreneur and his business, and the entrepreneur is evaluating the venture capitalist and his business.

HOW TO APPROACH VENTURE CAPITALISTS

An entrepreneur can approach a venture capitalist either through a "cold call," a letter, or through an introduction by an investment banker, accountant, lawyer, banker, friend or another entrepreneur the venture capitalist knows.

Introduction by the Venture Capitalist's Friend

An introduction by a friend is an excellent way to begin with a venture capitalist. The business community is small and closely knit, and personal contacts often serve as the strongest endorsement an entrepreneur can receive. However, the friend shouldn't attempt to represent the business proposal to the venture capitalist, (no one knows the business better than the entrepreneur); rather, the person making the introduction should bring the entrepreneur's company to the attention of the venture capitalists, and then allow the two parties to meet to discuss the details of the business.

The experience and reputation of the entrepreneur's friend will effect, negatively or positively, the first impression the venture capitalist has of the entrepreneur and his new venture. The entrepreneur should carefully consider who to ask for help in such situations.

Investment Bankers

Investment bankers are also an excellent source of leads to venture capitalists and advice concerning venture funding. Some investment bankers even sponsor their own venture capital funds. The investment banking community will sometimes help new ventures find capital, because if and when the company needs additional financing, the investment banker has a ready-made client. It is the investment bank's way of building its business.

Large investment banking firms have excellent reputations in the financial community, and an introduction from a large firm to a venture capitalist may lend credibility to the new venture. The size of the investment an entrepreneur requires generally dictates the size of the investment banking firm with whom he should work. The smaller bankers usually handle investments from $1 million to $10 million, while the larger firms handle investments for $10 million and more.

Accountants

Many of the large accounting firms, such as Arthur Young, have specialists in venture capital who can assist entrepreneurs through the process of finding financing. Specialists in these firms can help in the development and review of the business plan, including its financial statements and projections. They also make referrals and introductions to appropriate potential investors and help management understand company valuations. Accountants shouldn't function directly as the selling agent, though, as in all cases, this role is best left to the entrepreneur.

Lawyers

Many lawyers also have good venture capital contacts. A lawyer who is experienced in putting together venture capital deals will best assist the entrepreneur with introductions and act as an advisor, as a critic of the business plan, and by drawing up the term sheet and other final agreements, when appropriate. Opinions vary; some sources say the attorney should not attend meetings between the entrepreneur and the venture capitalists until after the investors agree to finance the deal and a price has been set. Until then, the attorney's presence is unnecessary, or may complicate matters. Other sources recommend the attorney be present to assure that the entrepreneurs, who are almost always new to structuring the deal, get a fair shake. An attorney may also lend an experienced perspective to proceedings, helping the entrepreneur to discern between common practices and topics requiring negotiation.

Generally speaking, an attorney who is knowledgeable about structuring venture capital deals is critically important to the company's success down the road, and is therefore one of the entrepreneur's most important consultants. He can advise the entrepreneur about what to expect in his meetings with the venture capitalist, as well as how to behave and respond in the process of negotiations. See Chapter 5, "Negotiating the Deal," for more information about working with attorneys.

Cold Calls

Once the entrepreneur has determined which venture capitalists will best help him meet his professional goal, he may wish to contact them directly to briefly describe his company. Venture capitalists receive many unsolicited executive summaries and business plans, and these documents can get lost or misplaced. If the entrepreneur calls before sending information, he can quickly determine if there is any interest at all in his idea. He will learn whether or not the venture capitalist is investing in companies such as his, how much money is available for making investments, and if the firm is accepting proposals at the present time. If the venture capitalist is interested, the entrepreneur can send his information to the individuals with whom he spoke and call shortly thereafter for an appointment. Generally, the venture capitalist will want to see an executive summary or a business plan before setting up an introductory meeting. In this case, the entrepreneur's follow up phone call will help distinguish his plan from the other plans the investor receives.

A word of caution here: "cold calls" may be inconclusive. Too frequently, venture capitalists are inundated with responsibilities to existing investments, and may not have time to return phone calls, or may lose messages in the shuffle. The entrepreneur can spend a lot of time playing phone tag. Often, the recommendation of someone known to the venture capitalist moves the deal to the top of the pile. Getting the venture capitalist's "real attention" is the key in the first step.

GETTING THE VENTURE CAPITALIST'S ATTENTION—THE COVER LETTER AND EXECUTIVE SUMMARY

During his initial call, the entrepreneur must find out to whom he should send the executive summary, a two-to-four-page condensation of the business plan. Depending on individual preference, the venture capitalist will sometimes ask to see the full business plan immediately, but we will confine our discussion here to the executive summary, which is most often the entrepreneur's first sales tool.

Based on his conversation with the venture capitalist, the entrepreneur should prepare a cover letter that is tailored to each individual firm. The letter should be brief, about three-quarters of a page to one page in length. Usually it makes reference to the phone conversation and outlines the contents of the package the entrepreneur will send to the venture capitalist. Again, if the entrepreneur is unable to reach the venture capitalist by phone, he might talk with the investor's assistant or secretary to get the name of the person to whom the plan or executive summary should be sent.

Because the executive summary may be all the venture capitalist ever reads, it is the most important of all the documents. It should pique the venture capitalist's imagination and inspire him to pursue the deal further. It should introduce the entrepreneur and his venture in an exciting light, stressing the originality of the product or service and its place in the market, and focusing on the company's management strengths. The summary should also describe market sizes, growth potential, and mention any of the entrepreneur's outstanding successes. In short, the summary should convince the venture capitalist of the viability of the proposed business, and spur him to action—namely to read the business plan and call the entrepreneur in for an interview.

The basic ingredients of an executive summary include name, address, phone number and contact for your venture; a description of your company and product or service, detailing its unique qualities or distinctive competence; a list of key executives with a brief description of their backgrounds and capabilities; a description of the market and marketing strategy; a description of the competition; the amount of funds required and their proposed use; brief financial data; and financial projections. In addition, the entrepreneur should include any information on key technologies and his "unfair" advantage. Although the summary should be no longer than two to four pages, it must be clearly written. Technical and esoteric concepts can be boiled down to plain English and included in greater detail in the business plan.

Company Name, Address, Phone Number and Contact

Even if the address and phone number appear on the cover letter, it is a good idea to include this information again on the first page of the executive summary, simply because the cover letter may get lost or misplaced.

Description of the Company and Its Product or Technology

In this part of the executive summary, the entrepreneur should clearly define his proposed business and its product or technology in just a few sentences. What does the company do? If an entrepreneur has difficulty explaining his business briefly and in simple terms, perhaps he is still uncertain about the company's mission or goal. In this case, it is doubtful that the venture will ever get off the ground.

Even if it is still on the drawing board, the entrepreneur should describe the product's unique qualities, its "unfair advantage," and the attributes that give it an edge on the competition. What is really important here is the marketplace potential for the product, the barriers to entry, and the key to the business's success. If he has an operating business, the entrepreneur should describe the uniqueness of his company, and the factors that he feels will account for its growth. He should provide enough information to give the venture capitalist a clear picture of his goals and how he plans to attain them. He must show the venture capitalist how his company will meet investment objectives. If the entrepreneur is entering a highly competitive field, it is essential to establish a real need for the product coupled with the existence of a large growing market. Without those assurances, the venture capitalist probably will not invest.

Description of Key Executives

Almost without exception, venture capitalists believe that the experience and track record of management is the most important element in a new venture. A new company may have an excellent product, but poor management curtails its chances to succeed. Venture capitalists know that even with an average product, good managment will find a way to win. Much as "location, location, location" is the credo in the real estate business, "managment, management, management" is the byword for new ventures. Good management is more than one superstar, it's a balanced team.

It is important to describe the expertise of the executive team that will run the company. It is especially important to highlight any experience that is directly related to managing the new venture. Nobel prizes might be nice, but they have little to do with building and running a profitable business.

Markets and Marketing

The entrepreneur will immediately instill confidence in the venture capitalist if he demonstrates a clear understanding of the market for his product and the best ways to reach that market. He should also describe how big the market will get in the next five years, what its chief characteristics will be, and how he expects to modify his plan in response to changes in the marketplace.

The entrepreneur should list the names of any existing clients, especially if they are large well-known companies. If not, he should explain their position in the marketplace he is targeting. If some of the clients are leaders in a particular field, or the largest firm of their kind, the entrepreneur should state this so the venture capitalist will better understand the market. Who will buy the product and why? To cite shares of growing markets, without saying something specifically about how and why a particular buyer will purchase the product, is not persuasive.

The entrepreneur should describe the major applications for his product and compare them with the competition. He should include in the discussion a description of new developments expected to enhance the product and any new patents or trademarks the company has developed that will effect the product or service.

Finally, the executive summary might include a section discussing major trends in the industry, since the venture capitalist is always looking for products with virtually unlimited potential. Obviously, very few products have such appeal. It is, however, important for the entrepreneur to describe the potential of his product by indicating its market share and the percentage of the market he thinks he will be able to capture within a specific period of time (see Chapter 3). Referring again to our analogy from horticulture, the business must have the potential to grow multiple stems and blossoms, or several viable products, rather than just one. The entrepreneur's business plan must indicate how he will achieve market acceptance and penetration. He should explain why he feels confident that his product will achieve the projected market penetration.

Competition

The entrepreneur should briefly mention any important competitors. Knowing his competition is as important as knowing his market, and he should investigate this area until he can safely say that he has identified all major competitors, and future competitors, as well. The entrepreneur should indicate how he compares with his competition. He should focus on his strengths in the sales, marketing, manufacturing, or service areas. The entrepreneur should also indicate the market share of his competition, comparing this information against growth projections to determine if he has a realistic estimate of his company's potential.

Funds Required and Their Uses

How much money does the company need? This figure can be determined only after the company's financial projections are complete. To prepare this part of the executive summary, the entrepreneur should consider using the services of an accountant. Frequently, an outsider brings realistic perspective to the company's assessment of its capabilities and needs, and an accountant can assist in the organization and presentation of the data.

The Small Business Administration (SBA) states that the two most common reasons for business failures are poor management and undercapitalization. Although undercapitalization is a serious problem at any stage, its effects are especially devastating in the start-up stages, when the company is experiencing rapid growth. Nothing is worse than running out of money at a critical time. Our experience shows, businesses take longer and cost more to develop than anyone expects.

The entrepreneur should explain in this section of the executive summary how much capital he needs. Venture capitalists will be looking for a specific figure, not a range, and often they will want to know how much equity the entrepreneur is willing to surrender. However, asking the first question begins the negotiation of value. What is the company worth today, and how much can it be worth in the future? Can the investment of venture capital dollars help the company meet its potential?

How will the funds be used? Again, this information will come out of the preparation of the company's projections. For example, the entrepreneur will know what he needs for inventory, for capital expenditures, for research and development, for the purchasing of new equipment, and for expenses.

The entrepreneur should also indicate how much he thinks he might need in subsequent rounds of financing. He should draw a best case scenario—what would happen if he got twice as much financing, or if business was twice as good—and a worst case scenario—if he got only half as much financing, or if the business was only half as good as he thought. This "sensitivity" analysis will help the entrepreneur and the venture capitalist really understand risk and potential. (See Chapter 5, "Negotiating the Deal.")

Company Financial History

For the purpose of the executive summary, the entrepreneur should include a summary of key financial data and historical operating results.

Company Financial Projections

This paragraph of the executive summary is very important. Venture capitalists know that deals usually cost more and take longer than summaries or plans project. In fact, companies rarely do as well as their financial projections suggest. The entrepreneur will have to walk a tightrope, no matter how he approaches the projections. If he is too optimistic, the venture capitalist may think he doesn't know his business, or that he is not realistic. If the entrepreneur is too conservative, the venture capitalist may not have sufficient motivation; i.e., a large enough return on investment. It is best to develop projections that represent a reasonable, rather than an extreme, prospect for growth. Later on, when the company meets or does better than projected, subsequent rounds of financing are more easily accomplished because the venture capitalist has come to trust the entrepreneur's judgment.

The Exit

Venture capitalists are usually most interested in ventures that offer the greatest potential for large returns in the shortest period of time. Therefore, the entrepreneur should be aware of the venture capitalist's need to see valuations increase and opportunities to exit from the deal with a substantial profit. For more information on this important issue, see Chapter 3, "The Business Plan—A Process, Not A Document."

Summary

Although it might seem like an impossible task, the executive summary should touch briefly, in just two to four pages, on as many as possible of the points outlined above. Of course, not all of these points are applicable to all businesses, depending on the type of business and its stage of development. To give you a better idea of what an executive summary might look like, we have provided an example at the end of this chapter.

WHAT VENTURE CAPITALISTS CONSIDER WHEN REVIEWING AN EXECUTIVE SUMMARY—THE FACTORS IN A SUCCESSFUL BUSINESS EQUATION

Venture capitalists are busy people, with responsibilities to their own investors, to their portfolio companies, to their profession, and to their community. A few years ago, venture investors reported spending 60 to 80 percent of their time on new investment opportunities. Today, venture capitalists spend 60 to 80 percent of their time on portfolio management. That means only a small amount of time can be spent reviewing investment opportunities, conducting due diligence, and negotiating deals. One can see why a venture capitalist might not be able to spend more than five minutes or so reading the executive summaries and business plans that cross his desk. The venture capitalist must be selective about what he reads. When he looks at an executive summary, he generally considers the four factors that add up to a successful venture: the entrepreneur and his management team, the market, the technology or business, and the financing issues of the deal. It is the balance and mix of these elements that help the venture capitalist decide whether or not to pursue a particular venture.

The Management Factor

Arthur Young's Law #1: Teams win . . . Superstars lose.

Most venture capitalists will agree that good management is the most important factor for a high tech company's success. In some ways, you can compare a strong management team to a stool resting solidly on four legs of equal length and strength. The four legs are the key management positions, and they usually (but not exclusively) include an expert in technology or product development, someone knowledgeable about marketing and sales, someone with expertise in manufacturing and operations, and someone with proficiency in the area of finance and administration. The secret to a viable and effective management team is to find the absolute best person possible for each of the key positions. The team must meld the strengths of the various disciplines and compensate for any weaknesses. Like a stool with legs of equal length, the team must function in a balanced manner to attract, manage, and retain key employees and to build the business. Legs that are too short or too long provide a rocky foundation upon which to build a company.

There is an irony about the way management works in the environment of a high technology company. The irony emerges from the fact that these companies are science-driven entities, particularly in their earlier stages. Generally, they are conceived and formed by people who understand technology—researchers or even Nobel prize-winning scientists. Such individuals are tremendously gifted when it comes to scientific matters, and they place their confidence in the importance of making the technology work. However, they sometimes incorrectly assume that if the product can be made to perform a task more rapidly, more efficiently, or with some innovation, the world will beat a path to the company's door.

Certainly, without these creative and entrepreneural thinkers, high technology companies could never be founded, but the efforts of the technologists must be balanced by other team members. Companies have a goal beyond making the technology work. Companies often cannot exist without attracting investors, which means they must provide an adequate return on investment. The real task of the management of a high technology company is to take the work of the scientist and convert it, in a reasonable period of time, into products and company profits. Rendering the technology into a useable product requires skills very different from those exhibited by the scientist. It takes operational skills. The apparent irony concerning management is resolved once a company realizes that the people who may not understand the intracacies of making a laser work, will understand how to turn that laser into a useful product that is marketable and can finance the company.

The Marketplace Factor

Arthur Young's Law #2: If the product doesn't succeed in the marketplace, everything else is irrelevant.

This is the arena in which the merits and advantages of a product are finally tested by the people who count most—the buyers. Here, the attributes of a product are useful only from the standpoint of meeting the market's needs. For example, consider two different companies. The first one has a technically mediocre product, but a powerful product distribution chain, a good servicing arrangement, and brilliant marketing support. The second company has a technically superior product, but because it is a start-up, it has almost no distribution channels, a small advertising budget, and the prospective customers voice concerns about the company's ability to make repairs and replace parts. In this situation, the customer is more likely to select the first company's product, even though it is technologically inferior. Customers consider more than technical quality when reviewing product options. That's why good product positioning is vital to a company's success. To position products requires an understanding of the marketplace, distribution channels, and the competition.

Sometimes a company gets confused at the market window. It can arrive at the window too early, attempting to bring a product to market before the window is open—before the customers are ready or able to buy. Or the company can lag behind the optimum time, and bring a product to market when the competition is entrenched and thriving on its large, well-established market shares. Successful management teams understand the window of opportunity, position their products at the right time and place, and stay in touch with the market. They listen to what customers say about their needs, and determine the direction the company should take to solve customer problems. When management teams lose track of the market, they frequently get blind-sided by a competitor who develops a new solution. The key is to know the market well enough to solve real customer problems.

What is the market size? If it's small, it must be dynamic enough to provide the growth necessary to give the venture capitalist adequate return on investment. Venture capitalists need returns of 30 to 40 percent per annum in increased valuations on their portfolios to compensate themselves for the risk, and to attract capital for future investments. While some deals in the portfolio will fail, others will generate 50 percent to 100 percent returns; therefore, venture capitalists will seek to invest in market areas that grow fast enough to support such increases in valuation.

If the market is large and crowded with competitors, the entrepreneur should consider a niche marketing strategy. This is a particularly successful strategy for small businesses, which can move quickly to reflect changing market needs. These businesses usually establish a foothold and then grow a company around that base. For further discussion of marketplace issues, see Chapter 3, "The Business Plan."

The Technology Factor

Arthur Young's Law #3: Built-in barriers to market entry provide better product protection than patents and trademarks.

The third factor in the "successful company equation" is the technology or product, and the protectability of the idea itself. Nothing is worse than investing heavily in a venture, building up a market force and a market presence, only to discover that those efforts have helped the competition compete more effectively against the venture. This happens when the competition allows the entrepreneur to take all the risks of creating and developing a marketplace, so when circumstances are most favorable, the competing company can enter the market on such a grand scale that the entrepreneur cannot compete.

What makes a new product valuable really may have little to do with its patent or copyright. The most important element of an innovative product is a built-in barrier to entry, that is, a quality so intrinsic to the product that it would be impossible for someone else to replicate the idea in a short period of time, if ever. Another barrier to entry may be the high cost of developing the technology, making it prohibitively expensive or not cost effective to enter a particular market. For example, the barrier to entry in the pharmaceutical human therapeutics business is significantly higher than the barrier to entering the micro-computer software spreadsheet business. Human therapeutic products have a long product-to-market development time, they require substantial research-and-development (R & D) financing, and they may face stringent federal regulatory processes. While both industries can be adequately protected by patents and copyrights, therapeutic products have a higher barrier to entry and are therefore less likely to be replicated by a competitor.

The Finance Factor

Arthur Young's Law #4: Financing strategies dictate business strategies.

Has the entrepreneur considered how his financing strategy will influence his business strategy? (See discussion in Chapter 1.) Is venture capital the best choice for his business and does his plan reflect the logic of that choice? How will venture capital help the entrepreneur accomplish his business goals?

From his reading of the summary, the venture capitalist should have an estimation of the market's size. He will also want to know how the company's presence in that market translates into a projected return on investment. This projection will depend on the entrepreneur's calculations of how fast the company will grow, how fast the market is growing, and what market share the company can capture. The venture capitalist will want to see how the entrepreneur has substantiated figures concerning company growth. Are the figures too optimistic, or too conservative? Will the company capture a big enough market share and realize sufficient revenues in a short enough period of time to make the company an attractive investment? The venture capitalist will want to know how many rounds of financing the entrepreneur thinks will be required, and of course, how much capital will be needed in each round. Again, the critical issue here is whether or not the deal will give the venture capitalist an attractive return on investment.

In general, the venture capitalist reviews the financial sections to see how well the entrepreneur understands the ramifications of doing business. Do the numbers make sense on an intuitive level? Are the projections pragmatically feasible? Do the figures represent a best case/worst case scenario? Is the market growing fast enough to support the entrepreneur's projections? And does the entrepreneur have a common sense appreciation of how his business interacts with the marketplace?

The entrepreneur should seek financial advice when putting the summary's financials together. The numbers provide hard evidence of the entrepreneur's plans for his company, and good professional counsel will ensure that the figures make sense.

The Next Move . . . The Business Plan

If the executive summary does its job, the venture capitalist will be so enthusiastic about the proposed venture that he will request to see the business plan and review the proposal in greater detail. Chapter 3 describes how to write, market, and use the business plan as a guide to operations.

(Note: This is the actual executive summary Attain, Inc. wrote to attract mezzanine stage financing. Although the company succeeded in getting the next round of financing, we have one critique on this particular executive summary: it should have included more information on the company's management team.)

ATTAIN, INC.
EXECUTIVE SUMMARY

Attain, Inc. (the "Company" or "Attain") was formed to provide the next generation of linear automatic test equipment ("ATE"). The company was founded in June 1983 by a group of experienced managers and engineers from LTX Corporation, the current industry leader in linear ATE.

Attain has designed a new generation of systems for testing linear and combined linear/digital integrated circuits which are primarily sold to semiconductor manufacturers. Existing equipment does not provide the desired level of throughput (test speed), is not effective technically in fully testing newly-designed complex linear circuits, and requires extensive hardware and software modification to test new circuits. These test problems are exacerbated by the shortage of linear test engineers, pressure to reduce the increasing cost of test, and the critical economic need to reduce the time-to-market for newly-designed devices.

By employing an innovative architecture and the most advanced electronic components available, the Attain test system overcomes the inadequacies of existing ATE. Attain's system is designed to achieve higher throughput via parallel processing, higher accuracies and higher "quality of test" through tester-per-pin architecture, and dramatically reduced test development time for new circuits with its uniquely flexible test head design and powerful "C" based test language.

The market for linear test equipment, a subset of the semiconductor test equipment market, is projected by VLSI Research Inc. and Prime Data to double to approximately $600 million by 1989 from the 1985 level of $300 million. The market growth for linear ATE results from the rising volumes and increasing complexity of linear devices produced. Attain is ideally positioned to capitalize on this market growth, while existing linear ATE suppliers will continue to be faced with overcoming the current problems in linear test. Competitive ATE equipment is based on dated architectures which limit its test capabilities and performance. To achieve the performance capabilities of Attain's system, competitors would have to redesign their present system architectures, thereby obsoleting the large software libraries and hardware fixtures written and built for their installed base of machines, which is their primary competitive advantage over a new market entrant. Attain believes it unlikely that competitors will soon redesign their system architectures, which would force them to cannibalize their installed base. The Company therefore expects to retain its technological advantage in the marketplace for the foreseeable future.

In August 1985, Attain placed its initial beta site unit in a large, predominantly military semiconductor manufacturer. Results to date have confirmed the improved accuracy, higher throughput and reduced test development time in a high volume, production environment.

Based on an analysis of existing and projected competitive test systems, and projected growth in the linear ATE market, Attain has projected the following sales, earnings and market share:*

Attain has assembled outstanding professionals in design, engineering, development, manufacturing, finance, and sales and customer service capable of building Attain into a significant supplier of linear test equipment and of developing important follow-on products. With its experienced team,

---

*Certain sections of information were not included for proprietary reasons.

Attain will be well postured to capitalize from the next upturn in the semiconductor industry.

Attain is supported by a syndicate of six venture capital firms. The company has raised $X of financing for product development and market introduction. Attain has now raised second round financing of $X in working capital from existing and additional investors to fund the growth of the Company until Attain achieves a profitability and self sustaining cash position in mid 1987.

Chapter 3

The Business Plan—A Process, Not a Document

While the business plan is a key document in the process of finding venture capital, the most important element is the business planning process itself. Good business planning is absolutely essential to a successful business. The business plan is created as a repository for information derived from the planning process and as a means of allowing others to evaluate the process. So, what is it all about?

First, the business plan serves as a planning tool. Next, it serves as a tool to convince others to invest, and finally, it is a guide to operations. In the early stages of a business concept, the entrepreneur must assess the feasibility and the desirability of developing the proposed idea. The process of writing the plan forces the entrepreneur to objectively consider all of the elements that contribute to a successful enterprise and to quantify them for another person's review. It can be a time consuming process, taking up to six months to complete, but it is the most important thing you will ever do in building the business.

Once the plan is written, the entrepreneur frequently uses it to market his business to investors. Similar to the way in which a job seeker uses his resume to secure interviews with prospective employers, so an entrepreneur uses the business plan to secure interviews with prospective investors. Especially when there is no working prototype available to show potential investors, the business plan is the only tangible means of describing the nature of the business and projecting its success.

Finally, when the company is up and running, the business plan provides a guide for operations and a measurement of performance. In this capacity, the business plan serves as a meaningful overview, and it becomes the document that drives the budget and operating plans. How closely management can follow this guide is an indication of their professional abilities. Achieving critical milestones lends substantial credibility to management's understanding. It's important to remember that the business plan also serves as a document people will look back on to see where they expected to be and when.

THE BUSINESS PLAN AS A PLANNING TOOL

In its initial stages, the business plan is more useful as a process than as a document. Writing a successful business plan involves more than supplying prospective investors with a few facts and figures, a couple of graphs, and some resumes. The entrepreneur will need to consider such major issues as the quality of the management team, the climate of the marketplace and the competition, how the proposed business or product fulfills customers' needs, what the company's "distinctive competence" or "unfair advantage" is, and the company's estimated valuation. Through the discipline of committing ideas to paper, the entrepreneur has an opportunity to view his plans objectively, to focus in minute detail on every aspect of the venture, to challenge unexamined assumptions, and to make sure the various elements of the business fit together.

Most often, business plans that are written by management teams have a better chance of being funded. Such plans are the product of several different points of view and are more likely to cover all the bases.

In its earliest stages, the business plan also provides a vehicle for soliciting advice and comments from other professionals. Before sending the plan to venture capitalists or potential investors, an entrepreneur is wise to confer with other entrepreneurs, members of the financial community, accountants, attorneys, and bankers. Frequently, these professionals are excellent critics, experienced in reviewing business assumptions and asking appropriate questions. Generally, they are knowledgeable about the sources and requirements of venture capital financing. They are receptive to entrepreneurial ideas and often have time to meet, review plans, and recommend ways to make the plans more effective. These people will exercise their greater objectivity and think of things the entrepreneur has overlooked. They can offer counsel concerning the directions a new business might take and will suggest strategies and tactics necessary for building a more profitable enterprise.

At this stage of the business's development, an entrepreneur should incorporate professional comments into his plan, even if it means extensively rewriting parts of it. It is not unusual to revise the business plan several times, perhaps dozens of times, in response to the observations professionals offer. The business plan is a "living" document. It should change to reflect new information, changes in the marketplace, and changes in company management.

It is probable that in attempting to answer the key questions of a business plan, the entrepreneur will confront whether or not he should start the business at all. It is critical to distinguish between an interesting market play—a one-shot product with a limited lifetime in the marketplace—and the potential for establishing a commercially viable entity, one that is supported by a well-organized infrastructure and an expanding line of products. Many unique products and single market opportunities would better culminate in a licensing agreement with a large company, or in an arrangement that compensates the entrepreneur with royalties. Ultimately, one-time products lack the market potential or the substance to create an enterprise. In the process of preparing a plan, the entrepreneur often reaches the conclusion that his concept will not result in a viable company. In this case, the process of writing the plan is beneficial, because it frees the entrepreneur to develop other ideas for starting a business, or drives the entrepreneur to license the product, or to commercialize it in other ways. Not all products can build companies, nor are all companies viable for venture capital investment. Only a special few really make it through the process. However, if the entrepreneur thoroughly answers his own questions about the business, and the questions posed by those professionals who have reviewed the plan, it is likely he is developing a commercially viable entity.

From all of the above, it may be clear that the process of developing a business plan is not something an entrepreneur can delegate to someone else. Only he and members of his team know what the business must accomplish, what the schedule should be for important milestones, and how much funding is needed at each stage of development. Such decisions can't be made by a consultant or a freelance writer, for if the entrepreneur delegates writing the plan, he misses the benefits derived from engaging in the process. The person who develops the plan, in effect "owns" it, and understands best the factors that will make the business successful.

The entrepreneur must invest the necessary *sweat equity* it takes to put a plan together.

One of the first questions entrepreneurs ask about writing a business plan is "How long should it be?". The answer is that there is no prescribed length. The plan should fill as many pages as it takes to adequately describe the venture in a brief and concise manner. The quality of a plan is not in direct proportion to its length. In fact, if the plan is too long, it may suggest that the entrepreneur is confused about what are the critical components of the business. Or it may indicate a defensive posture, in which too much information is offered in an attempt to counter all skeptical responses. Of course, if the plan is too short, it will lack specificity about the nature of the business, its markets, and critical success factors. Regardless of length, a plan should be thorough, readable, and concise. A well-written plan will reflect the clarity of management's thought processes and their ability to communicate intelligently.

THE NUTS AND BOLTS—
WHAT A BUSINESS PLAN CONTAINS

The plan should also be well organized. Typically, business plans contain 12 basic sections that are usually presented in the following order:

Executive Summary
Table of Contents
Company Description
Market Analysis and Strategy
Technology and Research and Development
Manufacturing/Operations
Management and Ownership
Organization and Personnel
Funds Required and Their Uses
Financial Data
Administrative Considerations
Appendices or Exhibits

Each of these topics is discussed more fully below.

The Executive Summary

This is the most important part of the plan. As discussed in Chapter 2, it might be the only section the venture capitalist ever reads. It is the entrepreneur's first chance, and possibly only chance, to capture the investor's attention. Venture capitalists are deluged with business plans and look for any immediate reason to reject them and move on to the next one in the pile. Their time for studying a plan is limited. They may spend about only five minutes on their initial review and peruse the executive summary first to get a quick impression of the proposal's major thrust. Since less than 10 percent of the plans an investor reads passes the first review, the information the entrepreneur includes in the executive summary will determine whether or not the venture capitalist reads other sections of the plan. If he concludes he has no interest in any aspect of the proposal, he will either return the plan or trash it.

> In two to six pages, the summary draws a thumb-nail sketch of the business and emphasizes the key points of the plan. It positions the company by describing the basic product or service, and discusses which market needs the product fills. The summary says why the product is different from its competition and how it will succeed. It also introduces the management team, outlining the individual's relevant skills as well as any professional weaknesses and plans for correcting those weaknesses. It also briefly references financial projections for future years and provides a schedule regarding financial results. Finally, the summary should state the amount of funding the entrepreneur seeks and how he intends to put these funds to use. Because it is so comprehensive, the summary should be written last and after all the other difficult decisions are made. For more information about executive summaries, see Chapter 2, "How to Find Venture Capital."

The Table of Contents

If the executive summary piques the venture capitalist's interest, he will turn next to the table of contents to locate specific information. Venture capitalists usually flip through business plans to review the sections that are of immediate concern to them, especially information on the people, the markets, the competitive environment, and the company's distinctive competence. Including a table of contents will not only make the plan more accessible and streamline the review process, it will also function as an outline of the plan and help the entrepreneur to organize information under key headings. It is also a good idea to include a table of contents for illustrations and charts, if the plan contains these.

Most likely, a potential investor will turn first to the section describing the management team to determine whether the individuals possess the professional expertise and personal qualities required to build a company. The reader may then review the chapter regarding market strategy to learn whether a market for the product already exists, or whether one will have to be created. The reader will also want to learn how big the present market is and how large it is expected to grow. Also, what does the entrepreneur know about his competitors? Who are they, and what portion of the marketshare do they have? Usually, he will turn next to the section detailing the technology, the protectability of the technology, or the barrier to entry that technology or business presents. Finally, the reader will review the section on finances to determine how much money the company requires at what stages, what the potential return on investment might be, and what options he has for exiting the investment. He will also review this section to evaluate how sophisticated the team is; that is, how well they understand the financial considerations.

These sections of the plan are generally considered to be the most important, but venture capitalists emphasize key elements differently and establish their own priorities for reviewing a plan. Although the product of the proposed business is important, most venture capitalists feel that an outstanding management team is the primary consideration in any new enterprise. They also recognize that no matter how ingenious the technology, if it does not have a market potential, it will not sell. A competent management team will realize this before becoming too involved in a limited business concept.

Company Description

What is the nature of the business? This question can be more difficult to answer than might appear at first glance. If it takes an entrepreneur several pages to describe his company and his business, he may still be unclear about the precise nature of his business. The entrepreneur should be able to sum up the business in a paragraph—upon which he can elaborate. Frequently, while writing a plan, the entrepreneur will change his mind about the type of business he is developing. He may redefine the product so it appeals to a different or broader market, or decide to emphasize and develop an aspect of the technology or service he hadn't previously considered. Knowing what type of business the entrepreneur is about to enter and being absolutely clear on that point are critical to the success of the venture. Certainly, after writing this section of the plan, the entrepreneur will have a well-defined sense of purpose.

The company description should discuss the major product or services, and the product application. Prospective investors will review the business plan to determine the distinctive competence of the product, in other words, the chief factor that will account for its success. The product must bring something new to the marketplace, or fill a particular need that has gone unrecognized, or for technical reasons has not been manufactured until now. The product should have a unique feature that will give it a leg up on the competition. The plan should also mention why it is appropriate to introduce the product or service at the present time, and explain that "the window of opportunity" is now open. Here is a chance for the entrepreneur to exercise real salesmanship, since in this section he should clarify his objectives and give potential investors good reasons why he will succeed. Because all professional investors have excellent alternative investment opportunities, the entrepreneur must demonstrate that his chances for success are better than the venture capitalist's other investment alternatives. Therefore, it is important to describe the business's "unfair" advantage, that which distinguishes it from other products in the industry. Since the entrepreneur is probably about to enter a competitive field, successfully communicating his distinctive competence is vital.

Whether products that fit into an already existing market are more likely to receive financing than products for which a market must be created is an interesting issue. The necessity of creating a market adds extra risk to a venture, and even though the returns on such an investment would be high, investors are hesitant about such pioneering. (You know the definition of "pioneers" . . . they are the ones with arrows in their backs.) This does not mean to suggest that a bias exists toward financing "me too" products in already crowded fields, although products that offer a better solution to market needs always stimulate interest. Rather, in situations where markets presently don't exist and entirely new markets and distribution channels must be created, the success factor is more complex, but the rewards may be worth the risks. That is the venture capitalist's real question.

If the entrepreneur is writing a plan to obtain financing for a business already in existence, the company description should contain an historical analysis. This includes general information about the year in which the business was founded, a description of the founding team, and the organization's form; i.e., corporation, partnership, etc. If the company is incorporated, the history discloses information concerning the corporation's stock classes and the number of shares outstanding, as well as outstanding warrants or options. It should also discuss how equity is distributed, who has invested what amounts of capital in the business, etc. The history also describes existing products and discusses the general direction and progress of the company. In this situation, the real question is, is the company on track and doing what it is expected to accomplish? Or is it floundering and looking for money as a deferral on its way toward failure? All growing businesses need additional capital, so being defensive about needing additional capital is not the issue. Rather, this is the point at which to demonstrate that the management is and has been controlling the company effectively.

Market Analysis and Strategy

In all the talk about management teams and products, it is easy to forget that every business is market driven. The bottom line is making money, and that means selling the product or service. No matter how air-tight the technology/product, or experienced the management team, if a company usually doesn't dominate a segment of the market, it frequently cannot succeed. Business cannnot exist apart from the marketplace. What the entrepreneur understands about the market factors affecting his particular business will determine its success. Venture capitalists reading this section of the plan will be alert to the entrepreneur's level of understanding. A realistic assessment of the marketplace will indicate the entrepreneur's ability to make other kinds of business decisions.

In fact, the market analysis is probably the most challenging section to write. Not only is it lengthy, but in addressing the many issues in a market analysis, the entrepreneur may come face to face with the realization that the business lacks a critical element necessary for its success. Since this section covers so many different topics, it will be useful to divide it into six major subheadings.

The Industry Description and Outlook. What is the industry? How big is it now? How big will it be in five years? Ten years? What are its chief characteristics? Who are or will be the major customers? Specifically, are they FORTUNE 100, 500, or 1,000 companies, or are they small proprietorships? What are, or will be, the major applications of the product or service? What are the major trends in the industry? What changes are occurring inside and outside the industry that will effect the business?

Target Markets. What major segments will the business penetrate? The analysis of market segmentation is crucial, and major miscalculations are often made in this area. One of the most common errors is to assume that the number of customers is equally distributed and that the median equals the mean. If the distribution is not normal, 50 percent of the customers may not be above the average. If an "average-sized" customer can afford the product, this may only be 10 percent of the total customer base. Secondly, in many markets, 20 percent of the customers may represent 80 percent of the demand. Ignoring factors that prohibit penetration of this 20 percent may cripple the entire marketing effort.

Even very successful companies often have surprisingly low market shares. Consequently, market share assumptions should be realistic. A realistic market share assumption of 10 percent could really represent 50 percent if careful market definition and segmentation showed that only 20 percent of the assumed market "qualified" as potential customers. For instance, assuming that any business above the average size is a prime target, this situation could occur if careful analysis showed that only 10 percent, not 50 percent, of customers were above the mean.

Probably the most common single error is to assume the validity of a prediction about what the business will sell by gathering some general numbers on the size of the market, then projecting a market share. If an entrepreneur knows that he is entering a billion dollar industry, assumes he can safely have one percent of that market, and projects revenues of ten million dollars, he has failed to perform an adequate analysis. Venture capitalists are particularly wary of this kind of reasoning and are immediately tipped off to the entrepreneur's lack of experience or research. The real question is who will buy the product (and why)? What will competitors do? A bottom-up analysis based on projected sales to specific customers will be far more credible than an X percent of a Y-sized market. This means, the entrepreneur must pinpoint and describe specific niches, estimate their size, and determine what percent of those niches will be interested in the product. He must also be aware of the competitors' activities and compare his products with those of the competition. The entrepreneur should be clear in his definition of the business's products and services and accurate in estimates of the market potential of each product or service.

The entrepreneur's reasoning must be supported with detailed research, otherwise the analysis is unconvincing and probably wrong. He may wish to consider hiring outside consultants to collect data and develop the market analysis. Or he may be able to collect data from trade associations and state and federal government associations. For each major application, an entrepreneur should ask what are the requirements of the customer or regulatory agencies? What are the current ways of filling these requirements? What are the buying habits of the customer? What impact will using the product have on the customer? This question suggests some appreciation for user economics. For example, how much will it save the customer per year, and what return on investment will a customer derive? There are other impacts to consider, such as whether or not the customer will have to change habitual ways of doing things. Will the product necessitate buying other equipment, changing work habits, or modifying organizational structures? How will these segments and applications change over the next three to five years?

Competition. Even companies entering relatively new fields will compete with mature businesses that have greater resources. Most investors expect that the first few companies to create and enter a market will remain the industry leaders. Too many competitors in an industry reduce the venture capitalists' return on investment. Therefore, they are less willing to fund businesses that would be joining an already crowded marketplace—where five to ten competitors currently exist. If a new company hopes to succeed, it must overcome a variety of barriers to entry and establish its competitive advantage. This is as true for non-technical ventures as it is for high tech companies.

In order to achieve these goals, it is imperative that an entrepreneur understands his competition. This includes similar businesses who have not yet entered the market, especially when the market is young, dynamic, and subject to rapid change. How does the proposed business compare with other competitive companies? What competition exists in each product or service line? How does the product or service compare with others, (especially through the eyes of the customer)? Entrepreneurs should construct a matrix to compare products and pricing. What is the market share of each existing competitor? Does the proposed business threaten the major strategic objectives or self-image of the competition or just the financial results? How will the competition react? For instance, will it lower the price of its product, in an attempt to destroy that possible competitive edge, or will it outspend the proposed business in marketing and advertising? What leverage does the competition have on distribution channels and markets? Does the business interface with important, non-competitive equipment whose manufacturer might still be reluctant to support the product because of warranty, liability, or image considerations?

What are the new company's barriers to entering a particular market? And how difficult will it be for others to do what this company is doing? For instance, if the competition commands the loyalty of established customers and is readily identified in the marketplace, a newcomer will probably have to spend a substantial amount of money in advertising to create public awareness of its arrival and to differentiate itself from the competition. The expense of a large advertising campaign can present a barrier to entry for start-up companies with limited cash resources. Or, it may cost potential purchasers of the new product too much money to warrant making a change from the old one. Costs can be incurred not only by the actual purchase of a new system or product, but also by the necessity of retraining employees, the time associated with installing and testing a new system or product, and also by the purchase of any peripheral pieces of equipment.

Another barrier may exist in establishing distribution channels. For instance, if these channels already carry the competition's goods, a newcomer who wants to use such channels will have to sell distributors on the idea by giving them a price reduction, or some sort of incentive that will probably reduce profits for the new company. Furthermore, the competition may enjoy certain advantages that make it more difficult for newcomers to compete with them on an equal footing. These businesses may receive special government subsidies, or dominate access to important natural resources. Because they entered the market earlier, these companies may occupy the best locations, which have since become too expensive for newcomers. Again, because more established firms have years of experience in the business, their operations are often more efficient and produce goods at lower unit costs. They also have a demonstrated technology that is proprietary in nature. Finally, the federal government may limit a new business's activities, by imposing regulations or licensing requirements that restrict product development or control the delivery of a service. In meeting federal strictures, a new company can expend critical amounts of time and money.

Frequently, entrepreneurs maintain a static "snapshot" view of the marketplace and their competition, with unfortunate results. For example, after assessing the state of the market at a particular time, and taking a mental picture of it, an entrepreneur leaves to develop and complete his product. At a later date, he returns to the marketplace, only to discover it has changed. During his absence, the competition made substantial inroads, the customers' demographics shifted, and new solutions and alternatives to customer needs increased the competition. It is important to remember that markets are dynamic. Because they change, a picture of the market today will look different two years from now when the product makes its debut. The entrepreneur must remain aware of current developments in his industry.

Reaction From Specific Prospective Customers. The entrepreneur should talk with prospective customers to elicit their reactions, especially if the customers have tested a realistic prototype of the product or service. A synopsis of real life examples is persuasive. Entrepreneurs should remember that prudent investors will do their own due diligence, their own independent review of the business opportunity, before they invest. The opinions of customers or potential customers about the product are vital. Even if the product is new or exists in a new marketplace, it is possible to research who will buy it, for what purpose, and why.

As with all other sections of the plan, an accurate and honest assessment wins the respect of potential investors. An entrepreneur best serves his business when he correctly estimates the strength of the competition. Glossing over the facts results in a plan that cannot be used later as a guide for operations because its basic assumptions are wrong. And potential investors will hesitate to finance someone who is apparently out of touch with the marketplace. In the long run, underestimating the competition can only have a deleterious effect on the venture's development.

Marketing Activities. This section communicates an ability to translate a concept into a profitable reality. It outlines the steps management will take to hit the sales target, and it serves as a prototype for a detailed and long-term marketing plan the company will develop at a later time. It describes the marketing strategy in terms of who will do what needs to be done, and how they will accomplish it. Too often we hear the comment that "the product will sell itself." This is just simply not true for any product. Marketing strategy and understanding markets is the key.

How will distribution be handled—through a sales force or retail? What will be the geographical penetration—locally, regionally, nationally? Will the company market domestically or overseas? If the company is young, it may choose to sell to a narrow market on a national or international scale. On the other hand, management may prefer a gradual rollout of the product, selling it on a regional level in stages, and then expanding the base. What arrangements can be made for field service or product support?

How is sales appeal rated? Sometimes it's a good idea to test the market in various areas to assess consumer reaction to the product. Will the business benefit from some sort of promotional assistance, such as advertising, public relations, and attendance at trade shows? If management has selected a firm to assist with product promotion, the potential investors will want to know whom.

How will the pricing be structured? This is one of the most important decisions the entrepreneur will make. If the price is too low, the company has a restricted buffer zone in which to work in situations where things cost more than planned. Costs are often underestimated, and customers are less accepting of price increases than they are of price reductions. It is a mistake to design a product superior to the competition's and then tell the venture capitalists that management plans to undersell it. Investors will wonder if the entrepreneur is an inept salesperson and therefore unable to sell the product for its worth. The pricing must make the product competitive in the market, and generate profits for the company. Is demand pricing or cost-based pricing favored? Will there be volume discounts, and how will pricing change over time? How does the pricing compare with that of the competition and how will they react to the pricing?

Finally, the entrepreneur must determine his priorities among the segments, applications, and marketing activities. The limited human and financial resources in a new venture prevent the business from being all things to all people, regardless of the opportunities.

Selling Activities. How will the entrepreneur identify prospective customers? He should consider not just the companies, but the relevant decision-makers who can spend money on the product, either discretionary or budgeted funds. How will he decide whom to contact and in what order? In most markets, there are the innovative companies, who adapt early and set trends. Then there are the followers. How does the entrepreneur get to the early adaptors, the innovators who buy and lend their credibility to the product? What level of selling effort will be necessary? How many salespeople? And with what efficiency; i.e., how many calls per salesperson? What conversion rates will the entrepreneur be able to obtain? For instance, how many calls per demonstration, and how many demonstrations per sale? How long will each of the above activities take in person-days? In elapsed time? What will the initial order size be? What is the likelihood and size of repeat orders? Based on the above assumptions, what is the sales productivity of each salesperson? What is the commission structure for the salespeople? Does the selling cycle take months because of budget or approval requirements by buyers?

Does it have increasing or decreasing rates for exceeding quota? What will the average salesperson earn per year, and how long will that person have to wait to receive commissions? Will they receive a salary? What are the sales cycle milestones? Finally, what evidence will the entrepreneur have to support his answers to the estimates above?

Technology or Product Innovation, and Research and Development

Next, we will discuss the essence and status of the current technology. What is the basic idea? Is there a prototype? Has the entrepreneur conducted a small production run? What is the company's patent or copyright position? How much is patented or copyrighted? How much can be patented or copyrighted? How comprehensive and how effective will the patents or copyrights be? Is it smart to obtain patents or copyrights? Which companies have technology that is superior or equal to the entrepreneur's venture? Are there additional means of protecting the technology, such as secrecy or speed in putting out the product or service?

The real question is whether or not patents are an effective means for protecting a small company's technology. Quite often they are not. Ironically, patents may provide a blueprint for another company to modify and create its own version of the same product. Large companies with substantial resources can afford to hire personnel to review recently issued patents and adapt them, thus saving time and money on research. Also, if a small company decides to defend its patent, it must be prepared to handle large litigation costs. Usually, small businesses do not have sufficient funds to pay the legal fees that protecting their patents incurs.

Most often, companies protect their technology by depending on trade secrets, by building the secret ingredient for success into the technology itself. This creates a "barrier to entry" that is stronger than any legal pronouncement. An entrepreneur must carefully decide in how much detail he will discuss the technology with investors. It may be wisest to describe the product without dissecting every step of its production. This compels potential investors to focus their diligence and investigative efforts on the marketability of the product, which is appropriate since many investors are not equipped to make an investment decision based principally on their expertise in a technical field. Ironically, investors are wary of a product that is simple enough to be completely and readily understood, because it may have a low barrier to entry, and therefore easily replicated by the competition.

What new technologies or scientific approaches exist now that may become practical in the next five years? What factors limit their development or acceptance? What influence might they have on the technology being developed or its marketplace? One common pitfall here is to compare the technology the entrepreneur is working on now and will have on the market in a year or two with that which competition has now. Instead, the entrepreneur will want to compare what he will have by the time he is in the market with what others will have then. The development of new technologies is dynamic and change is accelerating. Notwithstanding the "lifetime" a technology may be granted through patents and other forms of legal protection, the economic or useful life of many products is short. Science is moving faster than ever, and ironically, technologies become obsolete even before products embodying them can be prepared for the marketplace.

What are key research and development activities and related milestones and risks? What new products, preferably derived directly from first generation products, does the entrepreneur plan to develop to meet changing market needs? Are there any regulatory or approval requirements, such as U/L, EPA, FDA, or FCC?

Manufacturing/Operations

An efficiently managed operation is vital to a company's success. How will the entrepreneur accomplish production or conduct service operations? There are two points to consider in answering this question. First, how much will he do internally and by what methods? Second, how much will he accomplish through subcontracts, both initially and after one or two years?

What production or operating advantages does the entrepreneur have? What is the nature and quality of the manufacturing facilities? What is the present capacity for production or operations? This part of the plan describes both plant and office space, equipment and machinery, storage areas, and land. If the business is in the start-up stage, the entrepreneur must discuss how and when he will obtain facilities, whether he will lease or purchase them, and what percent of the financing will be applied toward setting up shop. How will these facilities be expanded and at what cost? What is the timing for expansion activities, and are there tax implications? What are the critical manufacturing parts? Are any of these parts "single- or sole-sourced," or are there backup vendors? What are the lead times of these parts? Where is the best geographical location for manufacturing the product—is it more cost effective to move production to an offshore site? Is labor readily available, and what are the wage rates? Will labor have the skills to manufacture the product, or will it be necessary to train the workers? Do unions have a significant impact on production? What is the distance between the manufacturing site and the customers, and how does the business transport its goods? How do the state and local laws, taxes, and zoning ordinances effect production? If parts of the manufacturing are subcontracted, how will management choose the subcontractor; i.e., according to its proximity or through bids?

How much of the production process will the entrepreneur subcontract? In other words, what is his "make or buy" strategy, and with what documentation does he support his decision? What are the standard costs for production at different volume levels and how do overhead, labor, the price of materials, and purchased parts effect production costs? What are the capital requirements for manufacturing? How are costs recovered and over what period of time? How does the business set standards for quality and production control? How does it manage inventory?

Management and Ownership

One of the industry standards is that venture capitalists or other potential investors "invest in people." No matter how receptive the market, or how unique the product, it takes a good team to start a company and manage it through its various phases of growth. Although the presence of a key individual may be important, good management teams win. The team must be complete, comprised of a marketing expert, a financial manager, someone competent in the development of the technology or the product, and a person who understands manufacturing and production requirements. The people on the team should be personally different from each other and represent different strengths. Frequently, new management teams are formed on the basis of friendship. The logic is that good friends should be good business partners; however, good friends are so because of the similarities they share, and it's common for these arrangements to include, for instance, one too many engineers.

A young management team may have trouble finding a person to round out the group. If the venture capitalists have confidence in the existing team members or the technology, they will often help the entrepreneur find appropriate additional members. The venture capitalists may agree to invest in the enterprise on the condition that they can place someone they know and respect on the management team.

Investors prefer to finance people who have had prior experience in the same industry as the proposed venture, since those skills will be translated directly to the new business. The venture business is high risk, and investors look for all possible reassurances that the deal they finance will succeed. Backing a marketing specialist for a microprocessor venture who has experience in the microprocessor industry makes more sense than backing someone who previously sold refrigerators.

Venture capitalists also prefer to back people who have good track records. This seems like an obvious point, but the competition for venture capital money is extreme and the better track records win respect.

Entrepreneurs who have started and developed successful companies in the past are likely to receive funding for new ventures on the basis of their previous work alone. Sometimes their business plans sketchily outline the type of product or service they are proposing, but knowing that an entrepreneur with a proven track record backs the idea is often sufficient proof to a venture capitalist. In lieu of experience, a young or novice entrepreneur will have greater success if his resume mentions accomplishments, good schooling, and an outstanding job history in work that relates to the challenges of the venture. Sometimes, great academic or scientific credentials are completely unrelated to the needs of the new business.

Venture capitalists look for people of high integrity. An effective partnership between entrepreneurs and investors depends heavily on the honesty of the people involved. Starting and running a new venture during its inherent times of crisis is challenging, and the investor/management relationship must be strong, built on mutual trust.

Who are the key managers? How will the company attract and compensate key people? For instance, will the company use stock or incentive bonuses? What salaries will members of management receive? If the company is a start-up, investors want to know that management is willing to receive moderate salaries at a time when the company has limited cash reserves. Has management made equity investments in the business or loans, and what are the amounts and the terms? What are the key managers' skills and, particularly, their experience, and how do these relate to the success requirement of the venture? Do members of the team require training to surmount any particular weaknesses? These issues require careful consideration for a couple of reasons. First, it is extremely important to differentiate between ownership and management roles, even when assumed by the same individuals. Second, it may be better to hire a person whose skills exceed the present job demand, because those capabilities will be required as the company grows. This is preferable to hiring someone who may provide a perfect job-match currently, but who will soon fall behind the curve in a fast-growth company.

In addition, what is the prospective employee's track record and how does this relate to the company's requirements? The most common problem here is failing to relate the team's capability to the success requirement of the business. For example, the chief engineer might be described as having a fine M.I.T. education and important-sounding job titles with sophisticated companies, but with no mention of work he has actually done. This information does not directly substantiate that he really could design the complex product necessary for the company.

What staff additions does the entrepreneur plan, when, and with what required qualifications? For example, the entrepreneur may not now have a candidate for the vice president of Finance position—or even need one immediately—but it is important to state the plans to support this function when required. Do any managers have outstanding "noncompete" agreements with previous employers? If so, the entrepreneur will want to get the opinion of counsel regarding the validity or applicability of these agreements.

Who is on the board of directors? Should the directors have specific credentials that qualify them to offer technical counsel and serve as advisors? Where do the investors belong in the board's structure? It's important to think ahead about the role of the board when the company becomes operational. It may be inappropriate to have certain early investors serve on the board if their potential for nonmonetary contributions is not substantial. It is also important to remember that it is easier to get members on a board than to get them off it.

Organization and Personnel

Since people and their talents often represent a company's real assets, how a business administrates human resources may directly effect its success. In the Silicon Valley and other high-tech centers, competition among companies for key employees is strong. There are plenty of opportunities for people to find employment with a competitor. How does a company hire and retain its key people? What compensation method will be used by type: salary, stock, profit-sharing, etc? While some companies offer stock options to upper level management, others motivate all employees by making stock options available to everybody from the president to the administrative staff. Often referred to as "golden handcuffs," monetary incentives are really only one aspect of retaining professionals. Recognition is also important. Does the company confer special achievement and merit awards, or allow its technical staff to publish and make presentations to colleagues in academia? What is the company's "corporate culture"? Does the company sponsor Friday afternoon beer bashes for all employees, or does it favor a more traditional corporate hierarchy? How many employees will the company need by type? Does the company create separate career paths for its technical staff and its management, or does it expect its scientists to assume management responsibilities and vice-versa? Companies that respect the different talents and strengths of various employees gain an advantage by maximizing the employees true fortes. This section should include sample organizational structures for formative years and thereafter.

In this section, the entrepreneur will also want to consider who are the current stockholders, and how many shares does each own? Remember to include comments about options and related prices. While it may be necessary or expedient to permit investment by many small and/or unsophisticated investors, their presence may cause concern among professional investors or headaches or diversion of management effort during the evolution of the company. Also, what is the amount of stock currently authorized and issued?

Funds Required and Their Uses

This section of the business plan tells potential investors how much financing the entrepreneur needs and at what times in the company's development. How much money does the entrepreneur require now? How much will be required over the next five years, and when will it be required? What would the scenario be if the entrepreneur got twice the amount of funding he seeks—or half the amount of funding he requested? How will these funds be used? What portion of the funds are expected to be raised from debt sources rather than equity? The entrepreneur should build buffers into his cash request and outline his plans to defer payments of certain deferrable items, such as taxes and perhaps capital outlays, and so retain cash for the company's operating use.

Although the process of valuating a company will be discussed in Chapter 5, "Negotiating the Deal," it should be noted here that the price management places on the company says something about its level of knowledge and experience. Quite often, inexperienced teams place too high a valuation on the business and compromise their credibility with potential investors.

What are the terms? If this document is being used in an initial financing, the entrepreneur should prepare a scenario for attracting required capital, approximate price per share and timing, and show the dilution of percentage ownership of the initial and subsequent investors. What additional funds will be needed and when? How attractive will the company be at the time it requires another round of financing? What is the anticipated valuation? What will be the financing alternatives then?

When will the company go public? Or will it ever? A major concern of professional investors is both the future value and liquidity of their investments. A company that is not profitable enough or large enough (e.g., less than $20+ million sales) within five years might not be of interest. This is also true if management indicates an unwillingness to go public for fear of losing control. Investors generally won't invest without knowing an "exit" opportunity exists. To what extent will valuations and exit options increase over the near term and long term?

Financial Data

If applicable, entrepreneurs must provide historical financial statements for the past three to five years, if the company has been in existence that long, including balance sheets and profit and loss statements as well as current financial statements. The plan must also include monthly or quarterly profit-and-loss and cash flow projections for the next three to five years, at least until the break-even point, and then annually to cover a five-year period. It is common to present monthly statements for the first year, quarterly statements for the next two years, and then for two or three annual periods. This section also includes balance sheet forecasts for the end of each year, capital budgets for equipment and other capital considerations, and the manufacturing/shipping plan.

Cash flow projections are an important part of the financial data because they indicate how much money will flow into and out of the business and at what times. Knowing this is crucial to timing rounds of financing, since in its early stages a company usually cannot finance its operations through cash flow, nor does the inflow coincide with outflow. Cash flow projections indicate when major capital financing is required, and they also provide a way to track the types of financing and the terms of repayment.

Profit forecasts depend heavily on correct estimations of sales and expenses. A company's profit projections will only be as accurate as management's estimation of its market share, the unit pricing, and the projected number of units sold. These figures are derived from an awareness of the markets, the competition's strength, customer preferences, and general industry trends.

The balance sheets tell investors what assets the business will require and what liabilities are created by financing those assets. Investors will review the balance sheets to determine debt/equity ratios, the amounts of available working capital, and how quickly inventory turns over. The entrepreneur may wish to project three different scenarios for the company's performance in a strong, weak, and moderate market environment.

An analysis should show the results based on two different debt versus equity assumptions with resultant interest expense, assuming the debt is viable. The break-even point should be clearly identified, as well as the market value of the company based on a price/earnings ratio of similar companies. What key assumptions has the entrepreneur made in his pro formas, and how good are these assumptions? This section is especially important. Potential investors will want a description of the company's accounting principles, and a discussion of the assumptions made about sales and market share, accounts receivable, R & D costs, state and federal taxes, interest and payroll expenses, and the costs of materials. These assumptions should reflect industry standards and, if not, specific justification must be given. Key considerations are whether these are "best-case" numbers, "worst-case," or something in the middle, which is preferred. The data should be based on several different assumptions to determine the reasonableness of the information. It is important to note, however, that too much financial information can be worse than too little. Each company must project those points it believes are most appropriate.

Sometimes the venture capitalist will challenge the entrepreneur's assumptions and ask management to prepare new financial models based on numbers the investor thinks may be most appropriate for the industry. In some ways, this request is also a part of the due diligence process—a test to see how well the entrepreneur thinks and can respond to the investor's request for a different set of financials. For instance, is the entrepreneur confused by the request, reluctant to make changes, or perhaps unable to generate new figures accurately? The kinds of assumptions management makes will also reveal how sophisticated their perceptions are about running a business. For example, if the entrepreneur thinks receivables can be collected in 30 days, the investor can safely suspect other assumptions may be unrealistic.

Administrative Considerations

Careful thought should be given to naming the new company. The name, especially for a new company, should reflect the major thrust of the business or be distinctive in some way. In addition, possible trademarks and service marks should be identified. A subsequent search by an attorney to see if the name or trademarks are available for use must be undertaken early, and if available, reserved.

Mention should be made here about confidentiality. The business plan is a confidential document that contains sensitive information. Entrepreneurs must keep in mind that, through a business plan, their proprietary ideas and information about the status of their company can be disseminated to competitors. Although these ideas must be disclosed to potential investors, the entrepreneur should stress to recipients of the plan that it is not to be forwarded to other readers unless the entrepreneur grants permission to do so. Therefore, it is important to control copies of the plan and document distribution.

Appendices or Exhibits

As they are required, resumes of key managers, pictures of the product or prototype, professional references, market studies, and articles from trade journals may all be included at the end of the business plan. However, the plan needn't contain a plethora of this kind of information since it can always be provided at the request of potential investors. Although opinion varies, we recommend against providing copies of the patents for two reasons. This inclusion makes it easier to breach the confidentiality of the plan. Secondly, investors probably lack the technical expertise and the time to decipher the patent's meaning and do not need to know about the product in such detail.

IMPORTANT POINTS TO REMEMBER

There are 10 essential points the entrepreneur should consider as he is developing the business plan.

1. Emphasize the distinctive competence or differentiating characteristic of the business. Since businesses are driven by markets,

the proposed business must reflect a market need, and the product must have a unique ability to meet that need.

2. Identify and then concentrate on the strategic thrust. No business can provide a product or a technology for everyone. It is important to identify a specific market niche. This comes with being familiar with the industry in general. How large is the industry and how will it grow in the next five to ten years? The industry itself has unique characteristics, and the entrepreneur will benefit from knowing the industry's major applications and trends. It is equally important to know something about the customers and competitors, the size of the competing companies, their market share, and their projected growth.

3. Validate top-down results through bottom-up analysis. For instance, a business plan predicts that a market is growing at thirty percent, and because the business is projected to occupy X percent of the market, the company's sales will be $X,XXX,XXX. This reasoning often appears in business plans, and is a common example of the faulty logic of a top-down analysis. In reality, if the projected market shares of all the companies in a particular industry were combined, the market for that industry would have to be many times larger than it actually is. It is more accurate to do a bottom-up analysis that shows how a company plans to get an anticipated market share, and why those plans will succeed in the marketplace.

4. It is wiser to err on the conservative side of an estimate. Typically, entrepreneurs assume they will garner 20 percent of a market share, but this is unrealistic to the point of being hyperbolic! Most start up companies should plan to attract only a small percentage of the market. Such conservativism will help in the long run, since the entrepreneur will design his plan for a more limited cash flow situation. He will be prepared to operate the company on that basis, instead of being surprised by a small cash flow that jeopardizes the health of the company. Anticipating a smaller cash flow, the entrepreneur is more likely to request enough funding from the venture capitalist to meet the real needs of the company.

5. Show how the investors are going to make their money. It is important to remember that those people who put money into a venture expect to take that money out for a substantial return on investment, one that is commensurate with the level of risk. The business plan is used to secure financing for only a limited amount of time. If possible, the

entrepreneur's company should be profitable and large enough to give sufficient liquidity that investors can be bought out in about five years. However, the length of investment time will depend on the investing philosophy of the venture capitalists. Some venture capital firms work to build a company for several years before realizing a profit, while other firms are less patient, hoping to liquidate their investment in a few year's time.

How will the investment be liquidated? The business plan should state if the entrepreneur intends to take the company public and in how many year's time. Another way to liquidate the venture capitalists' investment is by selling the company to a larger entity. The business plan should mention the names of the companies or corporations who would most likely be interested in making the acquisition. A third common method for liquidation is the buyback. The company's management agrees to gradually buy shares from the investors according to a schedule both parties previously approved.

6. Outline the critical milestones and important completion dates. When will the company's goals be met in research, manufacturing, and selling? Venture capitalists will be more willing to invest at later stages, if the entrepreneur meets the critical deadlines and milestones contained in the business plan. Successfully observing those dates instills confidence. Missing those deadlines signals problems to the venture capitalist, either in the way the company is being developed, or in the business plan itself. Perhaps the document's projections are unrealistic.

7. Assemble and present a talented and balanced management team. Despite their different investment strategies, most venture capitalists "invest in people." They carefully review the management team to ascertain that the personnel is in place to make a real company run. Good management is essential to building a successful company, and it typically includes a CEO with operating experience, preferably in the same industry as the proposed business, an expert in finance, a marketing expert, and someone experienced in manufacturing. A strong board of directors should round out the team, provide differing points of view, and act as a sounding board in discussions with management. Everybody should work effectively together, since venture capitalists will not fund a shaky management team.

8. Don't underestimate the company's capital requirements. Most businesses fail when they tumble into the reality gap of overestimated

profitability and underestimated capital needs. Unrestrained exuberance and absence of painstaking attention to detail create a company that limps into the capital market. Financing is most easily obtained when the business is an attractive candidate. Ironically, entrepreneurs have a greater chance of obtaining capital financing at a time when the company doesn't need it.

9. Never underestimate the competition. In the rapidly changing marketplace, nothing is status quo. The conditions under which business operates today, will undoubtedly be different tomorrow. How well the entrepreneur anticipates the competition's twists and turns will effect the profitability of his company.

10. Don't be a technological flash-in-the-pan. A single product does not a company make. A company is built with a line of products. Therefore, to grow and prosper, a company provides follow-on products for its market, or provides products or modifications that appeal to a broader segment, or even develops products that appeal to new markets.

BINDING THE PLAN

The last step in completing the business plan is to bind it for presentation. Generally, too much emphasis is placed on slick production values. Many expensively produced and bound plans contain proposals that will never receive funding. Similarly, a plan that is simply typed on paper and held together with a paper clamp may have buried within it the idea for a profitable enterprise.

Since venture capitalists receive so many plans, the entrepreneur should make sure his plan is clear and easy to read, on paper that cannot be erased, but is strong enough to endure some wear and tear. The binding doesn't have to be expensive, but it should hold firmly, such as a plastic spiral binding, or even a sturdy paper cover with brads for three-hole-punched paper. Since many printing and binding techniques are inexpensive, it is easy and advisable to give the business plan a professional appearance. If possible, the physical design of the plan should convey a feeling for the company's image, possibly with a logo placed on the cover. How much the entrepreneur wants to get involved in the more cosmetic processes depends on time and money. Of course, the plan should be free of any typographical errors that might suggest sloppiness, inattention to detail, or ignorance of grammar basics.

THE BUSINESS PLAN AS A MARKETING TOOL

Once the business plan is complete, it becomes the marketing tool through which an entrepreneur sells the most important product, the company, to the most important buyer, the investor. At this point, the business plan functions as a calling card, a way for the entrepreneur to introduce himself to the venture capitalist or funding source.

A plan that is selectively promoted has a better chance for financing than a plan that is mass-mailed or hawked at every street corner. The venture capital community is close-knit. If its members suspect a plan has been sent out in a mass mailing, the investor will wonder why no one else has invested in the plan and suspect it may not be a good one, or will feel that he gains no advantage by investing in an idea that is available to everyone.

WHAT VENTURE CAPITALISTS EVALUATE WHEN THEY READ A BUSINESS PLAN

As noted earlier, once the venture capitalist receives the plan, he will spend a limited amount of time reviewing it. Venture capitalists have different priorities for critiquing business plans. Some investors do not have the expertise to judge the proposed technology, but their experience with managing companies and their intuitions about people lead them to make successful investments based on their appraisal of management teams. Other venture capitalists feel that if the market is ready for a particular product, they can afford to take a risk with a less experienced management team. Still other investors are familiar enough with the technology in an industry to recognize an important product development that will fill an available niche in the market. However, all these elements count heavily, and venture capitalists will rarely invest if they have doubts about the strength of the management team, the market, the product, or if the valuations are inaccurately derived.

When a knowledgeable investor reads a plan, he will look for a few key indications that this proposal is a winner. First, does the company expect a rapid growth in its revenues and high profit margins in comparison to its competition? Does the company have, or project to have, a better than average return on equity? Such projections indicate that the company has potential. (On the other hand, does the balance sheet reveal that the company is highly leveraged? If so, the investor will be less likely to fund the proposal.) If the company is in a high tech industry, is it one of the first businesses to enter a field with strong market potential, and does it occupy a dominant position, or have the capability to do so? Investors will also compare the amount of capital the company allocates to research and development against annual revenues. Is the company's activity subject to government regulation, and if so how does that regulation affect timetables and profits? Finally, investors will be shy about funding a company that depends on one major client, since that client can always take its business elsewhere, leaving the company to scramble for new clients and maintain revenues.

THE FOLLOW UP

About 10 days after sending business plans to five or six prospective investors, the entrepreneur should call the investor or ask the professional who introduced him to place the call. If the venture capitalist hasn't yet reviewed the plan, he may be prompted to do so. If he expresses interest in the plan, a discussion with him will determine to what degree he is interested, what time frame he is considering, and whether there is a sufficient interest to suggest an initial meeting.

THE INITIAL MEETING

If the venture capitalist is interested in a business plan, after his reading of the executive summary or his review of the document, he will call either the entrepreneur or the professional who made the introduction, to set up an initial meeting, usually in the venture capitalist's office. At this point, the negotiations have really begun. The first impressions formulated during this initial meeting will significantly influence how the deal is conducted, and whether it will happen at all. It is the venture capitalist's first opportunity to learn about the entrepreneur as a person, to learn more about the business, and to begin discussions concerning the venture. At the same time, the entrepreneur has an opportunity to size up the venture capitalists and to confirm what his earlier research indicated. For both parties, the initial meeting should address such questions as, would we like to work together? Do we have common interests and goals, and are we motivated by the same desire to build a company? What steps do we need to take to begin the investment process, and what key issues must be resolved to move forward? The entrepreneur will also want to know how much time will it take to secure the venture capitalist's commitment, and what evidence will he have, along the way, to know that the venture capitalist is really interested?

During this meeting, the entrepreneur is expected to make a presentation that is about a half hour long. The presentation need not be elaborately produced, but it should be well organized. It is a good idea to bring drawings, photographs, or even working models of the product. Setting up a demonstration shows off the advantages of the product. The entrepreneur should assume that at the time of this first meeting, the venture capitalist has only a cursory knowledge of the business plan. He may have glanced briefly at it, or read only the executive summary. Because the presentation may be the entrepreneur's only chance to sell his business plan to this venture capitalist, the presentation should be rehearsed, polished, and genuine—not slick. This is the entrepreneur's opportunity to explain why the venture capitalist will make money on the venture.

The presentation should be clear and concise, giving the venture capitalist the most important information about the business. What is the nature of the business? What is the company's objective? What is its distinctive competence? This is an extremely important point, because the business must have a unique aspect that can be demonstrated to set it apart from the competition. Without this, the investors will be less likely to finance the proposal. Who are the members of the management team, and how do their strengths contribute to the venture? What is the potential market and the market climate? What are the financial milestones, and when will they be reached?

The entrepreneur should also discuss some of the downside risks or potential problems of the business. Because the process of forming a partnership with an investor necessitates complete disclosure, openess should be practiced from the very beginning of the relationship. Every business has built-in risks, and venture capitalists already know this. They will trust and respect an entrepreneur who is aware of the pitfalls and honest enough to point them out. Candidly discussing these potential problems tells the venture capitalist that the entrepreneur is sufficiently knowledgeable to recognize future concerns. In the presentation, entrepreneurs should suggest possible solutions and strategies for overcoming these problems, and solicit the venture capitalist's suggestions.

During the presentation, the venture capitalist and his associates may want to get some feeling for who the entrepreneur is as a person. Venture capitalists often work from a "gut instinct" about people and businesses. During the initial meeting, the investor will ask questions, both about the entrepreneur's own life and about technical and managerial issues related to the venture. Sometimes these questions will put the entrepreneur on the spot, perhaps by exposing a discrepancy in the entrepreneur's thinking about the business, or by uncovering an area in which he is technically deficient. Sometimes too, the venture capitalist will ask elementary questions or skip over an issue the entrepreneur anticipated discussing. If the issue is important enough that it could create problems in the future, the entrepreneur should introduce the subject at this meeting and then offer his solutions. The entrepreneur must be ready for anything and able to make a favorable impression by being knowledgeable about every aspect of his business plan. If the entrepreneur doesn't have all the answers at hand, he should try to establish another meeting time to give his responses. Above all, the entrepreneur will want to express his integrity and commitment for the proposed business.

It is important not to bog down in technical details. Dissecting the intracacies of the technology pulls the focus away from more important subjects. Generally, venture capitalists hire professional consultants to assess the technological feasibility of a new product. Initially, the venture capitalists are more interested in meeting the management and evaluating their talents for running a company.

During this meeting, the entrepreneur also has a chance to size up the venture capitalist. Does the venture capitalist know something about the industry the entrepreneur is about to enter, and has the venture capitalist had experience running a company? This will determine to what extent the venture capitalist can give "added value" to the enterprise and how effective he will be on a board of directors. Venture capitalists who have lost and made money managing companies have a real world appreciation for what works and what doesn't.

Does the venture capitalist have direct experience with companies in the same stage of growth as the entrepreneur's? Companies in different phases have different needs. Venture capital firms often specialize in businesses at a certain stage of development. The entrepreneur must confirm that potential venture capitalists match the requirements of the proposed business deal.

Is the venture capitalist a leader, that is, can he attract other venture capitalists to form a group of venture capital investors? Entrepreneurs should first approach a venture capitalist that is strong and experienced enough to attract a group of investors to support its cause. Does the firm have sufficient capital for follow-on investments that will be required, and are its members willing to invest the necessary amounts at the necessary times? Experienced investors know that more likely than not, a new business, especially one in the product development phase, will require more capital than originally estimated and plan for it.

How long will the venture capital firm retain its investment in the company? Do the two parties like each other as people? A venture capital deal lasts for years, so management and investors should have a basic rapport, or chemistry, that will support them the difficult times of growing a company.

The entrepreneur should feel free to ask questions about the firm's investment philosophy, and the background of the venture capitalist and his areas of expertise. It is especially important for the entrepreneur to get the names of portfolio companies and research these references. A good venture firm will have no qualms about sharing the names of other entrepreneurs in their portfolio who have similar businesses in similar stages of growth. If the firms represent successful companies, the chances are greater that the new business can also be a success.

The most important question this meeting addresses is, "Are we going to structure a deal?" Although it is highly improbable that the deal will actually be made by the end of the initial meeting, the venture capitalist has gathered enough information and impressions to decide whether or not he's interested in pursuing the venture. In the course of preparing the financial projections for the business plan, the entrepreneur will have formulated some idea of the amount of capital the company will need and how much equity he is willing to surrender. The entrepreneur should discuss this, but should not surrender on issues that could eventually become important later. Discussions about valuation should only give the investor a general idea to confirm that the entrepreneur is considering a price that is reasonable. Formal negotiations develop as the due diligence process unfolds. During the initial meeting, the entrepreneur and the venture capitalist should draw up a calendar of activities and deadlines that will progress toward making an investment.

What if the venture capitalist is not interested in the venture? Entrepreneurs should listen for any suggestions that might be hidden in a gentle refusal. Even a ngegative response offers the possibility of learning something new that will help to improve the venture. If possible, the entrepreneur should clarify exactly what objections the investor has. If several different investors voice a similar concern, the entrepreneur knows he must change something about the business, and he may be able to reach an agreement with the investors that once certain conditions are met they will take another look at the proposal.

THE BUSINESS PLAN AS GUIDE TO OPERATIONS

There is a third major function of a business plan as a guide to operating the company. If the entrepreneur wrote it with sufficient thought and research that the assumptions and projections are accurate, it can be used as a guide to operate the company during the initial stages, and to develop the more detailed budgets and operating plans. We talked earlier about the importance of meeting the goals and milestones outlined in the plan. A good plan will also provide the blueprint for accomplishing those milestones, since they result from the steps leading up to those points. The business plan should include enough detail that the entrepreneur can refer to it periodically.

If the company falls short of its goals, there may be a timing problem. Perhaps the entrepreneur expected the business to develop faster than it can, given industry standards and averages. Perhaps the business is developing slowly because of operating problems that are created or unskillfully handled by management. If the business develops faster than anticipated, maybe the entrepreneur's projections were too conservative. If the company is not meeting its projected goals at the proper time, the investors will probably wonder what else may be incorrect about the business plan. Consequently, monitoring and evaluating company performance according to standards outlined in the plan are good ways to measure managerial capability. The conclusions gained from this process will effect the level of investor interest in future rounds of financing.

Chapter 4

Due Diligence

The process by which a venture capitalist investigates an entrepreneur, his management team, and his new venture is called *due diligence*. Since most new ventures are investigated with some degree of thoroughness, it is important that the entrepreneur be familiar with the due diligence process so that he can prepare for it; however, due diligence is a fluid process, like so many other aspects of finding venture capital financing. Although there are no hard and fast rules, each venture capital firm will have its own procedures and standards.

Very positive things can come from the due diligence process, one of which is a revised and improved business plan that represents improved chances for success; however, if the venture capitalist finds misrepresentations or discrepancies in what the entrepreneur has said or in the business plan, it is conceivable that the deal will be dropped. The entrepreneur should not oversell, nor should he omit important information about himself, his management team, his product or service, the market, his competition, his successes and his failures. The entrepreneur should make his presentation and business plan as accurate as possible because his chances of succeeding in the due diligence process are far greater than if he hedges.

The investigation may take four to six weeks or longer—and sometimes due diligence can take a shorter period of time. It is wise for the entrepreneur to assist the venture capitalist in any way he can throughout the investigation. Before the due diligence process begins, the entrepreneur should be sure that 1) he wants to do business with this particular venture capitalist; 2) the potential terms of any agreement are generally satisfactory to both parties, especially in terms of the approximate valuation; and 3) both parties understand and agree to a timetable for the completion of the process, and ultimately to the finalizing and signing of an agreement, including when and how the entrepreneur's company will receive the funds. Due diligence takes various forms, from informal initial inquiries to detailed analysis and corroborations, so the entrepreneur shouldn't be too concerned about nailing down all the details. What is important is that both parties wish to proceed.

In a typical case, however, there are a number of steps the venture capitalist takes when investigating the entrepreneur, his management team, his business and his industry. Let's look at these steps to see how the entrepreneur can best prepare for them.

THE MEETING BETWEEN THE VENTURE CAPITALIST AND THE ENTREPRENEUR

As discussed in Chapter 3, the first step to being funded is for the entrepreneur to meet with the venture capitalist. He can meet with him alone or with his management team. Basically, the purpose of this meeting is for the venture capitalist to get to know the entrepreneur and for the entrepreneur to get to know the venture capitalist.

The entrepreneur will want to bring his business plan, any background material he may have on himself and each member of his management team, any information he may have about his company, his industry and his specific market. It is during this meeting that the venture capitalist may decide to either pursue the venture or to drop it.

It is essential that the entrepreneur understand everything in his business plan. The venture capitalist will want to know that the entrepreneur is in control of his firm and that he has knowledge of every facet of his business. He may want to know everything about the entrepreneur from his high school days to the present, what he has done academically, in the community, and in business. He may want to know if the entrepreneur has a stable personal life and what his plans are for the future, for his business, and for himself and his family. He may want to know if his family is aware of the sacrifices he will have to make to develop this company and if they are behind him and his efforts.

The entrepreneur must be candid about his background and his abilities. Every aspect may be checked, so he must be quite certain of his facts. The entrepreneur does not want the venture capitalist to feel that he has misled him just because the entrepreneur forgot to mention something, or because he left out any part of an explanation. If the entrepreneur finds that he cannot answer a particular question and he has brought his management team to the meeting, he may want to indicate that a member of his team can best answer the questions and have him do so. The entrepreneur can later embellish the manager's answer. If the entrepreneur uses his managers wisely, the venture capitalist will get a clear picture of how he and his team operate.

It seems like a small thing, but being open and honest in this first meeting is the only way for the entrepreneur to succeed. Everything he says, every document he brings, and every representative with whom he is associated may be researched. The venture capitalist wants to know he can trust the entrepreneur because problems always arise in the due diligence process. If the venture capitalist trusts the entrepreneur, he is less apt to jump to conclusions and, therefore, less apt to kill the deal over a small misunderstanding.

ON-SITE TOUR OF THE ENTREPRENEUR'S BUSINESS

Frequently, the venture capitalist will visit the entrepreneur's place of business. (Of course, this step could not be taken if the company were in a conceptual or seed stage.) The venture capitalist will learn everything he can about the entrepreneur's business. Although most venture capitalists invest in businesses with which they have experience, each business is different and it is this difference that the venture capitalist wants to learn about and to understand. Many of his or her questions may seem elementary. The entrepreneur should take the time to answer each one. Many of the questions will center on the uniqueness of the product, the manufacturing process, the delivery system, the service system, the marketing program, the financial stability, and the culture of the entrepreneur's firm.

It is advisable for the entrepreneur to begin by walking the venture capitalist through his operation from the receiving of raw materials to the shipping department where the final product is packaged and crated for transport to his customers. The entrepreneur should take the time to walk through his operation before the venture capitalist arrives to refamiliarize himself with every process and every employee. The dry run will make him far more effective when he takes the venture capitalist through himself.

It is also a good idea for the entrepreneur to tell his employees that the tour will take place and that they might be asked questions about their job, the managers, and the company. The entrepreneur should explain the need for them to be open and honest and to answer the venture capitalist's questions as best they can.

WHAT THE VENTURE CAPITALIST WANTS TO KNOW WHEN HE VISITS THE ENTREPRENEUR'S BUSINESS

It may seem redundant to the entrepreneur, because he has already answered many of the venture capitalist's questions when he met with him at his office, nevertheless he should answer all his questions again giving as much detail as possible.

Here are some of the questions venture capitalists most frequently ask of entrepreneurs and their new venture:

- How was the business started?
- How was the product or service created?
- From where did the entrepreneur get the idea?
- What is unique about the product or service? What are the barriers to market entry?
- Does the entrepreneur have a patent, trademark, or copyright on the idea?
- What is this company's competitive advantage?
- Who owns the product, service, or company and in what percentage?
- Has the entrepreneur obtained any financing and from whom and how much?
- How much of the business do other people own?
- Did the entrepreneur have to take out any bank loans?
- How big a market does the business have? How big will the market share be in five years?
- What percentage of that market can the entrepreneur realistically capture?
- Who are the customers?
- What do they think of the product?
- Who is the competition?

- Who are the suppliers?
- Do the entrepreneur's suppliers own any of the company?
- Does the entrepreneur offer a service? If so, how good is it and what do his customers think of it?
- What does the entrepreneur think of his employees?
- What does the entrepreneur's employees think of him?
- Do the entrepreneur's employees belong to a union?
- If the entrepreneur's employees belong to a union, is he on good or bad terms with them?
- What does the entrepreneur think of his management team?
- What does the entrepreneur's management team think of him?
- What additional managers will be required? When and where will they come from?
- How often does the inventory turn over?
- How many orders does the business have? Does it have a backlog?

Also be prepared for some hard-hitting personal questions:

- Is the entrepreneur honest?
- Why does the entrepreneur think he is the right person to run this company?
- What are the entrepreneur's weaknesses?
- What is the entrepreneur's background? From where does he come?
- Is the entrepreneur willing to replace some key executives?
- Does the entrepreneur have a stable personal life?
- Does the entrepreneur's family realize the commitment he is making? Are they ready to cooperate?
- What is the entrepreneur's commitment to this company?
- Who in this company cannot the entrepreneur trust?
- What are the entrepreneur's personal goals?
- What does the entrepreneur do when he is not working?
- What are the entrepreneur's strengths?

Venture capitalists generally agree that entrepreneurs share some basic characteristics that distinguish them as winners:

Age

The average age of most entrepreneurs is from 25 to 35, yet investors will fund entrepreneurs with good track records who are in their 50s or more. The key qualities venture capitalists look for are experience, initiative, and the willingness to work hard. If the entrepreneur is any younger than 25, venture capitalists may feel the entrepreneur is too inexperienced; if he is any older than 40, the entrepreneur may have had experiences that might prevent him from taking the necessary risks required in managing a new venture. Thus the age range from 25 to 35 is considered the "hungry years," or the years in which the entrepreneur is sufficiently motivated to grow a company.

Education

Today's entrepreneur is well-educated. He usually has a college degree—frequently advanced degrees. In the late 1890s and early 1900s, an entrepreneur could launch a business with little more than a grade school or high school education. While this may be true still for some businesses, these types of individuals rarely attract venture funds. The venture capitalist is looking for the best and the brightest. During the due diligence process, the entrepreneur's background is thoroughly checked. The venture capitalist looks for educational degrees in a related area of expertise, whether it is undergraduate or graduate work, and any specialized education the entrepreneur may have received. Many venture capitalists believe that success in school is a good barometer of success in business, and they may even inquire about the entrepreneur's gradepoint average and extracurricular activities.

Experience

The venture capitalist looks for entrepreneurs with 5 to 10 years or more of successful business experience, preferably in a field directly related to the business for which he is seeking venture financing. A good track record is one of the most important factors venture capitalists look for; in many cases it determines the first cut when the venture capitalist reviews new ventures. Venture capitalists aren't looking so much for scientists with impressive academic credentials, or executives who've held big management jobs. Instead they want people who have experience building companies, people who have successfully put together all the elements of a company and made it run.

Integrity

A mutual trust must develop between the entrepreneur and the venture capitalist, or the deal won't happen. This shared feeling of integrity must survive throughout the interview process and the investigations that are necessarily part of due diligence. If the venture capitalist discovers a misrepresentation, made either in conversations with the entrepreneur, or in the business plan, he may drop the deal. It is therefore best for the entrepreneur to be scrupulously honest in all his statements and plans.

Intuition

There is a subtle area of knowledge that all venture capitalists look for in the ideal entrepreneur. This is the awareness the entrepreneur has about his competition, the market, the future of his industry, and where his business fits into the big picture. It is not enough for the entrepreneur to know just his own company. A venture capitalist will look for the entrepreneur who also has intuition, a special insight that will help the company creatively through the hard times and to capitalize on new opportunities.

High-Energy

Because starting a business entails long hours and hard work, entrepreneurs must have high energy levels, and successful entrepreneurs have learned how to channel their energy to maximize productivity. An entrepreneur cannot dilute his or her energy by attempting to control every aspect of business. He must concentrate on those areas in which he excels and delegate other tasks. High-energy translates into the now-famous concept of *sweat equity*. The real "sweat" the entrepreneur and his management expend for the company is, in one sense, more valuable than money.

Motivation

Because starting a business is a rocky road, an entrepreneur must really want to do it, and usually more than anything else in the world.

He must be motivated by his vision of running a successful company. Successful entrepreneurs are winners because they are driven to achieve. The process of finding financing, in itself, is sufficiently arduous that it often weeds out the faint-hearted from the truly dedicated.

Leadership

The entrepreneur of a new venture assumes responsibility for his investors' capital, for the future of the business, and for the lives of his employees. He must have the necessary leadership qualities to make sure the job gets done. Can he motivate his employees and management team, give them directions they can follow, and instill a vision of the company's future? Is the entrepreneur willing to be ultimately responsible? What type of culture is he creating?

Management Ability

Entrepreneurs are innovative and serve as the driving force behind new ventures, but too often they are not experienced managers. At some point in the company's development, the venture capitalist may be compelled to replace original members of the management team with more seasoned players. As you might expect, this can be difficult and painful, and venture capitalists would rather avoid it. The investors' assessment of the entrepreneur's management skills can make or break a deal. It is important for the entrepreneur to realistically assess his management skills before he contacts a venture capitalist. If he feels he needs a strong general manager to back him up, he should hire, or locate, one before he starts to look for venture capital, or he should consult with the venture capitalist and other advisors and request help in recruiting a strong manager.

Attitude

An entrepreneur must have a positive attitude in order to achieve his personal goals, as well as the goals of his company. The venture capitalist needs to know that the entrepreneur is truly sold on the company and its future. And he needs to know that the success of the company is the entrepreneur's primary goal. A positive mental attitude is extremely important because it takes years for a company to grow and ultimately succeed. If the entrepreneur is not an optimist and committed to the venture, it will be difficult for him to lead his management team through the hard times the company will encounter.

Risk Taker

An entrepreneur is a risk taker. He is the one who stands to gain or to lose the most in any new venture. He puts himself on the line, commiting his time and resources. As a risk taker, the entrepreneur is a special individual in the business community. If successful, he is respected for his innovation, management skill, and creativity. The risks he takes bring new products and services to our economy.

Goal Oriented

An entrepreneur must have focus and a list of specific goals that he wants to accomplish within a given time frame. He does not understand the word "no." Instead, he understands that small achievements add up to a major achievement, and this is what he wants: the big success. A good entrepreneur will be willing to sacrifice nearly everything to achieve his established goal.

Innovative Problem Solver

Good new ventures offer creative solutions to old problems. The value of an innovative technology or service is its ability to give an answer, or to provide a new way to do something more efficiently. The venture capitalist sees the entrepreneur's role as being the catalyst for creating new developments in all areas of business.

Realist

Most entrepreneurs are positive thinkers. They know what they want, and they believe they will get it if they are smart enough and if they work hard enough. While venture capitalists share in that dream, they also want to back entrepreneurs who are realists, who understand that starting a new business is tough, and that most companies do not live up to expectations. If in his professional experience, an entrepreneur has confronted and overcome problems, he will have a more realistic assessment of his own capabilities and those of his management team. He knows the odds, yet is excited about taking a measured risk.

Capable of Living With Ambiguity

Starting a new venture is difficult at best, and the entrepreneur has to be able to live with a high degree of ambiguity. To begin with, finding financing is uncertain. If the company is a start-up, usually its product has not proven itself capable of capturing a large portion of the market. The size of the company may greatly increase in a very short period of time, creating a chaotic atmosphere in which the future looks bright one day and gloomy the next. At some point, the management team may be totally replaced, and the structure of the company may change. New competitive products will be introduced, and the market can shift from the time funding is first sought to when funding is actually received. Everything is tentative within the dynamic paradigm, and the best entrepreneurs have learned to live with this uncertainty, and, in fact, thrive on it.

Tenacity

Anyone who has tried to raise venture capital will tell you to "stick with it." Raising venture capital usually is a long and arduous process of meetings, phone calls, presentations, interviews, facility tours, and meals. The venture capitalists are keenly aware of the entrepreneur's needs, but there is a good reason why the system takes so long and is so highly selective: because it takes years to build a successful company. The venture capital process is difficult because, over the years, venture capitalists have found that only the really worthwhile companies pass the test. Venture capitalists sift through the available ventures until they find a solid candidate. Only those entrepreneurs with the best company, the best business plan, and the best management team receive funding. And the only way the entrepreneur can expect to be among those who do receive funding is by "sticking with it." Not only is it important to have tenacity during the funding process, it is equally important to exercise that quality throughout all phases of the company's growth and development.

Knowledgeable

The venture capitalist is looking for an entrepreneur who knows his business so well that he can anticipate certain problems, predict how the market will respond to new products and services, and know when the market is changing. The venture capitalist expects the entrepreneur to understand the manufacturing process, distribution, marketing, sales and service, finance—every aspect from the start up to the delivery of the product to the customer.

MEETING THE ENTREPRENEURS' EMPLOYEES

If the venture capitalist is to get a realistic picture of the company and its employees, the entrepreneur should discuss with his employees the investor's visit. The entrepreneur should explain the importance of the visit and try to answer any questions the employees might ask about what they should do or say. The entrepreneur should make it clear that neither the company nor their jobs are on the line, and that many other prospective investors will be taking a similar tour.

The entrepreneur should not put words in his employees' mouths. The venture capitalist will want to see that the entrepreneur's employees like their jobs, like the company, and believe in the entrepreneur, his management team and his product or service. Only honest answers given by the entrepreneur's employees to his questions will give the venture capitalist confidence.

MEETING THE MANAGEMENT TEAM

Entrepreneurs often pick friends, relatives, and investors as their key executives. The venture capitalist knows this. He also knows that with an infusion of capital the company will be growing rapidly and that the present management team may have to be replaced with qualified professionals. If the entrepreneur has picked friends, relatives and investors for his top management posts, he too should be aware of the possibility of a need for a change. If the entrepreneur feels that the people he has hired for these top level management posts are not qualified, he should let the venture capitalist know this before he visits the entrepreneur's business.

The best procedure for the entrepreneur to follow is to let his key managers demonstrate their knowledge and expertise to the venture capitalist. This can be accomplished by setting up meetings between the venture capitalist and each of his managers. Without the entrepreneur's presence and guidance, the venture capitalist will quickly draw his own conclusions about each manager.

After the venture capitalist has met all the managers, it is advisable to set up a meeting so that the venture capitalist can ask questions of the whole team. This will enable him to see how well the management team works together and where its strengths and weaknesses lie.

The venture capitalist will be particularly interested in the CEO or operations manager (if he is not the entrepreneur), the marketing/sales director, the people in charge of manufacturing and technology or product development, and the financial manager. These are the key positions in any firm, and the venture capitalist will look carefully at these managers to determine whether he will have to replace any of them.

As is true for entrepreneurs, management teams also embody certain characteristics that earmark them for success.

Relevant Business Experience

Each individual on the team should have successful experiences that are relevant to the company's endeavor. They should demonstrate a history of increased sales, productivity or efficiency, regular promotions, and their past income and perks should reflect their successes on the job. Often members of the management team are drawn from larger companies, but success in small companies is very different from success in big companies. Therefore, it is wiser to look for creative thinkers who show a willingness to work hard, than to find someone who has a history of delegating tasks to a large staff. The venture capitalist will study the managers' backgrounds. He will check their references and contact former employers to get a solid idea of the strengths and weaknesses of the team.

Commitment

The venture capitalist is looking for personal commitment to the venture from every member of the management team. This commitment can be ideological or financial. Naturally, a financial investment made by a manager to the venture is an excellent way of demonstrating belief in the company. This does not always exist, though, so the venture capitalist relies on personal interviews, the track record of each manager since joining the company, and the recommendations of the entrepreneur.

Balanced Management Team

A great entrepreneurial truism is "superstars don't win . . . teams win." No matter how skillful a player is, he cannot carry the game alone. In high technology companies, the management team may be led by a technological wizard, but he will need equally strong support from people in the financial, marketing, and production sectors if the company is to succeed. If any department is weak, the venture will suffer. All the players on a winning team must be talented and experienced. Referring again to the analogy of the chair with four sturdy legs of equal length, the company will rest firmly on a solid foundation created by four managers of strong, yet equal, talents in their areas of expertise.

Ability to Work Well Together

Managers must understand their roles clearly and communicate with each other easily. A team that respects and combines its diverse talents has a greater chance to succeed than one filled with discord. Although it is common for team members to disagree with each other, especially during times of stress and change in the business, the venture capitalist will evaluate the management team on its apparent ability to work together.

Flexibility

By its very nature, a new venture requires each manager to be flexible. Team members will be asked on many occasions to pitch in on various projects not directly related to their position, or to expand their job descriptions to include various ancillary roles. A growing company needs best effort from all the managers, and each manager must be ready to help out in a variety of circumstances.

Ability to Adapt to Change

Business is always changing. New markets open up, products and services become obsolete quickly, and the climate in every industry seems to change more rapidly than ever before. Managers responsible for the stability and well-being of a new venture must know how to respond to change. They must anticipate change and use it to their advantage. The venture capitalists will look for dynamic people who roll with the punches and stay on top of every new situation.

Leadership

Does the manager carry the venture's big-picture goal in his mind—the company "mission"—and instill other employees with the same big picture view? Can he interact with employees at all levels in the organization to direct their activities, motivating them to fulfill the company's objectives? How well does he understand the fine art of reprimand and reward, and the need to match employee goals with those of the organization? Venture investors look for managers who are leaders.

Risk Takers

Many management teams are composed of people who resigned from comfortable, if not luxurious corporate positions for the challenge and excitement of growing a young company. These people initially became successful because they willingly took the professional risks that won them the corner office. Eventually, they got bored and realized that it was time to take a new risk. Such managers have the vigorous courage and go-get-'em optimism that is inexpressibly valuable to a new venture.

CHECKING BACKGROUNDS ON
THE ENTREPRENEUR AND HIS KEY MANAGERS

Once the venture capitalist has visited the entrepreneur's business and met all the top managers, he may conduct an investigation into the entrepreneur's background and the backgrounds of his management team. He will look for successes and failures, related experience, management skills, education, personal information such as credit records and whether the entrepreneur or any one of his key managers have trouble with alcohol or drugs, and any other information that will help him decide whether to invest or not.

As we stated in Chapter 2, the venture capitalist knows that the success of a new venture depends largely upon the knowledge and skills of the management team. He is looking for top level managers with directly-related experience, and with successes in the field or in a related field. He is also looking for managers who have overcome adversity, but most of all, the venture capitalist is looking for a management team with a proven track record of successfully running a business. An average product or service backed by a solid management team can still be successful. A good product backed by a poor management team will most likely fail.

The entrepreneur should keep in mind that nobody is perfect, but it is easier to explain shortcomings or potential problems in the beginning rather than after the venture capitalist has turned them up in his investigation. If something does come up in these background checks that concerns the venture capitalist, the entrepreneur should cooperate in every way so that the problem does not become a deal breaker. The easier it is to resolve any problem that might arise, the sooner a deal can be made.

RESEARCHING THE BUSINESS

The primary question on the venture capitalist's mind when he begins investigating a business is, "Is this a viable business?" What a new venture appears to be is not always what is found in a thorough investigation. Now that the venture capitalist has visited the entrepreneur's business and met his management team and some of his employees, he has some idea of the kind of business the entrepreneur runs. Now he must find out if the business is good enough to warrant the major investment the entrepreneur requires of him . . . and whether it will provide the opportunity for the desired return or not. Understanding the business and the markets is crucial.

The Industry

To get a clear idea of a particular industry, the venture capitalist will contact experts, consultants, and industry specialists with professional associations, universities, and also read trade publications. On occasion, he may even talk with other business owners in the industry. These experts will explain how the industry works and where the entrepreneur's company, with its product or service, might fit into the overall picture. The venture capitalist may order industry reports from the major financial publishers and generally avail himself of all possible industry knowledge.

The Product or Service

The venture capitalist may wish to determine if the product or service the entrepreneur sells actually fills a real need in the marketplace. He may begin by studying the industry to determine if the product or service is as unique as the entrepreneur says it is, and if the size of the market is as great as the entrepreneur believes. He may check with professional associations, consultants, industry publications, and even the entrepreneur's competition to obtain the information he needs. He may visit industry trade shows and meet with customers. He will also employ his own intuition about the product . . . would he buy the product or service and why?

The Suppliers

The venture capitalist may want to talk with the entrepreneur's suppliers about the entrepreneur and his company. He may ask what the suppliers think about the product. Do they think it has potential? Do they believe that the company will grow? Are they agreeable to extending credit to the entrepreneur's company? Suppliers are often investors and the venture capitalist will be particularly interested in talking with those firms that have invested in the entrepreneur's company.

The Customers

If the company has sufficiently matured to have customers, the venture capitalist may talk to them to determine if the entrepreneur's product or service is as good as he says it is. The venture capitalist could ask the customers why they buy the product, and specifically, what special features the product has that attracts them to it. How does the entrepreneur's product stack up against competition? What does the customer think of the price, the company, the delivery time, and of course, the service?

This information will help the venture capitalist determine if the entrepreneur's evaluation of the response he is getting to his product or service is accurate. The venture capitalist may discover that the customer is buying the product or service for entirely different reasons than the entrepreneur perceives. This could effect the venture capitalist's opinion of the product or service and may indeed determine his interest in investing.

While interviewing the entrepreneur's customers, the venture capitalist may also learn what they think about the company, in general. Some products or services succeed despite the company that produces them; this is something in which the venture capitalist is genuinely interested. What he wants to hear is that the customer believes in the company, its products and/or services, and the company's future. The venture capitalist wants to know that the customer is satisfied with the products and services and that the entrepreneur and his people are working to keep each customer satisfied whether through effective service support or customer education. The customers are the heart of the entrepreneur's business and if the venture capitalist learns that the entrepreneur fully understands the value of his customer base, he will be positively effected.

The Competition

The most realistic appraisal of the entrepreneur's new venture may come from his competition. They perceive the business in economic terms: how much revenue will the entrepreneur pull away from theirs with his new venture? The entrepreneur's competition will have a realistic idea of the size of his market, the types of customer to whom he is catering and the growth potential of his company. The venture capitalist will want to learn as much from the entrepreneur's competition as possible, depending upon how much either side is willing—or can safely disclose.

The Market

The entrepreneur knows his market, but the venture capitalist should be convinced that the market is well-defined. The venture capitalist may consult with industry experts to determine the size of the market and whether or not it is growing or will remain stable. Sometimes the size of the market is less important than the market penetration the company has achieved. In other words, the venture capitalist may want to know if the entrepreneur is selling his product or services to a large percentage of the market or only a fraction of the market. What percentage of the market does the entrepreneur command and what is the probability that, with an infusion of capital, the entrepreneur will be able to garner a greater market share? Other important market factors include the product's or service's price, and the price of competitive products or solutions. The entrepreneur should have some predictions about how the market will behave after the introduction of his company's product.

In addition to researching the business, there are a number of other people with whom the venture capitalist may want to talk.

The Controller/Financial Manager

When talking with the company's financial personnel, the venture capitalist may ask specific questions about company conservatism, the company's systems, procedures, and controls. For instance, how does the company recognize revenue, and to what extent do they capitalize expenses. Does the company properly account for and classify its expenses? Are all of the liabilities and assets properly recorded? Does the company take a conservative or more aggressive approach in its accounting and tax positions? In essence, the venture capitalist may use his time with the controller to see if there are any "hidden bodies" he should know about. The venture capitalist may want to know if the controller is confident about the projections stated in the business plan. Does the controller think the company is financially solid and well run?

The Accountant

Usually, an entrepreneur does not commission a professional audit to be included in his business plan, nor does the venture capitalist expect it. Audited financial statements are generally deemed too expensive for start up entities; however, when available, they should be included. Otherwise, the most current financial information should be given.

Seasoned venture capitalists know to review the financials to determine how the company arrived at certain figures and how the projections were calculated. The venture capitalist will usually ask the entrepreneur's accountant about the various business and accounting practices. He will also ask for a review of projections and related assumptions, and for personal references.

In general, the entrepreneur should develop and maintain a complete set of accounting records of his new venture. By doing so, he demonstrates an understanding of an important business practice, and he helps himself by speeding up the venture capitalist's investigation. The absence of good accounting records makes it more difficult for the venture capitalist to verify the numbers in the business plan, if he chooses to do so. In general, good accounting records from the time of the company's inception, simplify all future financing procedures and are a sign of truly professional management. Sometimes, if the entrepreneur is not meticulous about keeping his books, the venture capitalist will call for an audit to verify the financial statements included in the business plan.

The Banker

If the company is in a stage of growth that involves relations with bankers, the venture capitalist will usually want to talk to the banker to determine the entrepreneur's general business practices. He will also want to learn what the banker thinks about the entrepreneur's honesty and business reputation, and whether he is a good credit risk or not. The entrepreneur's relationship with his banker is important to the extent that the quality of that relationship will be reflected in the reference the banker gives during the due diligence investigation. And, the venture capitalist is very interested in the debt capacity the banker may provide to effectively leverage the venture capital funding.

The Lawyer

The venture capitalist will also contact the entrepreneur's lawyer for a reference and to ascertain the quality of the entrepreneur's legal representation. In addition, the venture capitalist will want to know if the entrepreneur has been sued, if he is now being sued, or if he is suing anyone and for what reasons. He usually wants to know if the securities have been appropriately authorized and issued. Also, if the entrepreneur has recently left another company, the venture capitalist will want to know about the entrepreneur's exit. Was it made on good terms or bad, and what restrictions may exist on the entrepreneur's activity? Can any legal issues arise about the person and his knowledge taken from earlier employers? In short, the venture capitalist will want to learn about the general state of pertinent legal affairs.

The venture capitalist will frequently contact the entrepreneur's patent lawyer to determine the validity of the patents, trademarks, or copyrights.

If the entrepreneur owns patents, trademarks, or copyrights, the venture capitalist will probably want to know when he received them, whether or not they are still in force and valid, and if the lawyer is aware of competition that the venture capitalist has not yet discovered in his investigations. Because a patent and trademark search is so thorough, the lawyer should know about patents and trademarks that compete with those owned by the entrepreneur. If one of the entrepreneur's patents or trademarks is being contested, this will greatly affect the venture capitalist's decision to continue or to stop his investigation.

To ensure that all the bases are covered before final agreements are signed, the venture capitalist will consult with his own attorney. The attorney will try to determine if the company's existing legal documents will have any particular impact on the new venture and ultimately upon the deal. The venture capitalist may review, or have his lawyers review, contracts, supplier and customer agreements, investments, personnel agreements, insurance papers, loans, patents, trademarks, copyrights, initial investor agreements, and corporate or partnership papers.

RESEARCHING THE NUMBERS

The venture capitalist may take a careful look at the numbers, the projections, and the claims that the entrepreneur has made in his business plan. The venture capitalist may compare what he has found in his investigations with the information contained in the business plan. Although few businesses live up to their projections, the entrepreneur must strike that delicate balance between being too optimistic and failing to project an attractive potential return on investment. If the entrepreneur's projections are too optimistic, the venture capitalist may doubt other assertions in the business plan. On the other hand, if the figures aren't sufficiently exciting, the entrepreneur runs the risk of not piquing the venture capitalist's interest.

Because it takes time to raise venture capital many venture capitalists find that business plans need to be updated to reflect the changes that have occurred since the plan was originally drawn up. This is to be expected, and usually these financial modifications will not scare off the venture capitalist unless the projections, market estimates, and industry analyses have changed so much that the business plan is quite different and the opportunities are less exciting.

The best business plans are those that reflect the new venture's present financial situation, as well as projections that are in line with its industry. If the industry is new, the projections should reflect careful consideration of the size of the market, the time and expense of delivering the product or service to the market, marketing costs, labor costs, and the price the entrepreneur intends to charge. If the venture capitalist determines that the projections are unrealistic and that the entrepreneur will need more time to deliver his product to the market or that he will need a far greater amount of capitalization, the entrepreneur's credibility and the deal may be compromised. That is why it is so important to develop a well-researched, well-thought-out business plan.

The venture capitalist's goal is to learn all he can about the entrepreneur, the management team, and the new venture. He is not on a witch hunt. Nothing would make a venture capitalist happier than to find everything in order and to receive positive reviews from everyone he speaks to about the entrepreneur's new venture, but this is rarely the case. As was stated earlier in this chapter, no one is perfect and no business is perfect. The venture capitalist will probably find something unexpected. In fact, it is this important information that the entrepreneur and the venture capitalist can use to improve the business plan and to increase the entrepreneur's chances for success. The entrepreneur has nothing to worry about if he has been honest from the beginning. It is smart to establish an understanding that whenever the venture capitalist is concerned about something the due diligence process reveals, he will check with the entrepreneur. In this way, the entrepreneur can address that concern quickly and to the satisfaction of the venture capitalist, rather than let the information cause the entrepreneur or his firm any undue delay.

Nevertheless, it is frequently during the due diligence process that new ventures are made or broken. The venture capitalist can receive all the right signals, but if a sufficient number of discoveries in the investigation indicate that a major problem exists, the deal may be dropped. If the entrepreneur's business plan is filled with errors and blue sky, if the entrepreneur's place of business is too plush, or if the deal is "too rich"—in other words, overvalued—the venture capitalist might simply walk away from the deal. For any number of reasons, the deal may not coalesce, but the hope is that the venture capitalist and the entrepreneur will emerge from the due diligence process "married."

Chapter 5

Negotiating the Deal

Several factors come into play when negotiating the deal. The key issues
are:

- The structure of the financing, that is the selection of investment vehicles
- The risk involved in making the investment, which often reflects the
  stage of the business's growth
- The anticipated return on investment
- The pricing or valuation of the company and ownership
- Voting control
- The timing for the rounds of financing
- The structure of the board of directors
- The anticipated exit the venture capitalists will take from their
  investment

Also, it is important to consider how the structure of the initial
arrangement will affect future financings and business decisions. All of
these elements dovetail and work interdependently, but we'll look at them
separately. Entrepreneurs should note that structuring a venture capital
deal is usually very complicated. Generally, negotiating the terms requires
expert counsel from an experienced attorney in venture capital deals, and
entrepreneurs are advised to refer to legal counsel throughout the
negotiations.

THE STRUCTURE OF THE DEAL

Basically, there are four different securities used most frequently
in structuring venture capital deals. They are preferred stock, common

stock, various types of debt instruments, and warrants or options. Both the preferred stock and the debt securities, also frequently called "senior securities" will normally be convertible into common stock.

Convertible Preferred Stock

So named because it gives the holder some preference over the common stockholders, this security is extensively used to structure venture capital investments. It is extremely flexible, and it can be established in a variety of ways to offer the investor some protection for the recovery of the investment. Convertible preferred stock confers special rights over those of the common shareholders (common stock is usually held by the founders and the management team). The special rights of preferred stock holders include having priority as to dividend payments, special voting rights, the rights to convert preferred stock to common, having special provisions to protect the preferred stock from dilution of its equity interest resulting from subsequent stock issues at lower prices, having preferences in liquidation, special redemption rights (at particular times), and having normally preemptive rights to participate in future financings.

Preferred stock may come in several classes, generally identified in series (e.g., series A, series B, etc.), which distinguishes the different rights of the stock for investors who want different characteristics in the type of stock they own, or who purchase stock at different times and prices.

Dividends

Dividends on preferred stock are paid before common share dividends, are frequently measured as a percent of the par value of the stock, but are not tax deductible like interest. If the company doesn't earn enough to pay dividends on its preferred stock, and if the dividends are "cumulated," they must be paid to preferred stockholders before any dividends are paid to the common stockholders. However, paying dividends on a backlog of cumulated dividends could create cash problems for a young company. Increasingly, either the dividends are noncumulative or a class of preferred stock is created wherein the dividends are noncumulative at first, and then later become cumulative. After all, if the company is in a start-up phase, the investors, themselves, may prefer to create a class of preferred stock wherein dividends are not distributed to shareholders, but are reinvested in the company. Otherwise, at this stage, the investors would really be paying themselves dividends out of their own pockets. Even if the company is in a position to pay dividends, the board of directors will have to decide if those payments actually will be made. If the board of directors decides against a dividend payment and the dividends are cumulative, they must be paid in future years to the preferred stock shareholders before they are paid to the common shareholders. If the dividends are noncumulative, the shareholders lose them.

Frequently, dividend rights and preferences are included as a vehicle to assist in the venture capitalist's recovery of his investment should failure result and liquidation occur.

Voting Rights

The special voting rights give preferred shareholders leverage through which they can effect the management of the company. Convertible preferred stock generally allows the shareholder a vote per share of common stock into which the preferred is convertible. The different series of preferred stock also carry particular voting rights pertaining to the election of the board of directors, as well as to issues affecting the business, such as a merger, sale of the company, or an amendment of the articles of incorporation. Voting rights may become an important issue to the entrepreneur if the investors who hold preferred stock really control the company's board of directors. The entrepreneur may become concerned about losing control of his company to investors through their superior voting rights. On the other hand, the venture capitalist will want this ability to control the company's direction, especially if it is a start-up and things begin to go wrong. How important the issue of control is will be discussed later in this chapter.

Conversion To Common

Usually, preferred stock is convertible to common stock at the preferred shareholder's option, and automatically in specific cases, such as when the company reaches a particular financial benchmark or goes public.

Anti-Dilution Protection

Anti-dilution provisions (see the "Glossary") are designed to protect the preferred stockholders from the effects of dilution if the company issues new stock at a price below a specified level (generally the level at which the venture capitalist bought), or if a stock split occurs. In these instances, the provisions stipulate more stock will be issued automatically to the investors, or that the ratio of conversion must be changed to preserve the investors' stock value. Different types of anti-dilution provisions are used, including the "ratchet-down," "formula," and "weighted average" provisions. Entrepreneurs should seek an attorney's advice before agreeing to an anti-dilution provision that might be punitive in some way. Many investors realize harsh anti-dilution provisions are short-sighted because they reduce the effectiveness of stock incentives for the management group. Therefore, many experienced venture capitalists take dilution of their holdings along with management. Anti-dilution provisions can also create a reserve of stock that the company can issue to key employees without necessitating anti-dilution adjustments.

Liquidation Rights

Preferred liquidation rights give the venture capitalist a chance to recoup some of his investment if the entrepreneur's company falters. This is appropriate because the investors have contributed significant funds to the deal. In the event that the company is liquidated, the preferred stock has a right to the proceeds before common stockholders. Investors sometimes may be restricted to at most the original price they paid for the stock. Preferred shareholders may also receive distributions of the company's assets or qualify to receive payments of accumulated dividends. Liquidation rights may be different for separate classes of stock.

Redemption Rights

Investors will sometimes arrange a schedule whereby the company buys back the stock at certain intervals of time. Either the investors or the corporation may exercise this option upon request, or redemption may occur automatically in certain circumstances. Mandatory redemption provisions are an ever-present potential liability for the company. In the case of a stock redemption, entrepreneurs should be entitled to a minimum

30-day advance notice of the investors' intention to redeem their stock holdings. The price of the redeemed stock should also be negotiated, and is usually established as the price set for liquidation plus an added premium.

Preemptive Rights

This provision helps the investor retain his desired percent of stock ownership by allowing him to participate, pro rata with other investors, in future rounds of financing. This can be a particularly attractive option if the company is successful; if the investor has the right of first refusal, he may choose to finance 100 percent of the next round. Alternatively, some suggest avoiding pre-emptive rights, as their administrative complexity combined with the power it vests in the holders to dictate pricing (thereby sometimes preventing the entrepreneur from getting a higher stock price), may make them undesirable.

If the business fails or does not do as well as anticipated, the venture capitalists will do better holding preferred stock than common. They will try to recapture as much of their investment as possible through the preferred stock's favorable liquidation and redemption rights. During the process of negotiation, investors and management should determine the liquidation value and distribution rights for each class of stock, and how unpaid dividends will be administrated.

Common Stock

This form of equity is not often used in structuring deals with venture capitalists because it offers no advantage to venture capitalists for making a risk investment, which a convertible preferred or convertible debt instrument would. Common stock confers no special voting, liquidation, antidilution, or redemption privileges for the shareholder, and common stock dividend payments are subordinated to payments made on the preferred. Structuring the deal using only common stock also puts the entrepreneur at a disadvantage, because he frequently gives up so much of the company. Because common stock confers no special advantage or protection, the venture capitalist will frequently want to offset his risk by taking more of the company. Common stock is usually issued to founders, management, and employees, but in later stage financings, common stock is frequently used by venture capitalists, too.

Convertible Debentures

A convertible debenture is a loan that bears interest and can be converted into common stock. It is subordinated to loans made by other financial sources and is sometimes unsecured. Most businesses finance their growth through a mixture of equity and debt, and convertible debentures are a flexible combination of the two. They are popular with SBICs because SBICs borrow a substantial amount of their investable funds from the government and need to service their own interest payments on that debt. By issuing convertible debentures, an SBIC can take the interest it collects from investments and apply it to service its debt.

For a young company, one that is in the start up or early growth stages, traditional debt financing is an impractical idea. Usually, the cash flow situation for these companies is tight, and generating extra funds to meet interest payments takes away from money that would be better allocated to the development, manufacturing, and sale of the product. To the extent that rates on convertible debentures are lower than on straight debt or that interest can be deferred for a period of time, convertible debentures offer a compromise solution for managing this situation. First, they give the investor a chance to convert his loan to common stock shares. If the company is successful, the investor stands to make more money than he would through a straightforward repayment of the loan. Second, convertible debentures give the negotiators an opportunity to determine when the conversion takes place, at what price, the interest rate of the loan, and the structure of the loan itself. Thus, some of the differences in valuation that frequently drive investors and entrepreneurs apart can be resolved through effective use of conversion rights, given certain performance parameters. Convertible debentures may also confer to the investor a seat on the company's board of directors.

Warrants With Straight Debt Instruments

Sometimes an entrepreneur can secure a loan if he offers the investor an additional inducement, an option/warrant to buy stock in the company. Even after the loan is repaid, the investor may have the opportunity to buy stock through his holding of the warrant. Again, the terms for exercising the warrant, specifically at what time and at what price will be negotiated. True debt financing is not typically available until a company can give reasonable assurance it can meet its debt service responsibilities. Usually, therefore, debt financing tends to be available only for companies in later stages of growth. At this point, the company's sales are strong, the company is seeking to expand its operations, and the investor risk is low. From the entrepreneur's point of view, warrants also have the attraction of being another source of capital. Upon exercise, warrants really represent another stock sale and proceeds go to the company.

Which Securities Are Best?

In the early stages of a company's development, the entrepreneur has little choice. Security decisions will be made largely by the venture capitalist, with a take-it or leave-it offer. However, as the company grows, financing options are more varied, (see Fig. 1-2 under "Financing Influences Business Strategy" in Chapter 1). The company's stage of growth, how the money will be used, and the market climate determine the nature of the financing. Deals structured for start-up companies are usually negotiated on an equity basis only—and usually with preferred stock. Equity is used in situations where the risk factor is extremely high. If the company is successful, the investor's equity holdings will grow and provide incentive and reward for risking capital. Because young companies have limited cash flow, they are generally unable to make interest payments, so their debt capacity is more limited. (See Appendix A, "Alternatives to Venture Capital").

Well-established and more secure companies, such as those with sales that seek expansion funding, may be able to service debt, but as with all financing methods, debt financing has positives and negatives. Through debt financing, management is able to retain the company's equity and often more control of operations. Management can also avoid dilution of share valuation. However, the more leveraged a company is, the more interest it pays, and therefore the higher its break-even point. Clearly, a company must plan carefully when walking the tightrope between having enough cash to pay a loan and assuring that enough funds exist to continue the company's progress.

On the other hand, creditors have liquidation preference over stockholders, so investors who use debt instruments in structuring a deal have a better chance of recouping their capital. Investors who use debt instruments also have cash flow from interest payments the company must make on its loan. These payments are more secure than the payment of dividends, which need to be declared by the board of directors and capacity depends upon the availability of capital.

RISK

The risk/reward ratio is a critical element in negotiating the deal, when risk is as tangible as money itself. Venture capitalists expect to be compensated in proportion for the risk they take through a greater portion of equity or a higher return on investment. If the company's management team is unproven, if the technology is especially complicated or needs further refinement, or if a market doesn't currently exist and needs to be developed, the venture capitalists will want a larger portion of the company, and consequently greater control, to offset the higher risk factors.

If the company is in a seed financing stage, the investors may expect the entrepreneur to contribute his own finances to the deal in its earliest rounds. Few deals are financed totally on "other people's money." For the entrepreneur, this initial seed investment can mean borrowing from relatives, mortgaging the house, and taking out a personal bank loan. Venture capitalists know the entrepreneur is committed to the deal when he has invested both "sweat" and "real" equity and is in a position to lose money along with the venture capitalist if the business crumbles. The entrepreneur's willingness to go out on a limb tells the venture capitalist that he, the entrepreneur, has great faith in the venture.

Generally speaking, the capital the entrepreneur receives in the seed "rounds" will be the most expensive ever. The further the entrepreneur can finance the company on his own, through contracts, sales, licenses, friends, and other sources of capital, the better off he'll be. Using too much venture capital money too early is too expensive.

In today's environment, venture capitalists often form syndicates to fund deals and diffuse their risk. It is quite common for the major venture capitalist—the one who is willing to make the largest dollar investment—to adopt the role of the *lead investor*, then contact his venture friends to build a pool—or syndicate—of investors. Everybody in the pool contributes funds to the deal and reaps the rewards commensurate with their level of participation. The lead venture capitalist takes the largest slice and acts as the "manager" overseeing the deal, usually joining the board of directors. Syndication also benefits the entrepreneur, since it brings together many different ideas and viewpoints. If a number of experienced venture capitalists join together and offer counsel at a critical time in a company's development, the entrepreneur will be able to consider that many more alternatives, instead of being limited to the perspective of a single firm.

Some venture capitalists have a policy against ever taking the lead investor position, while other firms always require it. Ironically, even if an entrepreneur captures the interest of a venture capital firm, he generally will not receive financing until he finds a lead investor, who will volunteer to oversee and help manage the investment on behalf of the other venture capitalists. It is not uncommon for venture capitalists who would otherwise have a strong interest in investing in a specific venture to decline a chance to participate simply because they lack the time. Only if the entrepreneur can find a lead venture capitalist with whom he is comfortable will the investment happen.

RETURN ON INVESTMENT

Return on investment, or ROI, is usually the venture capitalists' incentive to place capital in a high risk investment. The greater the risk, the greater return on investment the venture capitalist will want. Because of his own investors' objectives, and because of the high risk factor, a venture capitalist requires his investments to provide a superior return—clearly to make more money than if he had invested in other things. For example, in 1985-86, returns on money market accounts averaged 7 percent, bond portfolios—24 percent, common stocks—30 percent, residential real estate—11 percent, and collectibles—4 percent (*Wall Street Journal*, January 2, 1987). Venture capitalists set their own standards for acceptable projected returns, but to attract capital themselves, and to compensate for the risk element, they generally require portfolio returns of over 30 percent. To achieve this rate of return, venture capitalists take into consideration and balance various factors: the company's stage of growth, the period of time for which the funds are invested, the industry in which the investment is made and the growth rates of companies in that industry, and the growth potentials suggested by market conditions.

The company's stage of development will vary the expected return on investment. Since companies in their seed and start-up phases represent the highest risk, investors expect them to generate a higher rate of return, frequently over 50 percent compounded per annum. Companies seeking financing for a turn-around situation also represent high risk, and the return on investment is frequently expected to be over 50 percent compounded per annum. Mid-stage companies who have a steady cash flow and may be seeking mezzanine financing for expansion can generate an ROI of 30 percent—40 percent compounded per annum. Investors hope that later stage companies will produce returns of about 25 percent—30 percent per annum, still significantly higher than investing in publicly held common equities.

Keep in mind that not every company in the venture capitalist's portfolio is a success. When the overall ROI is averaged, the companies that realize high returns on investment compensate for those ventures on which the venture capitalist loses money or breaks even. Venture capitalists are also aware that start-up companies require more management time, especially if the venture capitalist emphasizes the value-added approach. Sheparding a start-up over the rough terrain of its early years is time-consuming and often stress producing. For those venture capitalists who have the expertise and dedication to nurture a young company, a high rate of return is reasonable and appropriate compensation for their efforts.

Money has value in terms of the length of time it is used. If the investor sees a ten-fold return on investment in ten years, his ROI is 26 percent compounded annually, but if he sees the same ten-fold return in only five years, he's getting a 58 percent return—a much more attractive prospect. The length of time a venture capitalist is willing to stay with an investment varies, although five years is a derived average.

Venture capitalists invest in companies they think will benefit from their contribution. In other words, venture capitalists seek to build a company's value. To meet the objectives of their investors and to meet their own objectives, venture capitalists will fund a company whose growth rate will dramatically increase value, or "ramp up," as a result of the capital infusion. The company should be poised and ready to take off with the help of venture funding. A few years later, the growth rate usually slows, when the benefits of the capital infusion are maximized. At this point, the venture capitalist may decide to do a follow-on round of financing, if it will continue to increase the company's value. Alternatively, the venture capitalist may decide to exit the deal, before the company's growth rate slows. Successful venture capitalists intend to enter and exit a deal when the growth rate curve is the steepest.

As mentioned earlier, the venture firm's investment philosophy will depend on how the firm itself is funded. If the venture capitalist is funded through the wealth of a private family, liquidity may not be a driving issue, and he may be able to invest with companies for a longer period of time. In this case, the venture capitalist is managing money that is committed to the long-term development of companies. Such firms can often afford to wait for higher returns while nurturing the company at a slower rate.

Most venture firms, however, are structured as limited partnerships and have a relatively short life span of seven to ten years. They pool capital resources by obtaining investments from financial institutions (pension funds and insurance companies), and large private investors, who invest money with venture capital firms as a portion of their overall investment strategy. The venture firm's general partners act as managers and make money for their limited partner investors. The general managers take, as compensation, both a management fee and a percentage of the partnership's capital appreciation. Normally, however, the general partners can take their percentage only after returning all of the initial investment capital to the investors. Venture firms generally seek high returns in a short period of time and look for investment opportunities that will grow rapidly and provide quick liquidity opportunities, usually within three to five years. Of course, this perspective must be balanced. The fast-growth, quick liquidity philosophy is common when strong market conditions prevail; for example, in 1983 and again in 1987, when the market was fueled by an increase of initial public offerings. However, the depressed after-market of 1984 resulted in a more conservative attitude for both public and private investors. Many venture firms now wait five to seven years before liquidating their investments, giving their deals more time to mature. Some firms have developed a reputation for sticking through thick-and-thin with their companies for many years before realizing a return on investment. Others cut and run, eliminating losses by divesting early, if possible, or by refusing to make follow on investments of time and money in deals that have fallen short of expectations.

VALUATION

Ultimately, the key to the entire negotiation process is valuation. Since negotiation always entails giving up something to get something, the entrepreneur must be willing to surrender equity in exchange for the venture capitalists' investment money. Usually, the more funding the entrepreneur requests, the more equity he must offer to the investor to balance the investor's risk. Negotiations strike a delicate balance between the amount of money the company will need to reach its important benchmarks and the willingness of investors to invest, given the risk profile. Failing to raise enough funds threatens the company's development, but equity is most expensive at the time of the first deal. What management retains becomes the resources for future rounds of financing or for stock used to attract future management.

So, the question really is, how much should the entrepreneur give up today, and how does it effect his future financing? Looking back, if the entrepreneur did a perfect job of financing the venture, he would finance every time the company crossed over a major risk step-down point. That is, after the risk profile changes because the company meets a milestone, a financing happens that propels the company toward its next goal. To finance at each risk step-down point is probably not feasible, but ideally, as the risks change, subsequent financings should become less expensive. In retrospect, to do a perfect job, financings should have occurred at major risk step down points. Ultimately, then, the entrepreneur should have financed with the least amount of dilution. Unfortunately, when structuring the deal, the entrepreneur doesn't have the benefit of hindsight and may take the risk of getting too little money. How much the entrepreneur needs and how much equity he is willing to give up becomes the operative question.

Valuation asks, "how much is the company worth?" Finding the answer involves more art than science. Formulating an estimate requires a little "crystal ball" thinking, but industry standards do exist. While researching the investment opportunity, the venture capitalist weighs two major factors against each other: the risk he is taking with his capital (the downside) versus the profit he may make, or the upside. Some of the items he considers have already been discussed, such as the quality of the management team and the kind of technology and market opportunity the deal involves. The venture capitalist will try to reach a conclusion also by using both subjective business instincts and quantitative analysis. Some of the standard valuation models are:

- Comparisons of a company to others in the market
- Discounted cash flows
- Asset valuations
- Valuations based on sales multiples

Valuation is not just an objective consideration. It varies to what extent a firm relies on the quantitative assessments of proposed ventures. In the end, gut instinct about a particular business will really determine valuation, because it is all conjecture anyway.

Before investing in a deal, the venture capitalist estimates what his profits could be when he decides to liquidate his holdings, assuming the company is successful. Whether or not he can anticipate large profits depends, not only on the growth of the company, but also on the receptivity of the market when he wants to exit. This research also helps him more accurately value the stock, if he decides to negotiate a deal. Will the market allow and accommodate high growth for a company in this particular industry? To determine this, the venture capitalist frequently checks price earnings ratios for similar companies in the marketplace. If they are valued at high multiples, it is an indication that other companies offering the same service or product could command similar market valuation.

Company Comparisons

To establish a reasonable valuation for a business, venture capitalists look at market comparables—other companies in the same industry—to see how they are being valued today. (It is similar to buying or selling a house. Other comparable houses that have been sold recently are the best measure of "market" value.) Venture capitalists review companies at similar stages of growth. They check their market valuations, their price/earnings ratios, and other indicators. By comparing the projections given in the business plan with the operating statistics and ratios of other large and small companies, both public and private, the venture capitalist will generate some understanding for a particular industry and its present market valuation. Although the entrepreneur normally has a valuation in mind, the venture capitalist realizes it is probably too high, a reflection of the entrepreneur's enthusiasm. Studying comparable companies helps the venture capitalist put projections into perspective. If the company seeking financing has an operating history, those statistics will also be compared to the history of other companies. For example, as of March 31, 1987, the companies representing the Dow Jones Industrial average were selling at about 18 times their latest 12-months earnings. Companies in the technology business were averaging about 34 times their latest 12-months earnings (Source: Hambrecht & Quist, Inc.). By December 31, 1987, the Dow Jones Industrials were selling at 15 times their earnings, and technology companies were averaging 21 times their earnings. Given this, the entrepreneur can get a good handle on his company's valuation by taking his earnings five years from now and estimating the stock price then. Discounting this back, this market comparison will prove to be an effective valuation device.

Discounted Cash Flow

Generally, the entrepreneur's business plan contains sales and growth projections for at least the first five years of the venture. For instance, a company might project $100 million in sales by the fifth year. If the cost of goods sold is $60 million, the company realizes a gross margin of $40 million. Subtract a hypothetical $20 million to cover operating expenses, and the company has cleared $20 million pretax. Deduct 50 percent for taxes, and in year five, the company should show net earnings of $10 million. Let's say at this point the venture capitalist refers to the current market figures and notes that comparable public companies today are selling at a price earnings ratio of 20. If the venture capitalist applies this P/E multiple to the after-tax earnings of the entrepreneur's company, he derives a market value of $200 million. So, on this basis, the company will be worth $200 million in year five, if all things go as projected.

Most venture capitalists do appreciate that the projections entrepreneurs give in their business plans are usually optimistic. Based on his experience and awareness of industry standards, current market climate, and his estimate of the marketability of the product discussed in the business plan, the venture capitalist may reduce the projected sales figure by a certain percentage. In this case, he knows that the entrepreneur can't capture 10 percent of what would be a billion dollar industry, so he reduces the projected sales by 50 percent and projects the company will actually be seeing sales of approximately $50 million in its fifth year, and if the P/E multiple of the companies currently in the market remains at 20, the company should be valued at $100 million, in year five. If he has a 20 percent investment in this company, he knows his investment will be worth $20 million in year five. To figure out its net worth today, simple discounting at 50 percent will move this to a valuation of approximately $2.6 million.

Sales Multiplies

Although it is an inexact valuation, frequently the best measure of a company's worth comes from analysis and projections of its revenue base. If a business is in a service area, for example advertising, then its value may best be expressed in terms of gross billings or revenues, rather than in terms of a net earnings or price/earnings ratio. The important thing to consider when establishing value for such companies is the volume of business they do and the revenues their sales generate. Some companies sell at one or two times their revenues; others sell for even more.

Asset Valuations

Companies with large capital bases—i.e., extensive property, plant, or equipment holdings—are frequently valued more in terms of their asset values than in terms of a sales or price/earnings relationship. Interestingly, these companies' component pieces may have greater value when considered as separate and distinct parts, without accounting for the actual service or product the company renders. Asset valuation is frequently used as a valuation device in conjunction with other methods.

PRICING

Each venture capital firm establishes its own standards, based upon its own objectives. In our example, if the company is projected to be worth $100 million in the fifth year, what is it actually worth today? Assume the venture capitalist discounts the $100 million in the fifth year valuation, at the 50 percent per year, which is the return he may require. Using a standard discounted cash flow technique, this business would be worth approximately $13 million today. If the discount rate was 100 percent per year, this would be valued at $3 million. However, this assumes no additional financing. So if our entrepreneur needs $8 million today, and that's all the company will need during the next five years (an unlikely scenario), he should be able to expect to give up about 60 percent of the company for the $8 million, (assuming the 50 percent discount factor) . . . or, it is not financable, assuming the 100 percent per year discount factor.

Working the analysis from the other direction, one can see that if a venture capitalist purchases 60 percent of a company for $8 million, the remaining 40 percent, which is the percent the entrepreneur retains, is therefore worth approximately $5 million. Add this up and the total present value of the company is worth $13 million. The 40 percent, or $5 million, management keeps is known as the *pre-money valuation*, because that is what the company was considered to be worth before the capital infusion. The $13 million represents the company's value after financing. The pre-money valuation is a constant, and if the company had raised $5 million, the pre-money valuation would have remained $5 million, but management would then own 50 percent of the company's stock, rather than 40 percent, as previously calculated using the $8 million investment. In establishing the valuation of the company, the entrepreneur trades equity for funding, and so the more funding in proportion to the pre-money valuation, the more equity the entrepreneur surrenders. Experience shows that in most first round deals the venture capitalist takes 40 percent to 60 percent, and the valuations seldom exceed $1 to 3 million.

To get confirmation of a reasonable valuation for his company, the entrepreneur should talk to a couple different venture capitalists at the same time. As has been discussed, all venture firms are not alike, and an entrepreneur should not necessarily select the investor that offers to give him the highest valuation, but should also consider one that provides value and a better chance for the company's success. Has the venture capitalist built other successful companies, and does he know something about the entrepreneur's industry? Is the investor willing and able to finance later rounds, and does he have the necessary clout to attract other venture capitalists or to attract good investment bankers to take a company public? Whatever may be lacking in a valuation may be more than compensated for if the entrepreneur receives assistance from an experienced investor.

The percent of ownership management or the founders carry will be used later on to do future financings, or will provide stock option reserves with which to attract new management. If the company is growing, stock values should rise, the risk element should diminish, and management should be able to sell a smaller percentage of the company's stock for more money.

Ownership is not as important an issue as entrepreneurs sometimes think, however. Venture capitalists frequently ask for as much as 60 percent of the company in the first round in return for their sizeable capital risks. It is more important to increase the overall value of the company than to worry about control. The traditional reminder is that 100 percent of nothing is nothing. Instead of exercising great concern over the amount of equity he owns, an entrepreneur will profit by applying that concern to growing his company and increasing the value of the stock.

CONTROL

Discussion about valuation and ownership usually calls into question the issue of control, which is defined as one's percentage of voting interest. In some cases, the entrepreneur believes he should receive generous capital funding and still retain the greater percentage of equity. Similarly, the venture capitalist wants a substantial amount of equity so that he can protect his investment; in fact, control is not just a matter of equity holdings: in real life cases, the issue of control is also coupled with the power of "the golden rule" of venture capital, which states that "he who has the gold . . . rules." No matter how much equity the entrepreneur holds, the venture capitalist holds the purse strings. If the entrepreneur accepts venture financing, he automatically forfeits absolute control because decisions about the company's fate must be shared with the venture "partners."

Concerns about control are actually semantic rather than practical. By gaining control of the company, the venture capital investor is looking for enough influence to have a decisive voice in the direction and operation of the company and to appropriately compensate himself for the risk. However, he is not looking for day-to-day operating control of the business.

Venture capitalists maintain a number of companies in their portfolios and do not have time to exercise such management. Nor do they wish to, since the management team should demonstrate that ability if the investment is sound. Venture capitalists want only to influence management when, in their judgment, it needs guidance; however, if things are not happening as planned, the venture capitalist will try to protect his investment through voting control or hands-on management. At the most extreme level, the investor exercises control by replacing management. This may be difficult to accept for the entrepreneur who starts a company to "become his own boss," but he would be wise to defer to the investor's direction. At certain crisis moments, the concept of "value-added" becomes real when good venture capitalists employ their business experience to rescue failing companies. At such times, it should be clear that the entrepreneur's and investor's goal are one and that all decisions are made for the health of the company.

Remember that in exchange for a controlling percentage of equity, the entrepreneur gains the value-added many venture capitalists bring to a deal. The old adage, "It's not how much money, but whose . . . ," assumes meaning in this regard. Receiving funds from a firm that is experienced in a particular industry, or with companies at a certain level of growth, the entrepreneur benefits twice. First and most obviously from the financing, and secondly from the assistance a venture capitalist can offer, through his knowledge and network, via executive searches, management consulting, and marketing and business advice. This is why it is so important to find an investor who has hands-on knowledge about company operations, especially companies that have experienced operational difficulties.

Entrepreneurs should also be aware that after a series of financings, the issue of control will virtually disappear. Over time, the financiers will own substantially all of the company while the founders retain a relatively small part of it. The question is not if the founders give up control, but when, at what price, and how. Ideally, the founders or early management will own 10 percent to 15 percent of the company's equity at the time the company goes public or gets its fourth or fifth round of financing.

Note that how much the founding entrepreneur achieves is a function of the success of the company, or its value. Surrendering control may be a psychological hurdle in the early stages of financing, but shouldn't become a major obstacle to financing, since the entrepreneur will end up with less than majority ownership anyway.

The entrepreneur should remember that control is generally in the hands of the funding power, regardless of the percentages held . . . "He who has the gold, rules." Even if the entrepreneur has 100 percent of the vote, if the company is dependent on the venture capitalist's investment, the venture capitalist calls the shots. Without his investment, the company would be non-operational.

TIMING

This refers to the schedule of financings, and there are two major approaches. One method is to seek a single large financing, and the other method is to seek smaller amounts of capital to be infused at critical growth phases. Both methods have advantages and disadvantages. For instance, the entrepreneur may seek enough capital to bring the company through a couple initial growth stages. The advantages to this approach are that he will be less likely to run out of cash at a crucial moment in the company's development. Secondly, the management team won't have to devote significant amounts of their time to organizing future rounds of financing. The disadvantage is that the venture capitalist is faced with a substantial amount of risk. To offset the risk factor, the venture capitalist will request a significantly larger share of the company's equity at a time when it is most expensive. As a result, the entrepreneur will have less stock left over for subsequent rounds of financing and is more diluted now. If the entrepreneur seeks a large first financing, he will have to be quite accurate about how far the initial financing will go—or else, he may be in real trouble. He will have given up a large percentage of the company without hope of meeting his next milestone. Single large financings are rarely done. Even after careful analysis, things always seem to take longer and cost more than anticipated.

The typical approach to financing is by stages of growth. This method is more common than the one mentioned above because it has a built-in system of checks and balances. Capital is infused after the company meets critical benchmarks. Whenever the company reaches a new milestone, the risk factor is reduced, and everybody's confidence in the company's success increases. As a result, management can sell stock at increasingly higher prices.

In the case of a start-up company, frequently venture investors give a company between $1 million and $3 million to operate for a year to two years. This is the average time it takes for start-up companies to demonstrate technical proof of reaching the next important benchmark. The disadvantage to this approach is that the company may run out of cash before reaching its next crucial milestone. If this happens, investor confidence wavers, and the price of the stock goes down. The interim financing will be expensive for the entrepreneur, and because his request for cash comes at an unscheduled time, capital may not be available. In such cases, he is forced to seek alternative forms of financing, which could be scarce.

Knowing this, one can appreciate how important it is to develop accurate projections of a company's financial needs. To avoid unnecessary dilution of his holdings, the entrepreneur must accurately anticipate the number of financings and in what amounts his company will need capital to become successful. If he trades a large portion of equity for an inadequate amount of money, at some point in the future, when the company needs another capital infusion, he has less available equity to leverage. Second, if a number of financings are scheduled to occur before the venture capitalist plans to exit the deal, he will want more equity initially because with each successive round of financing, the value of his equity holding is diluted. Although dilution cannot be prevented, deals should be structured with an awareness of the effects it will have on the value of stock holdings. The legal documentation involved in finalizing negotiations includes anti-dilution provisions, which are discussed earlier in this chapter.

THE BOARD OF DIRECTORS

The company's board of directors should be structured, not by asking who has a right to sit on the board, but who will contribute the most to the company's success. For a start-up company, a small board of about five members works best for a variety of reasons. From a practical standpoint, the board of a start-up must convene more often during the formative years of the company. If there are too many members, it's difficult to find a time when everybody can meet.

The five-person board may consist of one or two representatives from management or from the company founders, one of whom should be the company president. The board may also include two representatives from the venture capital firm, and one outsider who has operating experience and can act as an advisor to the president. Preferably, the two company representatives are both founders and on an equal footing in the company's hierarchy, so that they will not be afraid to challenge each other's ideas during meetings. If the president asks somebody who is his junior to join him on the board, the junior individual may feel compelled to agree with him in all matters, rather than engage in a productive dialogue. The venture capitalists who sit on the board should be chosen for their expertise and knowledge about the company's business. Each firm has its own industry experts, and the entrepreneur should identify the individuals who can be most helpful.

THE EXIT

How a venture capitalist anticipates liquidating his holdings in a company will determine whether or not he will invest in the deal. When he thinks about the exit, a venture capitalist will consider:

- Timing
- Price/market valuation
- Availability of liquidation options, including
    - —Later stage financiers
    - —An initial public offering
    - —A merger
    - —Sale of the company in a buyout

Timing concerns the company's stage of growth. The right time to exit is when, as a result of the various fundings,the company has reached the peak of its fast-growth phase, or *ramping up*, and is ready to move into a period of slower growth. At this point, the company has maximized its use of the venture capital. The venture capitalist can determine the best time to exit by measuring the dollar amount of the investment against the length of time for which the company had use of the capital. By exiting before the company reaches the slower growth stages, the venture capitalist can realize the best possible return on investment. See Fig. 5-1.

Timing also refers to cycles in the public equity market and the valuations the market places on various types of companies and on companies in general. If the market is strong and valuations are high,

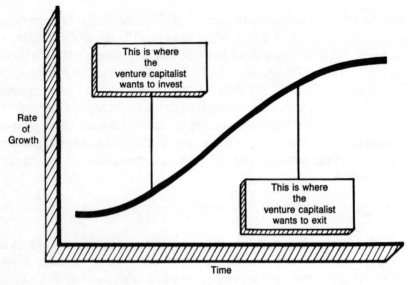

Fig. 5-1.

the venture capitalist may feel it is a propitious time to exit. He will be able to get a high valuation for his company and realize a substantial return. To meet his commitments and to make his own investors happy, the venture capitalist often prefers to pay investors by distributing public stock, which has more prestige and liquidity than private equity. (See Appendix A, "Alternatives to Venture Capital," Public Equity Markets.)

The venture capitalist may decide that he can most favorably exit a deal using a vehicle other than the public markets. Aside from going public, the basic methods for liquidation include selling the company to a larger corporation, arranging a leveraged buyout by management, or selling the company to other investors who have different investment objectives. Current market conditions determine which vehicles will bring the venture capitalist the highest return on investment at the time of exit. Not long ago, the most popular form of liquidation had been initial public offerings, but recently mergers and acquisitions achieved greater prominence.

PRINCIPLES OF SUCCESSFUL NEGOTIATION

Successful negotiating means walking the tightrope between giving up everything or surrendering nothing. Negotiating for a win-win scenario ensures that both sides leave something on the table, but come away with something neither party had before—a new venture.

Negotiation Cannot Be Delegated

In every negotiation of any substance, the principals must participate. Delegating the negotiation to subordinates is ineffectual because they lack sufficient knowledge about the proposed business, may not have everyone's best interests at heart, and don't have the necessary power to deal. The principals will always have the authority to revise any deal the subordinates arrange.

Compromise

Compromise is a useful strategy in every negotiation. Leave something on the table. Later on it can be leveraged to achieve closure on other key points. If the entrepreneur is willing to compromise on points that are less important to him, he builds extra space in which to push for the concessions he considers more crucial. Without that space, the entrepreneur's bargaining power is nil. Trust, fairness, and full disclosure cannot be compromised.

If one is entering into a long-term business venture with a partner, there can be no hidden agendas. The most destructive part of any negotiating process is the unexpected disclosure, the surprise, the hidden agenda that could emerge at an inopportune time. Full disclosure throughout the process of seeking venture capital is absolutely necessary for true negotiation to take place. Of course, this is smart from a legal standpoint, but it is also smart for the new venture. Being less than honest will eventually hurt a business, damaging the working relationship between management and the investors, and jeopardizing its operations. Once the venture becomes a reality, secrets are harder to keep.

Conduct The Negotiation In An Atmosphere of Equal Partnership

When the deal is structured and during the investment partnership, both sides must work together. It is crucial to create a non-adversarial environment in which management and venture capitalists feel they are striving toward the same goal, without the imposition of unreasonable or unbearable control mechanisms exercised on either party. Each side in the negotiation should feel as though they are doing business with equals, partners who stand to derive mutual benefits from a successfully managed company. An adversarial relationship at this stage will not transform later on into a good "marriage" between management and investors. As in a marriage, the people involved in the negotiation cannot assert their wills to achieve a gain at the other side's expense, without damaging their ability to function as a unit. To create a successful company, the partners must agree to a set of terms that meet both sets of objectives, the most common objective being the health of the company. This is the dynamic of a win-win scenario. Generally, it is wise to seek the counsel of an attorney, throughout the negotiation process. An attorney brings an objective point of view to the discussions and is capable of serving as an intermediary, representing the wishes of one side in the negotiations to the other.

Walk Away

Every negotiator should understand that at any time, he can walk away from the table. A deal should never be so critical that it becomes an absolute must for either side. Negotiating for survival is not negotiating from a position of strength. If a venture capital deal feels uncomfortable, or if the entrepreneur is not achieving what he thinks is most important through the negotiations, he should look for financing elsewhere. Perhaps he can try another venture capital group, or if through the negotiation process he realizes that venture capital money is not appropriate for what he wants to achieve with his business, he can successfully seek other forms of financing. These are discussed in the Appendix A, "Alternatives to Venture Capital."

RULES OF THUMB FOR NEGOTIATION

1. There are no rules of thumb; everything is negotiated.

2. Many entrepreneurs have to give up 60 percent of the company on first-round financing for $1.5 to $2.5 million.

3. During the first round, venture capitalists will not pay much more than 10 to 20 times the founder's price per share, (although in some cases there is no limit), and may not be interested in investing less than $500,000, except in "seed" deals.

4. The second round of financing will occur about a year after start-up and valuation will be at approximately 2 to 4 times the first round valuation if the company is doing well, and assuming the market is also doing well. In a poor market, second financings are sometimes done at almost no mark-up.

5. Venture capitalists want a minimum of 10 times their investment within five years.

$$\% \text{ ownership} = \frac{\$ \text{ investment} \times 10}{(\text{Expected sales (5 years)} \times \text{after-tax margin}\% \times \text{expected P/E ratio})}$$

For example, for a company "expecting" $50 million in annual sales in its fifth year with a 10 percent after-tax margin and a P/E ratio of 20, a venture capitalist would ask for at least 20 percent for a $2 million investment.

$$\% \text{ ownership} = \frac{10 \times \$2 \text{ million}}{(\$50 \text{ million} \times 10\% \times 20)} = 20\%$$

The fact that a venture capitalist may ask for 40 percent of the company may indicate that he will reduce the sales projections by 50 percent, a fact not to be overlooked by conservative entrepreneurs.

6. The founders and management should not expect to retain more than 10 percent to 15 percent of a company when it goes public.

7. Anticipating more than three rounds of financing before an initial public offering is not recommended. Ask for enough in two rounds to meet plans. Use the third round as a contingency.

8. Time the rounds of financing to correspond to major risk step-down points:

- Technical and sales team is in place
- Prototype works, technology is demonstrable
- Preproduction unit works
- Prestigious customers orders have been placed, or letter of intent based on performance
- Production units are being shipped in quantity

- Company has reached breakeven sales level

9. Founders may have to vest in stock over a three-year period at a rate of 33 percent/year; i.e., the company can buy back non-vested stock at the original price if the individual leaves. However, industry "norms" for this vary. Some stocks are immediately vested, while others vest at the end of five years.

LEGAL REPRESENTATION

Most entrepreneurs are starting a company for the first time, so they do not have experience with negotiating deals or understanding the venture capital process. On the other hand, venture investors structure numerous deals every year and have a sophisticated knowledge about the process and the long-term ramifications of contractual agreements. The importance of finding an attorney who specializes in venture capital deals cannot be sufficiently emphasized. In many cases, the attorney will be called upon to serve as a representative of the entrepreneur's best interests to the venture capitalist, providing his expertise during negotiations. In fact, an attorney who specializes in the legal needs of high tech or high growth companies can help the entrepreneur during the entire process of finding venture capital, through the early growth stages of the company, and later on as the company matures.

Initially, a knowledgeable attorney can be a good source of venture capital contacts. Also, he can review the business plan and make suggestions to improve it, he can assist in the negotiation process and so help to arrange a more favorable agreement, he can guide the entrepreneur in understanding the necessary legal process, and draw up necessary documents. For all these reasons, entrepreneurs should seriously consider hiring an attorney before going into negotiations with potential investors. The terms that are discussed in initial meetings often set the foundations for future negotiations. Entrepreneurs must be prepared by understanding the critical issues.

When seeking legal counsel, an entrepreneur should select a firm that is known to be experienced and knowledgeable in venture capital financings, preferably not the same firm that represents the venture capitalist for reasons of conflict of interest. It is important to choose a firm with a good reputation in the financial community and with whom the venture capitalists are familiar. The good reputation of the firm lends credibility to the entrepreneur's venture as well as providing some assurance of the firm's ability to handle venture capital deals.

Entrepreneurs should meet the attorney who will actually do the work, receive a commitment that this person will handle the case himself, and establish a good working rapport. It's not important that the attorney understand the technical side of a business. For instance, he will not need to know the whys and wherefores of microprocessors circuitry or monoclonal antibodies to adequately represent his client. He should be thoroughly knowledgeable about handling venture capital deals, however, since an inexperienced attorney can waste a lot of time and money focusing on minutia—or by missing an important point, create problems for the company down the road.

There are several issues in negotiating a deal that require particular attention from an attorney. Some of those issues are of greater importance to the entrepreneur than the investor and vice versa. One of the major concerns for the investor is the construction of the company's board of directors, the employee stock pool and its repurchasing and vesting rights, anti-dilution rights, and the right of first refusal, or pre-emptive rights. Entrepreneurs tend to be most concerned about the vesting schedule, the structure of the board of directors, and punitive anti-dilution provisions.

No one right way to finalize a venture capital agreement exists. Depending on how the deal is structured, the particular requirements of the entrepreneur and the investor, and which part of the country they are in, different legal documents are used to state the special terms of the deal. However, four key documents will probably be used. They are the term sheet, the investment agreement, the shareholders agreement (although not usually in West coast deals), and the stock purchase agreement. The term sheet is a non-legally binding document that is usually unsigned and is drafted by the investor's counsel to state the general terms of the deal, and frequently substitutes for the shareholder's agreement. The shareholder's agreement contains provisions that outline the way insiders are allowed to vote and sell their stock. The employee stock purchase agreement establishes a reserve of stock to be used as an incentive when hiring and retaining key employees. To give you a better idea of what these documents contain, we have included a sample term sheet and stock purchase agreement at the end of this chapter.

Usually, counsel will review the entrepreneur's company bylaws, the existing stock option plan, and probably rewrite the articles of corporation for the rights of the preferred stock; i.e., liquidation preference, dividends, and conversion rights. Sometimes a separate agreement is drawn up for registration rights, which allows the investors to add subsequent financings to the same registration rights, instead of creating new ones with each round.

From a legal standpoint, the process goes something like this. After the venture capitalist agrees to finance a deal and establishes the company valuation and the percent of ownership, he will call his attorney. The attorney will get in touch with the entrepreneur's law firm and secure pertinent documents concerning the new business, including the articles of incorporation, the bylaws, any existing stock option plans, and all previous agreements. The investor's attorney then sends the entrepreneur's attorney a term sheet. At this point, the entrepreneur's attorney will call the investor's counsel and both sides will meet to negotiate some of the terms and finalize the term sheet. As is true for most financial transactions, the side "with the money" is responsible for drafting the documents. When a deal is syndicated, the attorney for the lead venture capitalist represents the deal. If the investors invest in equal shares, they pick one firm to act as the lead.

From the legal standpoint, the actual time it takes to complete the paperwork is only about two to three weeks, but if there is extensive negotiation or many investors, the deal will take longer to close. It is important to remember that attorney's time is expensive, and the more either party uses legal services to review documents and negotiate fine points, the more expensive putting the deal together becomes. In some ways, too much time spent refining documents is wasted time. If the company is successful, most of the protectionary clauses will never be needed. If the company is not successful, the protectionary clauses are useless, since there will be no capital to divide, no company to liquidate. The items that must be clarified, such as the function of the preferred stock, can be administered simply, because experienced legal counsel routinely handles venture capital deals.

Some mention should be made concerning the differences between East and West coast in the way legal documents are drafted. The West coast law firms tend to be less formal in their approach to documentation.

The East coast law firms issue documents that often include lengthy positive and negative convenants and may be subject to rigorous negotiations.

Appendix B includes examples of an actual term sheet and stock purchase agreement, reprinted with the permission of Heller, Ehrman, White & McAuliffe, a law firm based in San Francisco. There is also a glossary in the back of the book.

Appendix A

Alternatives to Venture Capital

If after researching venture capital funding, the entrepreneur decides it is not an appropriate method for financing his business, alternatives are available. Such alternatives include public offerings, private placements, financing through government sources, research and development arrangements, and standard types of debt financing. One's choice of alternative financing methods will probably be determined by the stage of the company's development, the conditions in the financial marketplace, the strategic goals of the company, and even the kinds of products or services the company offers.

- At the stage when an entrepreneur is researching a concept for starting a young company, he has other financing choices in addition to venture capital. Very often, financing comes from the company founders and relatives; however, grants from governmental sources are also a possibility.
- If the company is in a start-up phase; i.e., if the management team is assembling and beginning to conduct market research for future product development, the entrepreneur may wish to consider making a private equity placement.
- If management is seeking first or second round financing, and if the team is ready to develop a prototype product or begin manufacturing, financing may be available through a private placement with institutional investors and industrial companies, or through an R & D Limited Partnership arrangement.
- When the company is in a pre-public expansion phase, companies should again consider making private equity placements with institutional and industrial investors.
- And when the company is more mature, a variety of financing options are available: through public equity markets, through joint ventures, and through bank financings and other debt financing sources.

GOVERNMENT SOURCES

Although applying for government funding involves wading through oceans of forms, it can be worth the effort, especially if it is "free money," as in the case of some grant programs. Government loans are available from a variety of sources including local governments, state governments, and at the federal level.

- At the local level, financing is available through tax-exempt bonds and notes that cities and counties issue to promote business development in their areas. Entrepreneurs should call their local governments to learn more about financing options in their municipality.
- Some states have established corporations that lend money for business expansion purposes, or distribute funds from the Department of Housing and Urban Development through Community Development Block Grants. Again, the entrepreneur should check with state government offices of commerce or economic development to learn about the specifics.

FEDERAL SOURCES FOR LOANS

Loans are available from several federal agencies and government sponsored programs including: the Small Business Administration, the Farmer's Home Administration, the Economic Development Administration, and the Small Business Innovation Research Program. The government often considers an application only if the entrepreneur has been refused by other lending institutions, and often, being turned down is a requirement to seeking federal funding.

There are two kinds of federal loan programs, direct and participation. When it grants a direct loan, the government agency determines the loan's interest rates and terms. The agency then gives the funds to a company, who repays the loan directly to the agency. Entrepreneurs can pursue a direct loan by getting in touch with an agency loan officer to discuss the nature of the loan and to ask for the forms. Since government officers only review forms that are complete, it is critical that all forms be filled out accurately and in detail. Direct loans are becoming more difficult to obtain, and in fact they may be discontinued in favor of participation loans.

Participation loans are joint loans that the government makes with another lender, for which the government's participation is qualified as either "Immediate" or "Deferred." In an Immediate Loan, the government supplies part of the funding along with the lender. With a Deferred Loan, also known as a *Guaranteed Loan*, the government does not actually contribute any funds, but guarantees to make repayments if the company defaults. The loan itself is granted by the commercial lender, with whom the entrepreneur works. The lender decides whether or not it requires support from the government to make the loan.

The Small Business Administration (SBA)

Congress created the SBA in 1953 to assist the growth of new ventures. Businesses who seek funds from the SBA must meet stringent criteria concerning the size, status, and purpose of the business. A variety of SBA loan programs exist, but the best known program is the 7(a), which is a guaranteed loan program, for up to 90 percent of the loan, with the guaranteed portion not to exceed $500,000. Companies who qualify for SBA loans must be independently owned and generally have 500 employees or less. The SBA will not loan money to a company that could get financing from a regular commercial lender, nor to a business that has assets that can be liquidated for capital, nor to a company lacking sufficient collateral.

The Farmer's Home Administration

This federal agency makes capital available to be used only in rural areas. Loans are usually made through a local lender and can be 90 percent guaranteed by the Farmer's Home Administration. The FHA offers two basic types of loans: for agricultural purposes or for business expansion in rural areas.

The Economic Development Administration

Recently the scope of the Economic Development Administration's activity has been limited. However, through both grant and loan programs, the EDA provides capital for business development, specifically for industries and commercial growth in economically depressed areas. The EDA is especially commited to the creation of new jobs, and loans are granted in part, on the number of new jobs a business will create per number of dollars being loaned. EDA loans are guaranteed for up to 90 percent, and must be applied for through a lender.

FEDERAL SOURCES FOR GRANTS

The Small Business Innovation Research Program

The Small Business Innovation Research Program (SBIR) was originated to encourage small businesses to conduct research and development activities for projects the government supports. This program awards small businesses a combination grant and service contracts. The government requires several agencies, such as the National Science Foundation and the Department of Agriculture, to allocate a portion of their research and development funds to the SBIR, which is supervised by the Small Business Administration. Each agency establishes its own terms for awarding grants.

The SBIR awards grants and contracts in three phases. In Phase I, companies may receive up to $50,000 to fund a research project. This capital is usually used to conduct a feasibility study of the research methodology and to ascertain the benefits of such research. In Phase II, companies may receive up to $500,000 to develop the best ideas over the next one or two years, and in Phase III, the agency involved will issue production contracts to help bring the product to market.

The entrepreneur must discern what the R & D requirements are for each agency and then send a proposal demonstrating the company's ability to meet those needs. Companies may send unsolicited proposals if the agency accepts them. However, generally, proposals should be sent in response to an agency's request for proposals, or in response to the periodic presolicitations that the SBA Office of Innovation, Research, and Technology issues to describe R & D projects currently of interest to particular departments.

EQUITY

For a variety of reasons, a company may decide it is not yet ready to go public, and venture capital financing may not be attainable or desirable. Instead, management may consider making a private placement. This is a good financing alternative because the company can get as much capital through an exempt offering as it would from a public placement without having to comply with stringent and expensive reporting procedures. Because the company sells stock to a few private investors, rather than to the general public, these offerings are exempt from registration with the SEC. Private placements require less paperwork, and save time.

There are different kinds of exempt offerings, known by the securities regulations that make the offerings possible, but the most famous is Regulation D. Under the Small Business Exemption, Rule 504 of Regulation D, non-public companies can sell up to $500,000 of stock to an unrestricted number of investors. Under Rule 505, companies both public and private can sell up to $5 million of stock to an unrestricted number of accredited investors, but to no more than 35 nonaccredited investors. (To be considered accredited, an investor must meet one of the criteria specified by Regulation D.) And under Regulation D's Rule 506, companies both public and private can sell as much stock as they wish to an unrestricted number of accredited buyers, and up to 35 nonaccredited purchasers who are considered "sophisticated," meaning, sufficiently knowledgeable to properly assess the benefits and risks of investing in private companies.

An offering may also be exempt from registration if it is made intrastate. Through an exempt offering, and usually without losing control to outside investors, management can quickly raise funds the company will not need to repay. Although exempt offerings are not subject to federal registration, state laws may require registration with state agencies. In addition, private placements are subject to securities laws and their anti-fraud provisions. A company making a private placement would be well-advised to provide accurate, complete, and unbiased information about the company to potential investors, so that they are equipped to make an intelligent decision.

Sometimes a company finds potential investors among friends, relatives, and professional associates. However, private placements are usually made through a broker who knows where to find investors interested in small companies. Depending on the nature of the company's business, there may be a built-in group of potential investors. Stock can be issued to them directly, instead of through an investment banker. Professional investors are also interested in the exempt offerings of small companies, especially if the company has an excellent management team. These investors are experienced and look for promising young companies in an industry with high growth potential. Another group of investors search specifically for companies that are making a private placement now, but who may go public at some point in the future. That the company is making an exempt offering now signifies it has strong potential in the marketplace. The investors hope to meet their objectives once the company does go public and the price of their stock holdings rise.

PUBLIC EQUITY MARKETS

Going public can be a successful method for raising funds and heightening the company's prestige, but being public also dramatically changes the way the company does business. Going public confers several advantages:

- As a result of the offering, the company has new capital that is available for general corporate purposes. By making the initial public offering (IPO), a company improves its financial situation through stock sales to the public. Generally, $3 to $5 million is the smallest offering a company would want to make; otherwise, the cost of the capital is too high. Potentially, an offering can be for as much as $100 million! This is money the company will not have to repay.
- Public companies enjoy greater prestige and improved business relations. Investors assume a public company is managed by an experienced team. Because they make frequent public disclosures, well managed public companies earn a positive reputation.
- Because the company's credibility is increased, it improves its borrowing power and can borrow funds at better interest rates.
- The company becomes a better instrument to use for making acquisitions.
- The public stock helps attract and retain employees, through stock option and ownership plans. Public stock used for employee compensation and incentives is more attractive than private equity because the market defines its value and the stock is highly liquid.
- The company provides liquidity for shareholders. Public stock usually trades at a higher value than private stock because investors are willing to pay more for the shares' increased marketability, and greater availability of information about the company.
- The share value may increase, so the company can obtain future capital on more favorable terms.

Going public also brings disadvantages:

- The biggest disadvantage is that the company's quarter-to-quarter business strategy must change to meet shareholders' and public expectations. This loss of privacy also influences the way management makes key decisions, because the management of public companies must seek approval from the board of directors and sometimes from the shareholders. Also in the process of keeping shareholders happy, the management of public companies must strike a balance between near-term objectives that will increase dividends and stock prices, and long-term goals that favor the company's healthy development over a period of years.

- There is a higher level of information disclosure, both in the present and in the future. The primary disadvantage is that public companies must disclose sensitive information about executive compensation and company operations. As a result, any special practices the company engaged in as a private company may have to change because they would not be well-regarded in a public setting.
- The process of going public is expensive, time consuming, and because management is redirecting its attention to the offering, there is a possibility that it will lose control of the company. Another disadvantage is the expense and time involved in maintaining public status, as reports and proxy statements must be prepared, filed, and mailed. Going public takes between two to six months and during that time management must continue to run the company. The success of a public offering depends on both good timing and good planning. Does management have the necessary qualities to manage a growing company, and is it well regarded by the financial community? Can the business's information systems produce accurate and timely information about the company's financial activities? Does the company have a history of steady growth that suggests the stock will continue to increase in value? Are conditions in the marketplace favorable for a public offering? The importance of picking the right time to go public cannot be overemphasized. Failing to do so can mean that an offering is cancelled before it is completed and the costs are absorbed by the company. The company may have to make more shares available at lower prices, or the price of its shares may tumble in a bad aftermarket and seriously compromise the company's credibility.
- If the stock price drops, the company may experience difficulty later on in raising future equity.
- Stock in public companies has a higher estate tax valuation.
- Public companies usually pay dividends.

R & D AND THE LIMITED PARTNERSHIP

When a company looks for ways to finance its research projects, it may consider arranging a limited partnership. The limited partners are those people who invest in the partnership, and their financial liability is generally limited to the sum of their investment. The company acts as the sponsor or general partner, or an independent third party may be the general partner. The general partner provides both the management and the research technology and capabilities. Limited partnerships can be offered publicly or privately, or established through joint ventures with corporations.

Since partnerships are not taxable, R & D limited partnerships were originally designed to pass the tax advantages along to the investor. Prior to the Tax Reform Act of 1986, all profits and losses from the partnership's activities were reflected on the limited partner's private tax return. Therefore, if the partnership lost money, that loss became a personal write-off. In essence, through this tax advantage, the investor could reduce the cost of his initial investment, or the tax advantage would improve the net return on investment if the project was successful. However, as a result of the passage of the Tax Reform Act, limited partners in R & D limited partnerships are no longer allowed to write off their "passive activity losses" from limited partnerships against other income.

As the general partner, the company licenses to the partnership the rights to the technology and retains the use of that technology for future projects through a non-exclusive royalty-free license. The R & D is performed with "best efforts," which means the limited partners understand the project may not be successful. The partnership agrees to make payments to the sponsor company by either reimbursing for the cost of the work, on a fixed-fee basis, or according to a cost-plus arrangement. The company who hopes to arrange an R & D partnership should place special emphasis on development, since financing research will not provide investors with a saleable product from which they can derive an adequate return on investment.

The company benefits from R & D limited partnerships because of the way it accounts for the partnership arrangement. Hypothetically, if the company raises $100 million in cash through a stock offering, the cash is entered on the balance sheet as an asset. If the company spends that cash on a research project, the expenditure is considered an expense. However, the company owns the technology it develops as a result of its research.

Now let's say the company raises money through an R & D partnership. In this case, the revenue and the expenses never hit the company profit/loss statement because this transaction happens under the aegis of the limited partnership. Thus this off-balance sheet financing has the benefit of being both "off-balance sheet" and "off profit and loss." The drawback is that the partnership also owns the technology, although the company can later buy the technology back from the partnership.

It is important to clearly distinguish one R & D effort from any others the business might engage in, and to specify exactly what a successful conclusion of the project will render. If the project is not successful, the partnership usually dissolves; however, the partnership may have the right to sell the technology or whatever product did result from the R & D work. In this case, the company would be wise to have the right of first refusal to purchase the technology and keep it out of the competition's hands.

The limited partners are compensated in a variety of ways. The company may purchase the exclusive rights to the developed products with cash or stock. The company and the partnership may agree to jointly market the products. The company may buy the exclusive rights to the technology and the products once the company starts paying royalties, offsetting part of the royalties against the price of the purchase. If the company becomes the exclusive manufacturer and marketer of the products, it will pay royalties to the partnership.

How the partnership is compensated will effect the individual's level of risk and reward, and consequently their interest in investing. For instance, if the royalties are paid when the product is profitable, the partnership must wait longer for compensation than if payments are based on the product's sales. Agreements concerning compensation should clearly define what constitutes a product's success, what the purpose of the product is, and how compensation will be paid.

R & D arrangements are complex and entail a variety of accounting, legal, and tax considerations. At the time of writing, the effects of the Tax Reform Act on the amount of capital available through limited partnerships is still uncertain. The expectation is that, without the motivation of a tax shelter, fewer people will want to invest. However, R & D limited partnerships will continue to be a viable financing alternative as investors redirect their efforts to locate projects with solid potential for compensating high risk investments with high returns. In fact, if a project succeeds, investors can anticipate substantially high returns—as much as 40 percent to 50 percent after taxes.

In summation, the advantages of an R & D Limited Partnership include:

* Large amounts of money become available to the research company—anywhere from $10,000 to as much as $100 million or more.
* Management retains control of the company because there is no equity dilution, and management also retains control over the direction of product development.
* There is no cost or risk to the company if the product cannot be successfully developed.
* The capital costs are low.
* The company enjoys the benefits of off-balance sheet financing.

The disadvantages include:

* The technology may be expensive to get back from the partnership of investors.
* R & D partnerships are complicated to structure.
* Management must spend time and associated costs to put together and maintain the deal.
* The tax advantages have been nullified by the Tax Reform Act of 1986.

The entrepreneur will want to consult his accountant and attorney when considering R & D financing. For more information, the reader is referred to *The Arthur Young Guide to Financing for Growth*.

DEBT FINANCING

Debt financing is not recommended for companies in the seed or start-up phases, but it is a good financing source for established companies, who have adequate cash flow to make loan payments. Typically, the loan is used as working capital or to expand the business. Most companies choose to borrow money when they want to preserve equity. Since the debtor does not own equity in the company, debt financing does not create dilution, nor can the debtor collect on earnings. Another advantage of debt financing is that the interest payments on the loan are tax deductible.

There are also disadvantages to debt financing. A company must first have the cash flow to meet the terms of the loan. Also, the more leveraged the company is, the higher the company's break even point. Further, if the debt to equity ratio is too high, making loan payments can hurt a company's profitability and severely effect its operating potential. Highly leveraged companies are considered riskier investments, and future rounds of financing may be more difficult to obtain.

The most common sources of debt financing are banks, finance companies, and savings and loans. Banks are the most traditional source and they offer a variety of financing options, both short- and long-term. Short-term financing typically covers unanticipated cash needs or is used to increase working capital. The company may need working capital to increase inventory or to finance sales. Short-term loans are either secured or unsecured, depending on the history of the company. If the borrower has a successful track record and a good cash flow, the lender is less likely to require collateral than if the company is relatively young. When a company is as yet unproven, the lender will probably require a pledge of assets to secure the loan. There are several ways to borrow working capital: through accounts receivable financing, through inventory financing, and with a revolving line of credit.

On the other hand, a company will typically use long-term financing to purchase capital assets, for expansion purposes, or to acquire another business. These transactions are frequently too expensive to finance through the regular company cash flow. The most common forms of long-term lending include capital loans, term-loans, and leases. Long-term financing is repaid over a number of years according to a regular payment schedule. Lenders make long-term loans only after carefully screening applicants, and the interest rates for long-term loans are higher than for short-term transactions. Capital loans are used to purchase capital assets, while a company uses a term-loan for expansion or acquisition purposes. If the company decides to acquire capital equipment, banks finance leasing arrangements in much the same way they do capital loans.

The advantages to debt financing include:

- No equity dilution.
- Debt financing can increase the return-on-investment/leverage.
- Establishing contact with a bank through a loan also accesses other bank services.

The disadvantages are:

- To secure the loan, a company needs financeable assets, such as inventory, fixed assets, accounts receivables, or other tangible items. Debt financing is not practical for financing "ideas."
- Leveraged financing is expensive and can hamper future financings if the company does not prosper.
- Banks and other debt sources traditionally do not understand the needs of high tech companies.
- The covenants with a source of debt financing can be restrictive.

For more information about these subjects, we encourage the reader to consult *The Arthur Young Guide to Financing for Growth*, published by John Wiley & Sons.

Memorandum of Terms for Private Placement of Equity Securities Preferred Stock Purchase Agreement

_____, 198__

MEMORANDUM OF TERMS FOR PRIVATE
PLACEMENT OF EQUITY SECURITIES
IN⁻

_____
_____
_____

      This memorandum summarizes the principal terms with
respect to a private placement of equity securities of
_____ (the "Company") by a group of investors.

Introduction

      The Company was incorporated in _____ on
_____, 19___. It presently has an authorized
capitalization consisting of _____ shares of Common Stock
("Common"), _____ shares of which have been issued to
_____ shareholders, and _____ shares of [type of
preferred stock, if any], _____ shares of which have been
issued to _____ shareholders.

      The _____ Founders of the Company have purchased
and paid for in full _____ shares of the Company's Common at a
price of _____ per share. As part of this private placement,
all of the Founders will execute Stock Restriction and Market
Standoff Agreements as described in "Stock Restriction and Market
Standoff Agreements" below. In addition there are outstanding
options to purchase in the aggregate _____ shares of Common at
prices ranging from $_____ to $_____ per share of Common.

Proposed Private Placement

      The Company and the investors propose a private placement
of shares of Preferred Stock on the following terms:

Amount:	$_____
Type of Security:	Series ___ Preferred Stock ("Preferred")
Price Per Share:	$_____("Original Purchase Price") Such price is to be consistent with the purchase of ___% of the Common on a fully-diluted basis after completion of the private placement.
Rights, Preferences, Privileges and Restrictions of Preferred Stock:	(1) Dividend Provisions: The holders of the Preferred will be entitled to receive dividends

Rights, Preferences,
Privileges and Restrictions
of Preferred Stock (cont.):

at the rate determined by the
Board of Directors ("Board")
from time to time, whenever of
funds are legally available and
when and as declared by the
Board. No dividend shall be
paid on the Common at a rate
greater than the rate at which
dividends are paid on Preferred
(based on the number of shares
of Common into which the
Preferred is convertible on the
date the dividend is declared).
Dividends on Preferred will be
in preference to dividends paid
on the Common. Dividends on the
Preferred will be noncumulative.

(2) Liquidation Preference: In
the event of any liquidation or
winding up of the Company, the
holders of Preferred will be
entitled to receive in
preference to the holders of
Commmon an amount ("Liquidation
Amount") equal to the Original
Purchase Price plus any
dividends declared on the
Preferred but not paid. A
consolidation or merger of the
Company or sale of all or
substantially all of its assets
shall be deemed to be a
liquidation or winding up for
purposes of the liquidation
preference.

(3) Redemption: 7 years from
the date of purchase of the
Preferred, the Company will
redeem the Preferred by paying
in cash the Liquidation Amount.

(4) Conversion: A holder of
Preferred will have the right to
convert Preferred, at the option
of the holder, at any time, into
shares of Common. The total
number of shares of Common into

Rights, Preferences,
Privileges and Restrictions
of Preferred Stock (cont.):

which Preferred may be converted
-initially will be determined by
dividing the Original Purchase
Price by the conversion price.
The initial conversion price
will be the Original Purchase
Price. The conversion price
will be the subject of
adjustment as provided in
paragraph (6) below.

(5) <u>Automatic Conversion</u>:
Preferred will be automatically
converted into Common, at the
then applicable conversion
price, in the event of an
underwritten public offering of
shares of the Common of the
Company at a public offering
price per share (prior to
underwriter commissions and
expenses) that is not less than
seven times the Original
Purchase Price in an offering of
not less than $7,500,001.

(6) <u>Antidilution Provisions</u>:
The conversion price of the
Preferred will be subject to
adjustment on a full ratchet
basis to prevent dilution in the
event that the Company issues
additional shares (other than
the Reserved Employee Shares
described under "Reserved
Employee Shares" below) at a
purchase price less than the
applicable conversion price so
that the conversion price will
be reduced to the lowest price
at which any additional share is
issued.

(7) <u>Voting Rights</u>: Except
with respect to election of
Directors, a holder of Preferred
will have the right to that
number of votes equal to the
number of shares of Common
issuable upon conversion of its

Rights, Preferences,
Privileges and Restrictions
of Preferred Stock (cont.):

Preferred. Election of
Directors will be as described
under "Board Representation and
Meetings" below.

(8) Protective Provisions:
Consent of the holders of at
least a majority of the
Preferred will be required for
any action which (i) alters or
changes the rights, preferences
or privileges of the Preferred
materially and adversely,
(ii) increases the authorized
number of shares of Preferred
Stock, (iii) creates any new
class of shares having
preference over or being on a
parity with the Preferred, or
(iv) involves sale by the
Company of a substantial portion
of its assets, any merger of the
Company with another entity, or
any amendment of the Company's
articles of incorporation.

Information Rights:

So long as an investor holds
Common issued or issuable upon
conversion of Preferred
(collectively, "IOC Common"),
the Company will deliver to such
investor annual and quarterly
financial statements.

So long as the investor holds at
least 5% of the IOC Common, the
Company will timely furnish such
investor with budgets and
monthly financial statements.
The obligation of the Company to
furnish budgets and monthly
financial statements will
terminate upon a public offering
of Common.

Registration Rights:

[If the Company has shares
outstanding with registration
rights] (1) Merger of
Registration Rights: It shall
be a condition of closing that

-4-

Registration Rights (cont.):

the registration rights provisions of the agreement dated _____, 19___ between the Company and certain purchasers of the Company's [Common or Preferred] Stock will be merged with the registration rights of of the investors. All shares subject to such registration rights provisions shall be deemed "Registrable Securities." [Note: If this paragraph is used, the term "Registrable Securities" should be used as applicable in the remaining paragraphs dealing with registration rights.]

(2) Demand Rights: If, at any time after the earlier of the Company's initial public offering and the date three years from the purchase of the Preferred (but not within 6 months of the effective date of a registration), holders of at least 50% of the IOC Common request that the Company file a Registration Statement for at least 20% of the IOC Common (or any lesser percentage if the anticipated aggregate offering price, net of underwriting discounts and commissions would exceed $2,000,000), the Company will use its best efforts to cause such shares to be registered. The Company will not be obligated to effect more than one registratration (other than on Form S-3) under these demand right provisions.

(3) Registrations on Form S-3: Holders of at least 25% of the IOC Common will have the right to require the Company to file an unlimited number of Registration Statements on Form S-3 (or any equivalent successor form).

Registration Rights (cont.):

(4) Piggy-Back Registration:
The investors will be entitled
to "piggy-back" registration
rights on registrations of the
Company, subject to the right of
the Company and its underwriters, in view of market
conditions, to reduce the number
of shares of the investors
proposed to be registered in the
Company's first registered
public offering.

(5) Registration Expenses: The
registration expenses (exclusive
of underwriting discounts and
special counsel fees of a
selling shareholder) of one
demand registration and as to
three piggy-backs will be borne
by the Company, and all other
expenses of registered offerings
shall be borne pro rata among
the selling shareholders and, if
it participates, the Company.

(6) Transfer of Registration
Rights: The registration rights
may be transferred to a
transferree (other than a
competitor of the Company) who
acquires at least 20% of the
shares of a holder of IOC
Common. Transfer of
registration rights to a partner
of any investor will be without
restriction as to minimum
shareholding.

(7) Other Registration
Provisions: Other provisions
will be contained in the
Purchase Agreement with respect
to registration rights as are
reasonable, including cross-
indemnification, the Company's
ability to delay the filing of
the demand registration for a
period of not more than 120
days, the agreement by
purchasers of the Preferred if
requested by the underwriter in
a public offering not to sell

-6-

Registration Rights (cont.):

any unregistered Common they hold for a period of up to 90 days following the effective date of the Registration Statement of such offering, the period of time during which the Registration Statement will be kept effective, underwriting arrangements and the like. The registration rights will only apply to Common issued upon conversion of Preferred and the Company shall have no obligation to register an offering of Preferred.

Board Representation and Company Meetings:

The corporate documents of the Company will provide that the authorized number of directors will be not less than _____ nor more than _____. So long as 50% or more of the Preferred issued in the financing remain outstanding, the Preferred (voting as a class) will elect ____ directors, the Common (voting as a class) will elect ____ directors, and the remaining ____ directors will be elected by both the Common and the Preferred, each voting separately as a class. So long as more than 25%, but less than 50% of the Preferred remain outstanding, the Preferred (voting as a class) will elect ____ directors, the Common (voting as a class) will elect ___ directors, and the remaining directors will be elected by both the Common and the Preferred, each voting separately as a class. If at any time, 25% or less of the Preferred remains outstanding, all of the directors will be elected by the Preferred and Common voting together as one class, and the Preferred will be entitled to vote as if all of the Preferred were converted to Common. The Board will meet at

Board Representation and
Company Meetings (cont.):

least quarterly. The bylaws
will provide that any two
directors or holders of at least
25% of the Preferred may call a
meeting of the Board of
Directors.

Employment Agreements;
New Hires:

The Company has or will have
employment agreements with the
following persons: _____.
The Company will elect persons
acceptable to the investors to
the following positions:

_____.

Key Man Insurance:

As determined by the Board of
Directors.

Right of First Refusal:

So long as an investor is a
holder of not less than __% of
the IOC Common, if the Company
proposes to offer any shares for
the purpose of financing its
business (other than Reserved
Employee Shares, shares issued
in the acquisition of another
company, or shares offered to
the public pursuant to an
underwritten public offering),
the Company will first offer
such shares to such investor on
a pro rata basis and in such
amount as will enable such
investor to maintain its
percentage ownership of the
Company on a fully converted
basis as of the day prior to the
sale of such shares. The right
of first refusal will terminate
upon an underwritten public
offering of shares of the
Company.

Stock Restriction and Market
Standoff Agreements:

(1) Stock Restriction Agreement:
The Founders and all other
holders of Common of the Company
who are employees of, or
consultants to, the Company will
execute a Stock Restriction
Agreement with the Company
pursuant to which the Company

Stock Restriction and Market
Standoff Agreements (cont.):

will have a repurchase option to
buy back at cost a portion of
the shares of Common Stock held
by such person in the event that
such shareholder's employment
with, or consulting to, the
Company is terminated prior to
the expiration of 48 months from
the date of the purchase of the
Preferred or date of first
employment or consulting,
whichever is later (the
"Measuring Date"). A portion of
the shares will be released from
the repurchase option based upon
continued employment by the
Company as follows: 25% will be
released from the repurchase
option at the end of 12 months
from the Measuring Date, 25%
will be released at the end of
24 months from the Measuring
Date and thereafter 1/24th of
the remaining shares will be
released from the repurchase
option per month. In addition,
the Company will have a right of
first refusal with respect to
any employee's or consultant's
shares proposed to be resold.
The price at which the Company
may exercise its right of first
refusal will be equal to the
lower of (i) the price offered
by the proposed third party
purchaser and (ii) the price
most recently set by the Board
of Directors as the fair market
value of the Common. The right
of first refusal will terminate
upon a public offering. The
Stock Restriction Agreement will
also contain a right of co-sale
providing that, before sale of
Common, the investors must be
given an opportunity to
participate in such sale on a
basis proportionate to the
amount of securities held by the
selling shareholder and the IOC

Stock Restriction and Market
Standoff Agreements (cont.):

shares held by all of the
investors.

(2) Market Standoff Agreement:
It will be a condition of
closing that the Company will
cause all present holders of the
Company's Common and all present
holders of options to purchase
the Company's Common to execute
a Market Standoff Agreement with
the Company pursuant to which
such holders will agree, if so
requested by the Company or any
underwriter's representative in
connection with the first two
public offerings of the
Company's Common, not to sell or
otherwise transfer any
securities of the Company during
a period of up to 120 days
following the effective date of
the applicable registration
statements.

Reserved Employee Shares:

The Company may reserve up to [a
number equivalent to 10-15% of
the Company's outstanding shares
of Common] shares of Common (the
"Reserved Employee Shares")
including shares presently
reserved for issuance upon the .
exercise of outstanding options
for issuance to Employees.

The Reserved Employee Shares
will be issued from time to time
under such arrangements,
contracts or plans as are
recommended by management and
approved by the Board. Issuance
of shares to employees in excess
of the Reserved Employee Shares
will be dilutive events
requiring adjustment of the
conversion price as provided
above and will be subject to the
investors' right of first
refusal described above.
Holders of Reserved Employee
Shares will be required to

-10-

Reserved Employee Shares (cont.):

    execute Stock Restriction
Agreements as described above.

Proprietary Information
and Inventions Agreement:

    Each officer, director and key
employee of the Company will
enter into a proprietary
information and inventions
agreement in a form reasonably
acceptable to the Company and
the investors.

The Purchase Agreement:

    The purchase of the Preferred
will be made pursuant to a Stock
Purchase Agreement drafted by
counsel to the investors and
reasonably acceptable to the
Company and the investors. The
Purchase Agreement will contain,
among other things, appropriate
representations and warranties
of the Company, covenants of the
Company reflecting the
provisions set forth herein, and
appropriate conditions including
qualification of the shares
under applicable Blue Sky laws,
the filing of a Certificate of
Amendment to the Company's
Articles of Incorporation to
authorize the Preferred, and
opinions of counsel.

Expenses:

    The Company and the investors
will each bear their own legal
and other expenses with respect
to the transaction (except that,
assuming a successful completion
of the offering, the Company
will pay at the Closing the
reasonable legal fees incurred
by a single counsel to all
investors).

Finders:

    The Company and the investors
will each indemnify the other
for any finder's fees for which
either is responsible.

Closing:

    The closing of the transaction
is expected to occur on or
before _____.

Counsel to the Company: _____
                                 _____
                                 _____
                                 _____

Counsel to the Investors: Christopher L. Kaufman, Esq.
                                 [Name of Associate]_____
                                 Heller, Ehrman, White & McAuliffe
                                 333 Bush Street
                                 San Francisco, CA 94104
                                 (415) 772-6000; or
                                 525 University Avenue
                                 Palo Alto, CA 94301
                                 (415) 326-7600

SERIES _ PREFERRED STOCK PURCHASE AGREEMENT

TABLE OF CONTENTS

EXHIBITS AND SCHEDULES

SERIES _ PREFERRED STOCK PURCHASE AGREEMENT

THIS SERIES _ PREFERRED STOCK PURCHASE AGREEMENT (the "Agreement") is made as of _____, 198_, by and among _____, a California corporation (the "Company"), and the persons listed on Schedule 1.1 who are signatories to this Agreement (the "Investors").

R E C I T A L S:

A.   The Board of Directors of the Company has adopted the Amended and Restated Articles of Incorporation ("Amended and Restated Articles") in the form attached hereto as Exhibit A which, among other matters, establish the rights, preferences and privileges of the Company's no par value Series _ Preferred Stock, (the "Preferred Stock").

B.   The Company desires to sell shares of Preferred Stock to the Investors, and the Investors desire to purchase shares of Preferred Stock, on the terms and subject to the conditions set forth in this Agreement.

THE PARTIES AGREE AS FOLLOWS:

1.   Purchase and Sale of Stock.

1.1   Sale and Issuance of Preferred Stock. The Company shall sell to the Investors and the Investors shall purchase from the Company, at a price of $_____ per share (the "Purchase Price"), an aggregate not to exceed _____ shares of Preferred Stock (the "Shares"). The number of Shares to be purchased by each Investor is set forth opposite the name of such Investor on Schedule 1.1.

1.2 <u>Closing</u>. The purchase and sale of the Shares
shall take place at the offices of Heller, Ehrman, White &
McAuliffe, _____, California _____, or at such
other place as the Company and the Investors mutually agree, on
such dates and at such times as the Company and the Investors
mutually agree (which dates, times and place are designated the
"Closing"). The first Closing shall take place at _____ _.m. on
_____, 198_, and the Company may issue and sell at subsequent
Closings Shares to additional Investors on an ongoing basis at any
time. At each Closing, the Company shall deliver to each Investor
a certificate representing the Shares which such Investor is
purchasing against delivery to the Company by such Investor at such
Closing of (a) an executed counterpart of this Agreement, and (b)
the Purchase Price of such Shares by wire transfer or by a check
payable to the Company.

2. <u>Definitions</u>. For purposes of this Agreement:

2.1 "Material Adverse Event" shall mean an
occurrence having a consequence that either (a) is materially
adverse as to the business, properties, prospects or financial
condition of the Company or (b) is reasonably foreseeable, and if
it were to occur might materially adversely affect the business,
properties, prospects or financial condition of the Company.

2.2 "Subsidiary" constitutes any corporation more
than 50% of whose stock (measured by virtue of voting rights) in
the aggregate is owned by the Company.

3. Representations and Warranties of the Company to the
Investors. The Company hereby represents and warrants to the
Investors that:

     3.1 Corporate Organization and Authority. The
Company:

          (a) is a corporation duly organized, validly
existing, authorized to exercise all its corporate powers, rights
and privileges, and in good standing in the State of California;

          (b) has the corporate power and corporate
authority to own and operate its properties and to carry on its
business as now conducted and as proposed to be conducted; and

          (c) is qualified as a foreign corporation in
all jurisdictions in which such qualification is required;
provided, however, that the Company need not be qualified in a
jurisdiction in which its failure to qualify would not have a
material adverse effect on the business, properties, prospects or
financial condition of the Company.

     3.2 Capitalization. Immediately prior to the
Closing, the authorized capital of the Company shall consist of:

          (a) Preferred Stock. _____
(_____) shares of Preferred Stock, none of which shall have
been issued prior to the first Closing.

          (b) Common Stock. _____
(_____) shares of Common Stock, of which _____
(_____) shares are duly and validly issued (including,
without limitation, issued in compliance with applicable federal

-3-

and state securities laws), fully-paid, non-assessable, outstanding
and held by the persons and in the amounts set forth on
Schedule 3.2.

(c) Other Securities. The Company has granted
options to purchase _____ shares of the Company's authorized
Common Stock. Except as contemplated by this Agreement or as set
forth in Schedule 3.2 hereto, there are no outstanding warrants,
options, conversion privileges, preemptive rights, or other rights
or agreements to purchase or otherwise acquire or issue any equity
securities of the Company.

3.3 Subsidiaries. The Company does not presently
own, have any investment in, or control, directly or indirectly,
any Subsidiaries, associations or other business entities. The
Company is not a participant in any joint venture or partnership.

3.4 Authorization. All corporate action on the
part of the Company, its officers, directors and shareholders
necessary for the authorization, execution, delivery and
performance of all obligations under this Agreement and for the
issuance and delivery of the Shares and of the Common Stock
issuable upon conversion of the Preferred Stock and the Shares has
been taken, and this Agreement and the Information and Registration
Rights Agreement (the "Rights Agreement") attached hereto as
Exhibit 6.8, and entered into with the Investors in connection with
this Agreement, constitute legally binding valid obligations of the
Company enforceable in accordance with their terms.

-4-

3.5 <u>Validity of Shares</u>. The Shares, when issued, sold and delivered in accordance with the terms and for the consideration expressed in this Agreement, shall be duly and validly issued (including, without limitation, compliance with applicable federal and state securities laws), fully-paid and non-assessable. The Common Stock issuable upon conversion of the Preferred Stock and the Shares, assuming such Common Stock is issued to the Investors, upon issuance in accordance with the Amended and Restated Articles shall be duly and validly issued (including, without limitation, issued in compliance with all applicable federal and state securities laws), fully paid and non-assessable.

3.6 <u>No Conflict with Other Instruments</u>. The execution, delivery and performance of this Agreement will not result in any violation of, be in conflict with, or constitute a default under, with or without the passage of time or the giving of notice: (i) any provision of the Company's Amended and Restated Articles or By-laws; (ii) any provision of any judgment, decree or order to which the Company is a party or by which it is bound; (iii) any material contract, obligation or commitment to which the Company is a party or by which it is bound; or (iv) to the Company's knowledge, any statute, rule or governmental regulation applicable to the Company.

3.7 <u>Financial Statements</u>. Attached as Exhibit 3.7 is the unaudited balance sheet of the Company at _____, 198_, together with an unaudited statement of income and expenses for the

period ended _____, 198_ (collectively, the "Financial
Statements"). The Financial Statements are complete and correct in
all material respects and fairly present the financial position of
the Company as of the date thereof.

     3.8 <u>Changes in Condition</u>. Except as described in
Schedule 3.8, there has not been since the date of the Financial
Statements:

     (a) any change in the assets, liabilities,
financial condition or operating results of the Company from that
reflected in the Financial Statements, except changes in the
ordinary course of business which individually, or in the
aggregate, do not constitute a Material Adverse Event;

     (b) any damage, destruction or loss, whether
or not covered by insurance, which might individually or in the
aggregate constitute a Material Adverse Event;

     (c) any waiver by the Company of a valuable
right or a material debt owed to it;

     (d) any satisfaction or discharge of any lien,
claim or encumbrance or payment of any obligation by the Company,
except in the ordinary course of business and which is not material
to the assets, properties, financial condition, operating results
or business of the Company (as such business is presently conducted
and as it is proposed to be conducted);

     (e) any change or amendment to a material
contract or arrangement by which the Company or any of its assets
or properties is bound or subject;

(f)   any material change in any compensation arrangement or agreement with any employee; or

(g)   to the Company's knowledge, any other event or condition of any character which might individually or in the aggregate constitute a Material Adverse Event.

3.9   Litigation. Except as described in Schedule 3.9, there is no action, proceeding or investigation pending or threatened, or any basis therefor known to the Company, that questions the validity of this Agreement or the right of the Company to enter into this Agreement, or that would result, either individually or in the aggregate, in any Material Adverse Event, including, without limitation, any action, proceeding or investigation involving the prior employment or consultancy of any of the Company's employees or consultants or their use of any information or techniques alleged to be proprietary to any former employer of any such employee or consultant.   There is no judgment, decree or order of any Court in effect against the Company and the Company is not in default with respect to any order of any governmental authority to which the Company is a party or by which it is bound.   There is no action, suit, proceeding or investigation by the Company currently pending or which the Company presently intends to initiate.

3.10   Title to Properties; Liens and Encumbrances. Except as described in Schedule 3.10, the Company has good and marketable title to all of its properties and assets, both real and personal, and has good title to all its leasehold interests, in each case subject to no mortgage, pledge, lien, security interest, conditional sale agreement, encumbrance or charge.

      3.11 <u>Patents and Other Proprietary Rights</u>. Except as described in Schedule 3.11:

      (a) To the knowledge of the Company: (x) the Company has sufficient title and ownership of all patents, trademarks, service marks, trade names, copyrights, trade secrets, information, proprietary rights and processes necessary for its business as now conducted, and as proposed to be conducted, and (y) such business does not, and would not, conflict with or constitute an infringement of the rights of others;

      (b) There are no outstanding options, licenses or agreements of any kind relating to the matters listed in subsection 3.11(a), nor is the Company bound by or a party to any options, licenses or agreements of any kind with respect to the patents, trademarks, service marks, trade names, copyrights, trade secrets, licenses, information, proprietary rights and processes of any other person or entity;

      (c) The Company has not received any communications alleging that the Company has violated or, by conducting its business as proposed, would violate any of the patents, trademarks, service marks, trade names, copyrights or trade secrets or any proprietary rights of any other person or entity;

      (d) The Company is not aware that any of its employees is obligated under any contract (including licenses, covenants or commitments of any nature) or other agreement, or subject to any judgment, decree or order of any court or administrative agency, that would interfere with the use of such employee's best efforts to promote the interests of the Company or that would conflict with the Company's business as proposed to be conducted;

(e)   Neither the execution nor delivery of this Agreement, nor the carrying on of the Company's business by the employees of the Company, nor the conduct of the Company's business as proposed, will, to the Company's knowledge, conflict with or result in a breach of the terms, conditions or provisions of, or constitute a default under, any contract, covenant or instrument under which any of such employees is now obligated;

(f)   The Company does not believe it is or will be necessary to utilize any inventions of any of its employees (or people it currently intends to hire) made prior to their employment by the Company.

3.12   *Taxes.* Except as described in Schedule 3.12, all federal, state, local and foreign tax returns required to be filed by the Company have been filed, or if not yet filed have been granted extensions of the filing dates which extensions have not expired, and all taxes, assessments, fees and other governmental charges upon the Company, or upon any of its properties, income or franchises, shown in such returns and on assessments received by the Company to be due and payable have been paid, or adequate reserves therefor have been set up and have been disclosed in the

Company's Financial Statements, if any of such taxes are being contested in good faith; or if any of such tax returns have not been filed or if any such taxes have not been paid or so reserved for, the failure so to file or to pay would not in the aggregate constitute a Material Adverse Event. The Company knows of no proposed additional tax assessment that is not provided for in the Balance Sheet.

      3.13 <u>Company's Contracts</u>. All of the contracts and agreements with expected receipts or expenditures in excess of $_____ or involving a license or grant of rights to or from the Company involving patents, trademarks, copyrights or other proprietary information applicable to the business of the Company, to which the Company is a party as of the date of the Closing are listed on Schedule 3.13. All such contracts and agreements are legally binding, valid, and in full force and effect in all material respects, and there is no indication of reduced activity relating to such contract or agreement (other than in the ordinary course of business) by any of the parties to any such contract or agreement.

      3.14 <u>No Defaults, Violations or Conflicts</u>. The Company is not in violation of any term or provision of any charter, by-law, or any material term or provision of any indebtedness, mortgage, indenture, contract, agreement, judgment, or to the Company's knowledge, any decree, order, statute, rule or regulation.

3.15   Insurance.   The Company has in effect
insurance covering risks associated with its business in such
amounts as are customary in its industry.   The Company is not aware
of any pending or threatened claims against the Company for
personal injuries or property damages.

3.16   Private Offering.   The Company agrees that
neither the Company nor anyone acting on its behalf will offer any
of the Shares or any similar securities for issuance or sale to, or
solicit any offer to acquire any of the same from, anyone so as to
make the issuance and sale of the Shares subject to the
registration requirements of Section 5 of the Securities Act of
1933, as amended (the "Securities Act").

3.17   Prior Registration Rights.   Except as provided
in the Rights Agreement attached as Exhibit 6.8, the Company is
under no contractual obligation to register under the Securities
Act any of its presently outstanding securities or any of its
securities that may subsequently be issued.

3.18   Full Disclosure.   Except as described on
Schedule 3.18, (the absence of such Schedule 3.18 indicating that
none was intended) the Financial Statements, the representations
and warranties of the Company contained in this Agreement, the
other provisions of this Agreement and the Business Plan dated
_____, 198_, (with the exception of projections or statements
regarding items to occur in the future) when read together, do not
contain any untrue statement of a material fact or omit any
material fact necessary to make the statements contained therein or

-11-

herein in view of the circumstances under which they were made not
misleading. The projections presented in the Business Plan and the
statements contained therein regarding items to occur in the future
have been prepared in a good faith effort by the Company to
describe the Company's present and proposed products, operations
and projected growth.

       3.19 <u>Distributions</u>. There has been no declaration
or payment by the Company of any dividend, nor any distribution by
the Company of any assets of any kind, to any of its shareholders
in redemption or as the purchase price of any of the Company's
securities.

       3.20 <u>Employee Compensation Plans</u>. Except as set
forth in Schedule 3.20 hereto, the Company is not party to or bound
by any currently effective employment contracts, deferred
compensation agreements, bonus plans, incentive plans, profit
sharing plans, retirement agreements or other employee compensation
agreements. Subject to applicable law, the employment of each
officer and employee of the Company is terminable at the will of
the Company.

       3.21 <u>Employee Relations</u>. The Company believes its
relations with its employees are satisfactory. The Company's
employees are not represented by any labor unions nor, to the
Company's knowledge, is any union organization campaign in
progress. The Company is not aware that any of its officers or
employees intends to terminate employment.

3.22 <u>Brokers and Finders</u>. The Company has not
retained any investment banker, broker or finder in connection with
the transactions contemplated by this Agreement.

3.23 <u>Transactions with Affiliates</u>. Except for
(i) transactions relating to purchases of shares of the Company's
Common Stock and Preferred Stock, (ii) regular salary payments and
fringe benefits under an individual's compensation package with the
Company, and (iii) the issuance and sale of the Shares pursuant to
the terms and conditions of this Agreement, none of the officers,
employees, directors or other affiliates of the Company are a party
to any transactions with the Company. There have been no
assumptions or guarantees by the Company of any obligations of such
affiliates.

3.24 <u>Corporate Documents</u>. Except for amendments
necessary to satisfy representations and warranties or conditions
contained herein (the form of which amendments has been approved by
the Investors), the Articles of Incorporation and Bylaws of the
Company are in the form previously provided to the Investors, if so
requested.

3.25 <u>Governmental Consents</u>. No consent, approval,
order or authorization of, or registration, qualification,
designation, declaration or filing with, any federal, state, local
or provincial governmental authority on the part of the Company is
required in connection with the consummation of the transactions
contemplated by this Agreement, except for the filing pursuant to
Section 25102(f) of the California Corporate Securities Law of

1968, as amended, and the rules thereunder, which filing will be effected within 15 days of the Closing.

    4. <u>Representations and Warranties of the Investors</u>. Each Investor severally represents and warrants to the Company as follows:

    4.1 <u>Authorization</u>. When executed and delivered by such Investor, and assuming execution and delivery by the Company, this Agreement will constitute a valid obligation of such Investor, enforceable in accordance with its terms.

    4.2 <u>Brokers and Finders</u>. Such Investor has not retained any investment banker, broker, or finder in connection with the transactions contemplated by this Agreement.

    5. <u>Securities Laws</u>.

    5.1 <u>California Securities Laws</u>.

    THE SALE OF THE SECURITIES WHICH ARE THE SUBJECT OF THIS AGREEMENT HAS NOT BEEN QUALIFIED WITH THE COMMISSIONER OF CORPORATIONS OF THE STATE OF CALIFORNIA AND THE ISSUANCE OF SUCH SECURITIES OR THE PAYMENT OR RECEIPT OF ANY PART OF THE CONSIDERATION THEREFOR PRIOR TO SUCH QUALIFICATION IS UNLAWFUL UNLESS THE SALE OF SECURITIES IS EXEMPT FROM THE QUALIFICATION BY SECTION 25100, 25102 OR 25105 OF THE CALIFORNIA CORPORATIONS CODE. THE RIGHTS OF ALL PARTIES TO THIS AGREEMENT ARE EXPRESSLY CONDITIONED UPON SUCH QUALIFICATION BEING OBTAINED, UNLESS THE SALE IS SO EXEMPT.

5.2   Securities Laws Representations and Covenants
of Investors.

(a)   This Agreement is made with each Investor
in reliance upon such Investor's representation to the Company,
which by such Investor's execution of this Agreement such Investor
hereby confirms, that the Shares to be received by such Investor
will be acquired for investment for such Investor's own account,
not as a nominee or agent, and not with a view to the sale or
distribution of any part thereof, and that such Investor has no
present intention of selling, granting any participation in, or
otherwise distributing the same. By executing this Agreement, such
Investor further represents that such Investor has no contract,
undertaking, agreement or arrangement with any person to sell,
transfer, or grant participations to such person or to any third
person, with respect to any of the Shares.

(b)   Each Investor understands and acknowledges
that the offering of the Shares pursuant to this Agreement will not
be registered under the Securities Act on the grounds that the
offering and sale of securities contemplated by this Agreement are
exempt from registration pursuant to Section 4(2) of the Securities
Act, and that the Company's reliance upon such exemption is
predicated upon such Investor's representations set forth in this
Agreement.

(c)   Each Investor covenants that in no event
will such Investor dispose of any of the Shares (other than
pursuant to Rule 144 promulgated by the Securities and Exchange

-15-

Commission ("Commission") under the Securities Act ("Rule 144") or any similar or analogous rule) unless and until (i) such Investor shall have notified the Company of the proposed disposition and shall have furnished the Company with a statement of the circumstances surrounding the proposed disposition, and (ii), if requested by the Company, such Investor shall have furnished the Company with an opinion of counsel satisfactory in form and substance to the Company and the Company's counsel to the effect that (x) such disposition will not require registration under the Securities Act and (y) appropriate action necessary for compliance with the Securities Act and any applicable state, local or foreign law has been taken. Notwithstanding the limitations set forth in the foregoing sentence, each Investor which is a partnership may transfer Shares to its constituent partners or a retired partner of such partnership who retires after the date hereof, or to the estate of any such partner or retired partner or transfer by gift, will or intestate succession to any such partner's spouse or lineal descendants or ancestors without the necessity of registration or opinion of counsel if the transferee agrees in writing to be subject to the terms of this Agrement to the same extent if such transferee were an Investor; provided, however, that each Investor hereby covenants not to effect such transfer if such transfer either would invalidate the securities laws exemptions pursuant to which the Shares were originally offered and sold or would itself require registration under the Securities Act or applicable state securities laws. Each certificate evidencing the Shares transferred as above provided shall bear the appropriate restrictive legend set forth in Section 5.3 below, except that such certificate shall not bear such legend if the transfer was made in compliance with Rule 144 or if the opinion of counsel referred to above is to the further effect that such legend is not required in order to establish compliance with any provisions of the Securities Act.

(d) Each Investor represents that: (i) such Investor has such knowledge and experience in financial and business matters as to be capable of evaluating the merits and risks of such Investor's prospective investment in the Shares; (ii) such Investor has received all the information it has requested from the Company and considers necessary or appropriate for deciding whether to purchase the Shares; (iii) such Investor has the ability to bear the economic risks of such Investor's prospective investment; and (iv) such Investor is able, without materially impairing its financial condition, to hold the Shares for an indefinite period of time and to suffer complete loss on its investment.

5.3 Legends.

(a) All certificates for the Shares shall bear the following legend:

"The securities represented hereby have not been registered under the Securities Act of 1933, as amended ("Act"). Such securities may not be transferred unless a Registration Statement under the Act is in effect as to such transfer or in the opinion of counsel for the Company, such transfer may be made pursuant to Rule 144 or registration under the Act is unnecessary in order for such transfer to comply with the Act."

(b) The certificates evidencing the Shares shall also bear any legend required by the Commissioner of Corporations of the State of California or required pursuant to any state, local or foreign law governing such securities.

5.4 <u>Reports Under Securities Exchange Act of 1934</u>. With a view to making available to the Investors the benefits of Rule 144 and any other rule or regulation of the Commission that may at any time permit an Investor to sell securities of the Company to the public without registration or pursuant to a registration on Form S-3, the Company agrees to:

(a) make and keep public information available, as those terms are defined in Rule 144, at all times after ninety (90) days after the effective date of the first registration statement filed by the Company for the offering of its securities to the general public;

(b) take such action, including the voluntary registration of its Common Stock under Section 12 of the Securities Exchange Act of 1934, as amended (the "1934 Act"), as is necessary to enable the Investors to utilize Form S-3 for the sale of the Common Stock issuable upon conversion of the Shares, such action to be taken, as required under the 1934 Act, after the end of the fiscal year in which the first registration statement filed by the Company for the offering of its securities to the general public is declared effective;

(c) file with the Commission in a timely
manner all reports and other documents required of the Company
under the Securities Act and the 1934 Act; and

(d) furnish to any Investor, so long as such
Investor owns any Shares or Common Stock issued upon conversion of
the Shares, forthwith upon request (i) a written statement by the
Company that it has complied with the reporting requirements of
Rule 144 (at any time after ninety (90) days after the effective
date of the first registration statement filed by the Company), the
Securities Act and the 1934 Act (at any time after it has become
subject to such reporting requirements), or that it qualifies as a
registrant whose securities may be resold pursuant to Form S-3 (at
any time after it so qualifies), (ii) a copy of the most recent
annual or quarterly report of the Company and such other reports
and documents so filed by the Company, and (iii) such other
information as may be reasonably requested in availing any Investor
of any rule or regulation of the Commission which permits the
selling of any such securities without registration or pursuant to
such plan.

6.   Conditions of Investors' Obligations at Closing.
The obligations of the Investors under Section 1 of this Agreement
are subject to the fulfillment at or before each Closing of each of
the following conditions, any of which may be waived in writing by
the Investors:

6.1 Representations and Warranties. The
representations and warranties of the Company contained in

Section 3 shall be true on and as of such Closing with the same effect as if made on and as of such Closing.

6.2 <u>Performance</u>. The Company shall have performed or fulfilled all agreements, obligations and conditions contained herein required to be performed or fulfilled by the Company before such Closing.

6.3 <u>Blue Sky Compliance</u>. The Company shall have complied with and be effective under all state securities or Blue Sky laws applicable to the offer and sale of the Shares to the Investors.

6.4 <u>Proceedings Satisfactory; Compliance Certificate</u>. All corporate and legal proceedings taken by the Company in connection with the transactions contemplated by this Agreement and all documents and papers relating to such transactions shall be satisfactory to the Investors, in the reasonable exercise of the judgment of the Investors. The Company shall have delivered to the Investors a certificate dated as of such Closing, signed by the Company's President, certifying that the conditions set forth in Sections 6.1 and 6.2 have been satisfied.

6.5 <u>Opinion of Counsel</u>. There shall have been delivered to the Investors an opinion of _____ in substantially the form of Exhibit 6.5.

6.6 <u>Patent, Copyright and Nondisclosure Agreement</u>. The officers and employees of the Company shall have executed and delivered to the Company a Patent, Copyright and Nondisclosure Agreement substantially in the form of Exhibit 6.6.

6.7 <u>Market Standoff Agreements</u>. Holders of all of the shares of Common Stock outstanding and holders of all of the outstanding options to purchase Common Stock of the Company shall have agreed that if so requested by the underwriters in connection with a registration of the Company's securities, such optionee shall not sell or otherwise dispose of shares issued upon exercise of the option for a period of up to ___ days following the effective date of such registration.

6.8 <u>Information and Registration Rights</u>. The Company and the Investors shall have entered into the Company's Information and Registration Rights Agreement attached as Exhibit 6.8.

7.   <u>Conditions of the Company's Obligations at Closing</u>. The obligations of the Company under Section 1 of this Agreement are subject to the fulfillment at or before each Closing of each of the following conditions, any of which may be waived in writing by the Company:

7.1 <u>Representations and Warranties</u>. The representations and warranties of the Investors contained in Sections 4 and 5 shall be true on and as of such Closing with the same effect as though said representations and warranties had been made on and as of such Closing.

7.2 <u>Blue Sky Compliance</u>. The Company shall have complied with and be effective under the securities laws of the State of California and any other applicable states as necessary to offer and sell the Shares to the Investors.

8.   Post-Closing Covenants of the Company.

8.1 Securities Laws Compliance. The Company shall
within 15 days of the Closing file a notice of the sale of the
Shares to the Investors pursuant to Section 25102(f) of the
California Corporations Code and shall make any other filings
required by the securities or Blue Sky laws of any other applicable
State.

8.2 Patent, Copyright and Nondisclosure Agreement.
Unless otherwise determined by the Board of Directors, the Company
shall require all future officers, directors and employees of, and
consultants to, the Company and its subsidiaries to execute and
deliver a Patent, Copyright and Nondisclosure Agreement in
substantially the form of Exhibit 6.6.

8.3 Key Man Life Insurance. The Company shall
procure and maintain key man life insurance, with proceeds payable
to the Company, as shall be determined by the Board of Directors.

8.4 Quarterly Board Meetings; Expenses; Budget.
The Board of Directors of the Company shall meet not less frequently than quarterly until otherwise agreed by holders of 66-2/3%
of the outstanding shares of the Preferred Stock. The reasonable
travel expenses of the directors incurred in attending board
meetings shall be paid or reimbursed promptly by the Company. The
Company shall prepare and submit to the Board of Directors for
approval 90 days prior to the end of each fiscal year an operating
budget and plan respecting the next fiscal year.

8.5 <u>Market Standoff Agreement</u>. The Company shall

cause all future holders of options to purchase, and all future

purchasers of, the Company's Common Stock to execute and deliver a

Market Standoff Agreement substantially in the form of

Exhibits 8.5A and 8.5B, respectively.

9. <u>Miscellaneous</u>.

9.1 <u>Entire Agreement; Successors and Assigns</u>. This

Agreement constitutes the entire contract between the Company and

the Investors relative to the subject matter hereof. Any previous

agreement between the Company and the Investors is superseded by

this Agreement. Subject to the exceptions specifically set forth

in this Agreement, the terms and conditions of this Agreement shall

inure to the benefit of and be binding upon the respective

executors, administrators, heirs, successors and assigns of the

parties.

9.2 <u>Governing Law</u>. This Agreement shall be

governed by and construed in accordance with the laws of the State

of California applicable to contracts entered into and wholly to be

performed within the State of California by California residents.

9.3 <u>Counterparts</u>. This Agreement may be executed

in two or more counterparts, each of which shall be deemed an

original, but all of which together shall constitute one and the

same instrument.

9.4 <u>Headings</u>. The headings of the Sections of this

Agreement are for convenience and shall not by themselves determine

the interpretation of this Agreement.

-23-

9.5 <u>Notices</u>. Any notice required or permitted
hereunder shall be given in writing and shall be conclusively
deemed effectively given upon personal delivery, or five days after
deposit in the United States mail, by registered or certified mail,
postage prepaid, addressed (i) if to the Company, as set forth
below the Company's name on the signature page of this Agreement,
and (ii) if to an Investor, at such Investor's address as set forth
on Schedule 1.1, or at such other address as the Company or such
Investor may designate by ten (10) days' advance written notice to
the Investors or the Company, respectively.

9.6 <u>Survival of Warranties</u>. The warranties and
representations of the parties contained in or made pursuant to
this Agreement shall survive the execution and delivery of this
Agreement and the Closing; provided, however, that such representations and warranties need only be accurate as of the date of such
execution and delivery and as of the Closing.

9.7 <u>Amendment of Agreement</u>. Any provision of this
Agreement may be amended by a written instrument signed by the
Company and by persons holding at least sixty-six and two-thirds
percent (66-2/3%) of the aggregate of (a) the then outstanding
Shares (assuming conversion to Common Stock at the conversion rate
then in effect) and (b) the then outstanding shares of Common Stock
into which the shares of Preferred Stock have been converted, other
than shares of Common Stock which have been sold to the public;
provided, however, that each Investor hereby agrees to amend this
Agreement at any time, without further action on the part of any

-24-

Investor, to include additional Investors purchasing Shares as if they were Investors purchasing Shares on the date of this Agreement.

9.8 <u>Finders Fees</u>. Each of the Company and the Investors will indemnify the other against all liabilities incurred by the indemnifying party with respect to claims related to investment banking or finders fees in connection with the transactions contemplated by this Agreement, arising out of arrangements between the party asserting such claims and the indemnifying party, and all costs and expenses (including reasonable fees of counsel) of investigating and defending such claims.

9.9 <u>Expenses</u>. The Company and the Investors will each bear their respective legal and other fees and expenses in connection with the transactions contemplated in this Agreement; provided, however, if the sale of any of the Shares is consummated, the Company shall pay at Closing the reasonable fees and expenses of a single counsel to the investors.

IN WITNESS WHEREOF, the parties hereto have executed this Agreement as of the day and year first above written.

The Company:

The Investors:

Directory

ALABAMA

Private Capital Corporation
2160 Highland Avenue, Suite 100
Birmingham, AL 35205
205-933-4618
Contact: Manager

ARIZONA

Camelback Capital Corporation
645 South Rockford Drive
Tempe, AZ 85281
602-894-6994
Contact: Manager

FBS Venture Capital Company
6900 E. Camelback Road, Suite 452
Scottsdale, AZ 85251
602-941-2160
Contact: Manager

Greyhound Capital
  Management Corporation
1408 Greyhound Tower
Phoenix, AZ 85077
602-222-8227
Contact: David A. Bays, Vice President

Norwest Venture
  Capital Management, Inc.
8777 East Via De Ventura, #335
Scottsdale, AZ 85258-3346
602-483-8940
Contact: Robert F. Zicarelli, Chairman

VNB Capital Corporation
15 E. Monroe, Suite 1200
Phoenix, AZ 85004
602-261-1577
Contact: John M. Holliman, III,
                 Managing Director

ARKANSAS

Worthen Finance & Investments, Inc.
Worthen Bank Building, 10th Floor
200 W. Capitol
Little Rock, AR 72203
501-378-1082
Contact: Ricor F. da Silveira,
                 Vice President, General Manager

CALIFORNIA

ACCEL Partners
One Embarcadero Center, #2102
San Francisco, CA 94111
415-989-5656
Contact: Arthur C. Patterson

Adler & Company
1245 Oakmead Parkway, #103
Sunnyvale, CA 94086
408-720-8700
Contact: Daniel C. O'Neill
       John Hamann

Advanced Technology Ventures
1000 El Camino Real, #210
Menlo Park, CA 94025
415-321-8601
Contact: Jos C. Henkens

Alafi Capital Company
P. O. Box 7338
Berkeley, CA 94707
415-653-7425
Contact: Moshe Alafi
       Managing General Partner

Alpha Partners
2200 Sand Hill Road, #250
Menlo Park, CA 94025
415-854-7024
Contact: Wallace F. Davis

Arscott, Norton & Associates
375 Forest Avenue
Palo Alto, CA 94301
415-853-0766
Contact: David G. Arscott
       Leal F. Norton
       Dean C. Campbell

Asian American Capital Corp.
1251 W. Tennyson Road, #4
Hayward, CA 94544
415-887-6888
Contact: Jennie Chien, Manager

Asset Management Company
2275 East Bayshore Road, #150
Palo Alto, CA 94303
415-321-3131
Contact: Manager

Associated Venture Investors
3000 Sand Hill Road
Building 3, #280
Menlo Park, CA 94025
415-854-4470
Contact: Manager

Avalon Ventures
1020 Prospect Street, #405
La Jolla, CA 92037
619-454-3803
Contact: Manager

Bancorp Venture Capital, Inc.
2082 Michelson Drive, #302
Irvine, CA 92715
714-752-7220
Contact: Paul R. Blair, President

Bay Partners
10600 North De Anza Blvd., #100
Cupertino, CA 95014
408-725-2444
Contact: John Freidenrich
       W. Charles Hazel
       John E. Bosch

Bay Venture Group
One Embarcadero Center, #3303
San Francisco, CA 94111
415-989-7680
Contact: William R. Chandler

Bessemer Venture Partners
3000 Sand Hill Road, #3-225
Menlo Park, CA 94025-7112
415-854-2200
Contact: Neill H. Brownstein

Beverly Glen Venture Capital
214 S. Beverly Glen
Los Angeles, CA 90024
213-272-7556
Contact: Manager

Brentwood Associates
11661 San Vicente Boulevard
Suite 707
Los Angeles, CA 90049
213-826-6581
Contact: William M. Barnum

Bryan and Edwards
3000 Sand Hill Road
Building 2, #215
Menlo Park, CA 94025
415-854-1555
Contact: Manager

Burr, Egan, Deleage & Company
Three Embarcadero Center, #2560
San Francisco, CA 94111
415-362-4022
Contact: Jean Deleage
        Shirley Cerrudo
        Brion Applegate

California Capital Investors, Ltd.
11812 San Vicente Boulevard
Los Angeles, CA 90049
213-820-7222
Contact: Arthur H. Bernstein
        Lynda S. Gibson

Carlyle Capital Corporation
444 South Flower Street, #4650
Los Angeles, CA 90017
213-689-9235
Contact: Dennis Stanfill
        Edwin A. Bowen

Carnegie Venture Capital Company
10880 Wilshire Boulevard, #1800
Los Angeles, CA 90024
213-208-1544
Contact: Manager

CDB Incorporated
4600 Campus Drive
Newport Beach, CA 92660
714-852-9000
Contact: Manager

CFB Venture Capital Corporation
Post Office Box 109
San Diego, CA 92112
619-230-3304
Contact: Richard J. Roncaglia,
            Vice President

R. H. Chappell & Co.
One Lombard Street
San Francisco, CA 94111
415-397-5094
Contact: Manager

Churchill International
444 Market Street, #2501
San Francisco, CA 94111
415-398-7677
Contact: Roy Helsing
        Robert Weeks

Citicorp Venture Capital Ltd.
Two Embarcadero Place
2200 Geng Road, #203
Palo Alto, CA 94303
415-424-8000
Contact: David A. Wegman
        Larry J. Wells
        Allen G. Rosenberg

Comdisco Venture Lease, Inc.
101 California Street—38th Floor
San Francisco, CA 94111
415-421-1800
Contact: James Labe
            William Tenneson
            Terrence Fowler

Continental Capital Ventures
555 California Street, #5070
San Francisco, CA 94104
415-989-2020
Contact: William A. Boeger, III

Crosspoint Venture Partners
1951 Landings Drive
Mountain View, CA 94043
415-964-3545
Contact: John B. Mumford
James F. Willenborg
Frederick J. Dotzler

Diehl & Company
18552 MacArthur Blvd., #305
Irvine, CA 92715
714-955-2000
Contact: Manager

Dillon Read & Co., Inc.
435 Tasso Street
Palo Alto, CA 94301
415-327-2600
Contact: Philip M. Young

**Draper Associates/
California Partners**
3000 Sand Hill Road
Building 4, #235
Menlo Park, CA 94025
415-854-1712
Contact: Tim Draper

Drexel Burnham Lambert Inc.
1940 Tice Valley Blvd.
Walnut Creek, CA 94595
415-932-7400
Contact: Manager

Dougery, Jones & Wilder
2003 Landings Drive
Mountain View, CA 94043
415-968-4820
Contact: Jeanne Mitchell

Early Stages Company
369 Pine Street, #723
San Francisco, CA 94104
415-986-5700
Contact: Woody Kuehn

EG & G Ventures, Inc.
700 E. El Camino Real, #270
Mountain View, CA 94040
415-967-2822
Contact: J. Rado

El Dorado Ventures
20300 Stevens Creek Blvd., #395
Cupertino, CA 94104
408-725-2474
Contact: Gary Kalbach, Partner

El Dorado Ventures
2 North Lake Avenue, #480
Pasadena, CA 91101
818-793-1936
Contact: Manager

Equis Management Company
Three Embarcadero Center, #2560
San Francisco, CA 94111
415-362-4181
Contact: Manager

Fairfield Venture Partners
650 Town Center Drive, #810
Costa Mesa, CA 92626
714-754-5717
Contact: Edmund M. Olivier
Randall R. Lunn

**General Electric Venture
Capital Corporation**
1020 Marsh Road, #220
Menlo Park, CA 94025
415-324-8092
Contact: Eric A. Young

Girard Capital, Inc.
4320 La Jolla Village Drive, #210
San Diego, CA 92122-1233
619-457-5114
Contact: E. S. Gudmundson
W. Creighton Gallaway

Glenwood Management
3000 Sand Hill Road
Building 4, #230
Menlo Park, CA 94025
415-854-8070
Contact: Tag Tellefsen

Golden Gate Investments, Inc.
2121 El Camino Real
San Mateo, CA 94403
415-345-9900
Contact: A. Larry Lindsey, President

Goldfarb Associates
3 Cotton Place
Menlo Park, CA 94025
415-329-0529
Contact: Norman M. Goldfarb

Grace Ventures Corporation
20300 Stevens Creek Boulevard, #330
Cupertino, CA 95014
408-725-0774
Contact: Dr. C. F. Horn

Hallador, Inc.
1435 River Park Drive, #505
Sacramento, CA 95815
916-920-0191
Contact: William T. Krieg

Hambrecht & Quist Venture Partners
235 Montgomery Street, 5th Floor
San Francisco, CA 94104
415-576-3300
Contact: Kenneth L. H Guernsey

Happ Ventures
444 Castro Street, #400
Mountain View, CA 94041
415-961-1115
Contact: William D. Happ

Henry & Co.
9191 Towne Centre Drive, #230
San Diego, CA 92122
619-453-1655
Contact: F. David Hare, President

Hillman Ventures, Inc.
2200 Sand Hill Road, Ste. 240
Menlo Park, CA 94025
415-854-4653
Contact: Philip S. Paul,
        Chairman and CEO

Hoebich Venture Management, Inc.
5770 Croy Road
Morgan Hill, CA 95037
415-326-5590
Contact: Christian Hoebich

Imperial Ventures, Inc.
9920 S. La Cienega Boulevard
Inglewood, CA 90301
213-417-5888
Contact: Donald B. Prell, President

Indosuez Technology Group
3000 Sand Hill Road
Building 4, #130
Menlo Park, CA 94025
415-854-0587
Contact: David E. Gold
        Philippe Sevin

Institutional Venture Partners
3000 Sand Hill Road
Building 2, #290
Menlo Park, CA 94025
415-854-0132
Contact: Sam Colella
        Reid Dennis
        Mary Jane Elmore

InterVen Partners
333 South Grand Avenue, #4050
Los Angeles, CA 90071
213-622-1922
Contact: Johnathon Funk
        Kenneth Deemer

Irvine Technology Fund
4600 Campus Drive
Newport Beach, CA 92660
714-852-9000
Contact: Manager

Julian, Cole and Stein
11777 San Vicente Boulevard, #522
Los Angeles, CA 90049
213-826-8002
Contact: James M. Julian

Kleiner Perkins Caufield & Byers
El Embarcadero Center, #3520
San Francisco, CA 94111
415-421-3110
Contact: Dina Downey

Leong Ventures
146 Atherton Avenue
Atherton, CA 94025
415-327-1169
Contact: Helen C. Leong
        Stephanie A. Leong-Geyer

Donald L. Lucas
3000 Sand Hill Road
Building 3, #210
Menlo Park, CA 94025
415-854-4223
Contact: Eileen Lepera

Matrix Partners
224 Airport Parkway, #395
San Jose, CA 95110
408-298-0270
Contact: David Douglass

Mayfield Fund
2200 Sand Hill Road, #200
Menlo Park, CA 94025
415-854-5560
Contact: Glenn M. Mueller,
        General Partner

MBW Management, Inc.
350 Second Street, #7
Los Altos, CA 94022
415-941-2392
Contact: James R. Weersing,
        Managing General Partner
        Robert J. Harrington
        Vice President

Melchor Venture Management, Inc.
170 State Street, #220
Los Altos, CA 94022
415-941-6565
Contact: Gregory S. Young
        Richard H. Frank

Menlo Ventures
3000 Sand Hill Road
Building 4, #100
Menlo Park, CA 94025
415-854-8540
Contact: Manager

Merrill, Pickard, Anderson & Eyre
2 Palo Alto Square, #425
Palo Alto, CA 94306
415-856-8880
Contact: Chris A. Eyre

Metropolitan Venture Company, Inc.
5757 Wilshire Boulevard, #670
Los Angeles, CA 90036
213-938-3488
Contact: Esther Lowy

The Mezzanine Fund
c/o Baldwin Capital Management
100 Pine Street, Suite 1700
San Francisco, CA 94111
415-421-8420
Contact: George H. Baldwin
        Paul B. Weiss
        Jane D. Lindner

Microtechnology Investments Ltd.
46 Red Birch Court
Danville, CA 94526
415-838-9319
Contact: M. M. Stuckey, Chairman

Mohr, Davidow Ventures
3000 Sand Hill Road
Building 4, #240
Menlo Park, CA 94025
415-854-7236
Contact: Larry Mohr
        Bill Davidow

Montgomery Bridge Fund
600 Montgomery Street
San Francisco, CA 94111
415-627-2000
Contact: Manager

Montgomery Securities
600 Montgomery Street
San Francisco, CA 94111
415-627-2454
Contact: Harold Shattuck
James L. Pelkey
Jeffrey A. Heimbuck

National Investment Management, Inc.
23133 Hawthorne Boulevard, #300
Torrance, CA 90505
213-373-8944
Contact: Manager

New Enterprise Associates
Building Four, Suite 235
3000 Sand Hill Road
Menlo Park, CA 94025
415-854-2660
Contact: C. Woodrow Rea, Jr.

New Enterprise Associates
235 Montgomery Street, #1025
San Francisco, CA 94104
415-956-1579
Contact: C. Richard Kramlich
Cornelius C. Bond, Jr.
Thomas C. McConnell

Newtek Ventures
500 Washington Street, #720
San Francisco, CA 94111
415-986-5711
Contact: Peter J. Wardle
Barry M. Weinman

Oak Grove Ventures
173 Jefferson Drive
Menlo Park, CA 94025
415-324-2276
Contact: Duane C. Montopoli

Oak Management Corporation
3000 Sand Hill Road
Building 3, Suite 240
Menlo Park, CA 94025
415-854-8825
Contact: David P. Best
Catherine A. Pierson

Olympic Venture Partners
101 California Street, #4035
San Francisco, CA 94111
415-362-4433
Contact: Denman Van Ness

Orange Nassau
Westerly Place, #540
1500 Quail Street
Newport Beach, CA 92660
714-752-7811
Contact: John W. Blackburn

OSCCO Ventures
3000 Sand Hill Road
Building 4, #140
Menlo Park, CA 94025
415-854-2222
Contact: J. G. Rudolph

Oxford Group, Inc.
33 Wilshire Boulevard
Santa Monica, CA 90401
213-458-2934
Contact: Manager

Pacific Venture Partners
3000 Sand Hill Road
Building 4, #175
Menlo Park, CA 94025
415-854-2266
Contact: Anthony T. Ellis
James C. Balderston
Rigdon Currie

Paragon Partners
3000 Sand Hill Road
Building 2, #190
Menlo Park, CA 94025
415-854-8000
Contact: Manager

Paribas Technology
101 California Street, #3150
San Francisco, CA 94111
415-788-2929
Contact: Manager

Alan Patricof Associates
1 Embarcadero Place
2100 Geng Road, #220
Palo Alto, CA 94303
415-494-9944
Contact: Manager

Peregrine Ventures
1299 Ocean Avenue, #306
Santa Monica, CA 90401
213-458-1441
Contact: Gene Miller

Princeton/Montrose Partners
2331 Honolulu Avenue, Suite G
Montrose, CA 91020
818-957-3623
Contact: Donald R. Stroben
          Managing General Partner

Reprise Capital Corporation
10000 Santa Monica Boulevard, #300
Los Angeles, CA 90067
213-556-1944
Contact: Norman Tulchin, Vice President

Riordan Venture Management
300 South Grand Avenue, #2900
Los Angeles, CA 90071
213-629-4824
Contact: J. Christopher Lewis

Robertson, Colman & Stephens
One Embarcadero Center
30th Floor
San Francisco, CA 94111
415-781-9700
Contact: Manager

Arthur Rock & Co.
1635 Russ Building
San Francisco, CA 94104
415-981-3921
Contact: Marie Getchel

Rogers & Whitney
3000 Sand Hill Road
Building 2, #175
Menlo Park, CA 94025
415-854-2767
Contact: Roy Rogers
          General Partner

**Rothschild, Unterberg,
   Towbin Ventures**
3000 Sand Hill Road
Building 3, #260
Menlo Park, CA 94025
415-854-2576
Contact: Manager

San Jose Capital
100 Park Center Plaza, #427
San Jose, CA 95113
408-293-7708
Contact: Robert Murphy

Schroder Venture Managers Limited
3000 Sand Hill Road
Building 2, #130
Menlo Park, CA 94025
415-854-8833
Contact: Robert J. Gailus
          Michael A. Hentschel

Security Financial
Management Corporation
100 Bush Street, #1905
San Francisco, CA 94104
415-981-8060
Contact: Manager

Security Pacific Capital Corporation
650 Town Center Drive
17th Floor
Costa Mesa, CA 92626
714-556-1964
Contact: Tim Hay, President

Security Pacific Capital Corporation
5 Palo Alto Square, #1038
Palo Alto, CA 94304
415-424-8011
Contact: James McElwee

Security Pacific Capital Corporation
155 North Lake Avenue, #1010
Pasadena, CA 91109
818-304-3451
Contact: John Padgett
         Tony Stevens

Sequoia Capital
3000 Sand Hill Road
Building 4, #280
Menlo Park, CA 94025
415-854-3927
Contact: Walter F. Baumgartner

Sierra Ventures
3000 Sand Hill Road
Building 1, #280
Menlo Park, CA 94025
415-854-1000
Contact: Manager

Sofinnova Inc.
3 Embarcadero, #2560
San Francisco, CA 94705
415-362-4021
Contact: Alain Azan

Southern California Ventures
9920 La Cienega, #510
Inglewood, CA 90301
213-216-0544
Contact: Manager

The Sprout Group
3000 Sand Hill Road
Building 1, #285
Menlo Park, CA 94025
415-854-1550
Contact: R. Pyne
         J. Stone

Stanford University
c/o Treasurer's Office
209 Hamilton Avenue
Palo Alto, CA 94301
415-723-1314
Contact: Rodney H. Adams, Treasurer

Sutter Hill Ventures
Two Palo Alto Square, #700
Palo Alto, CA 94306
415-493-5600
Contact: William H. Younger, Jr.
         General Partner
         Paul M. Wythes
         General Partner

TA Associates
435 Tasso Street, #200
Palo Alto, CA 94301
415-328-1210
Contact: Jeff Chambers, Manager

Taylor & Turner
220 Montgomery Street
Penthouse 10
San Francisco, CA 94104
415-398-6821
Contact: Bill Taylor
         Marshall Turner

Technology Partners
1550 Tiburon Boulevard, Suite A
Belvedere, CA 94920
415-435-1935
Contact: William Hart

Technology Venture Investors
3000 Sand Hill Road, #4-210
Menlo Park, CA 94025
415-854-7472
Contact: Mark Wilson
          Administrative Partner

3i Ventures
450 Newport Center Drive, #250
Newport Beach, CA 92660
714-720-1421
Contact: Frederick M. Haney,
       Managing Partner

Trinity Ventures, Ltd.
20813 Stevens Creek Boulevard, #101
Cupertino, CA 95014
408-446-9690
Contact: Gerald S. Casilli
       Noel J. Fenton
       David Nierenberg

U.S. Venture Partners
2180 Sand Hill Road, #300
Menlo Park, CA 94025
415-854-9080
Contact: Steven Krausz, General Partner
       Nancy Glaser, General Partner

Vanguard Associates
300 Hamilton Avenue, #500
Palo Alto, CA 94301
415-324-8400
Contact: Doug DeVivo
       Jack Gill
       David Rammler

Venrock Associates
Two Palo Alto Square, #528
Palo Alto, CA 94306
415-493-5577
Contact: Anthony Sun, General Partner

Ventana Growth Fund
1660 Hotel Circle North, #730
San Diego, CA 92108
619-291-2757
Contact: F. D. Townsen

Venture Growth Associates
3000 Sand Hill Road
Building 3, #125
Menlo Park, CA 94025
415-854-8001
Contact: Bill Welling,
       Managing Partner

Walden Capital
750 Battery Street, #700
San Francisco, CA 94111
415-391-7225
Contact: George Sarlo

Weiss, Peck & Greer
555 California Street, #4760
San Francisco, CA 94104
415-622-6864
Contact: Robert J. Loarie, General Partner

Westamco Investment Company
8929 Wilshire Boulevard, #400
Beverly Hills, CA 90211
213-652-8288
Contact: Leonard G. Muskin, President
       Scott T. Van Every, Vice President

J. H. Whitney & Co.
3000 Sand Hill Road
Building 1, #270
Menlo Park, CA 94025
415-854-0500
Contact: David T. Morgenthaler II
       Harry A. Marshall
       John W. Larson

Xerox Venture Capital
2029 Century Park E., #740
Los Angeles, CA 90067
213-278-7940
Contact: Stephen Taylor
       Al Talbot

COLORADO

Boettcher Venture Capital, L.P.
828 17th Street
Denver, CO 80202
303-628-8000
Contact: Foye F. Black, Jr.

**Centennial Business
Development Fund, Ltd.**
1999 Broadway, #2100
Denver, CO 80202
303-298-9066
Contact: David Bullwinkle, General Partner

The Centennial Fund Ltd.
1999 Broadway, #2100
Denver, CO 80202
303-298-9066
Contact: G. Jackson Tankersley, Jr.,
         General Partner

The Centennial Fund II, L.P.
1999 Broadway, #2100
Denver, CO 80202
303-298-9066
Contact: Mark Dubovoy, General Partner

Colorado Growth Capital, Inc.
1600 Broadway, #2125
Denver, CO 80202
303-831-0205
Contact: Debra Chavez

Colorado Venture Capital Corporation
4735 Walnut Street
Boulder, CO 80301
303-449-9018
Contact: Cliff Thygesen

Columbine Venture Fund, Ltd.
5613 DTC Parkway, #510
Englewood, CO 80111
303-694-3222
Contact: Mark Kimmel
         Sherman Muller
         Terry Winters

Graystone Capital, Ltd.
370 17th Street, #4290
Denver, CO 80202
303-573-8866
Contact: Manager

Hill, Kirby & Washing
885 Arapahoe Avenue
Boulder, CO 80302
303-442-5151
Contact: John Hill, General Partner
         Paul Kirby, General Partner
         Thomas Washing, General Partner

Intermountain Ventures, Ltd.
1100 10th Street, #401
Post Office Box 1406
Greeley, CO 80632
303-356-5721
Contact: Norman M. Dean, President

**Investment Securities
of Colorado, Inc.**
4605 Denice Drive
Englewood, CO 80111
303-796-9192
Contact: Vern Kornelsen, President

The Masters Fund
1426 Pearl Street, #211
Boulder, CO 80302
303-443-2460
Contact: Carl D. Carman
         Martin J. Chizzick

The Rockies Fund
8301 East Prentice, #202
Englewood, CO 80111
303-320-0090
Contact: Ed Pfohl

Weiss, Peck & Greer
1113 Spruce, #300
Boulder, CO 80302
303-443-1023
Contact: K. Dieter Heidrich,
         General Partner

Woody Creek Capital
Post Office Box 954
1919 14th Street, #330
Boulder, CO 80302
303-444-6000
Contact: Wayne Goss

CONNECTICUT

Abacus Ventures
283 Greenwich Avenue
Greenwich, CT 06830
203-629-4991
Contact: Yung Wong
       Charles Lee

**Cambridge Research
  and Development Group**
21 Bridge Square
Westport, CT 06880
203-226-7400
Contact: Manager

Fairfield Venture Partners
1275 Summer Street
Stamford, CT 06905
203-358-0255
Contact: Pedro A. Castillo
      Oakes Ames
      Eugene E. Pettinelli

First Connecticut SBIC
177 State Street
Bridgeport, CT 06604
203-366-4726
Contact: David Engelson

**General Electric Venture
  Capital Corporation**
3135 Easton Turnpike
Fairfield, CT 06431
203-373-2103
Contact: Suzanne Schuerman

**General Electric Venture
  Capital Corporation**
33 Riverside Avenue
Westport, CT 06880
203-373-3238
Contact: J. J. Fitzpatrick

James B. Kobak & Company
774 Hollow Tree Ridge Road
Darien, CT 06820
203-655-8764
Contact: Manager

MarketCorp Venture Associates, L.P.
285 Riverside Avenue
Westport, CT 06880
203-222-1000
Contact: E. Bulkeley Griswold

Memhard Investment Bankers, Inc.
Post Office Box 617
Old Greenwich, CT 06870
203-637-5494
Contact: Richard C. Memhard
      Laura M. Fleming

Oak Investment Partners
257 Riverside Avenue
Westport, CT 06880
203-226-8346
Contact: Ronald J. Verrilli

Orien Ventures, Inc.
36 Grove Street
New Canaan, CT 06840
203-966-7274
Contact: George Kalan

Oxford Partners
Soundview Plaza
1266 Main Street
Stamford, CT 06902
203-964-0592
Contact: Ken Rind

Prime Capital Management Co., Inc.
One Landmark Square, #800
Stamford, CT 06901
203-964-0642
Contact: Dean E. Fenton

Procordia Nova, Inc.
545 Steamboat Road
Greenwich, CT 06830
203-661-2500
Contact: Tord Carmel

Regional Financial Enterprises
36 Grove Street, 3rd Floor
New Canaan, CT 06840
203-966-2800
Contact: Manager

Saugatuck Capital Company
595 Summer Street
Stamford, CT 06901
203-348-6669
Contact: Norman W. Johnson

Ventech Partners, L.P.
Avon Park South
30 Tower Lane
Avon, CT 06001
203-677-0183
Contact: Manager

Vista Group
36 Grove Street
New Canaan, CT 06804
203-972-3400
Contact: Mary Lou Mitovich

Whitehead Associates
15 Valley Drive
Greenwich, CT 06830
203-629-4633
Contact: William E. Engbers
        Edwin C. Whitehead
        Joseph A. Orlando

Xerox Venture Capital
800 Long Ridge Road
Stamford, CT 06904
203-968-3383
Contact: L. J. Harris, Manager

DISTRICT OF COLUMBIA

Allied Capital Corporation
1666 K Street N.W.
Washington, D.C. 20006
202-331-1112
Contact: David Gladstone, President
        John Ledecky, Vice President

Broadcast Capital Fund, Inc.
1771 N. Street N.W.
Washington, D.C. 20036
202-429-5393
Contact: John Oxendine, President
        Ken Harris, Vice President

Malcolm Bund & Associates, Inc.
2000 L Street N.W., #200
Washington, D.C. 20036
202-293-2910
Contact: Malcolm Bund

Corporate Finance of Washington, Inc.
1326 R Street N.W. #2
Washington, D.C. 20009
202-328-9053
Contact: Peter W. Gavian, President

Ewing Capital, Inc.
1110 Vermont Avenue N.W., #1170
Washington, D.C. 20005
202-463-8787
Contact: Manager

Fulcrum Venture Capital Corporation
2021 K Street N.W., #701
Washington, D.C. 20006-1003
202-833-9590
Contact: Divakar R. Kamath, President

Middle Atlantic Ventures
655 15th Street N.W., #300
Washington, D.C. 20005
202-393-8550
Contact: William E. Simmons, Jr., Owner

**Minority Broadcast
Investment Corporation**
1820 Jefferson Place, N.W.
Washington, D.C. 20036
202-293-1166
Contact: Walter L. Threadgill

Pierce Investment Banking
1910 K Street N.W.
Washington, D.C. 20006
202-833-8031
Contact: John Clark
David Gregg

Wachtel & Co., Inc.
1101 14th Street N.W.
Washington, D.C. 20005-5680
202-898-1144
Contact: Sidney B. Wachtel

FLORIDA

Allied North American Company
111 East Las Olas Boulevard
Fort Lauderdale, FL 33301
305-763-8484
Contact: Edwin Harkness Spina

Caribank Capital Corp.
255 East Dania Beach Boulevard
Dania, FL 33004
305-925-2211
Contact: Michael E. Chaney, President
Elaine E. Healy, Investment Officer

Coastal Capital Resources, Inc.
3250 Mary Street, #202
Coconut Grove, FL 33133
305-442-4333
Contact: Lewis B. Freeman

First Tampa Capital Corp.
6200 Courtney Campbell Causeway, #340
Tampa, FL 33607
813-874-3112
Contact: Manager

Gold Coast Capital Corporation
3550 Biscayne Boulevard, #601
Miami, FL 33137
305-576-2012
Contact: William I. Gold

Hickory Capital Company, Inc.
615 Park Street
Jacksonville, FL 32204
904-356-2032
Contact: James L. Morrell

Interstate Capital Corp.
701 East Camino Real 9A
Boca Raton, FL 33432
305-395-8466
Contact: Manager

North American Company Ltd.
111 East Las Olas Boulevard
Post Office Box 14758
Fort Lauderdale, FL 33302
305-463-0681
Contact: Manager

Pro-Med Capital, Inc.
1380 NE Miami Gardens Drive
North Miami Beach, FL 33179
305-949-5900

South Atlantic Capital Corporation
220 East Madison Street, #530
Tampa, FL 33602-4825
813-229-7400
Contact: Donald W. Burton
Richard J. Brandewie

Universal Financial Services, Inc.
3550 Biscayne Boulevard, #702
Miami, FL 33137
305-573-1496
Contact: Norman Zipkin

Venture Management Associates, Inc.
One Southeast Financial Center
Miami, FL 33131
305-375-6470
Contact: Manager

GEORGIA

**Advanced Technology
  Development Fund**
430 10th Street, N.W., #N116
Atlanta, GA 30318
404-894-3575
Contact: Manager

Anatar Investments
235 Peachtree Street, #2218
Atlanta, GA 30303
404-588-0770
Contact: Douglas Hamilton

Grubb & Company
1500 Tower Place
3340 Peachtree Road
Atlanta, GA 30026
404-237-6222
Contact: Manager

Phillips J. Hook & Associates, Inc.
5600 Roswell Road, #300 North
Atlanta, GA 30342
404-252-1994
Contact: Manager

Investor's Equity, Inc.
2629 First National Bank Tower
Atlanta, Georgia 30383
404-523-3999
Contact: I. Walter Fisher, President

Mid-Southern Financial Corp.
Post Office Box 723355
Atlanta, GA 30339
404-458-0750
Contact: George Naterman, President

Noro-Moseley Partners
100 Galleria Parkway, #1240
Atlanta, GA 30339
404-955-0020
Contact: Charles D. Moseley, Jr.

North Riverside Capital
5775 Peachtree Dunwoody Road
Building D, Suite 560
Atlanta, GA 30342
404-252-1076
Contact: Thomas R. Barry, President

**The Robinson-Humphrey
  Company, Inc.**
3333 Peachtree Road NE
Atlanta, GA 30326
404-266-6075
Contact: Deborah Keel

Wellman-Thomas, Inc.
5775 Peachtree Dunwoody Road
Building D, Suite 640
Atlanta, GA 30342
404-252-8660
Contact: Manager

HAWAII

Bancorp Hawaii SBIC
111 South King Street, #1060
Honolulu, HI 96813
808-537-8557 or 808-521-6411
Contact: Thomas T. Triggs
                Vice President and Manager

ILLINOIS

Allstate Insurance Company
Allstate Plaza E-2
Northbrook, IL 60062
312-291-5681
Contact: Robert L. Lestina

Alpha Capital Venture Partners
Three First National Plaza, #1400
Chicago, IL 60602
312-372-1556
Contact: Andrew H. Kalnow

Amoco Venture Capital Co.
200 E. Randolph Drive
Chicago, IL 60601
312-856-6523
Contact: G. E. Stone, President

William Blair Venture Partners
135 South LaSalle Street
Chicago, IL 60603
312-853-8250
Contact: James E. Crawford, III
        Samuel B. Guren
        Scott F. Meadow

Business Ventures Inc.
20 N. Wacker Drive, #550
Chicago, IL 60606
312-346-1581
Contact: Milton G. Lefton, President

The Combined Fund, Inc.
1525 East 53rd Street, #908
Chicago, IL 60615
312-363-0300
Contact: E. Patric Jones, President

Comdisco Venture Lease, Inc.
6400 Shafer Court
Rosemont, IL 60018
312-698-3000
Contact: James Labe

**Continental Illinois
Venture Corporation
Continental Illinois Equity Corporation**
231 South LaSalle Street
Chicago, IL 60697
312-828-8021
Contact: John L. Hines, President

First Chicago Investment Advisors
Three First National Plaza
Ninth Floor, #0140
Chicago, IL 60670-0140
312-732-4171
Contact: Bart Holaday
        Managing Director

First Chicago Venture Capital
Three First National Plaza, #1330
Chicago, IL 60670
312-732-5400
Contact: Manager

Frontenac Venture Company
208 South LaSalle Street, #1900
Chicago, IL 60604
312-368-0044
Contact: Manager

Golder, Thoma & Cressey
120 South LaSalle Street, #630
Chicago, IL 60603
312-853-3322
Contact: Stanley Golder
        Carl Thoma
        Bryan Cressey

IEG Venture Management, Inc.
401 N. Michigan Avenue, #2020
Chicago, IL 60611
312-644-0890
Contact: Frank Blair
        Marian Zamlynski

Longworth Ventures
135 South LaSalle Street, #616
Chicago, IL 60603
312-372-3888
Contact: Andrew A. Beaurline
        General Partner

Mesirow Venture Capital
350 N. Clark Street
Chicago, IL 60610
312-670-6000
Contact: James C. Tyree
        Managing Director

North American Group, Ltd.
55 W. Monroe Street, #3500
Chicago, IL 60603
312-236-6800
Contact: Gregory I. Kravitt
           Vice President

Peterson Finance
  and Investment Company
3300 West Peterson Avenue, Suite A
Chicago, IL 60659
312-539-0502 or 312-539-0503
Contact: James S. Rhee, President

Prince Venture Partners
One First National Plaza, #4950
Chicago, IL 60603
312-726-2232
Contact: Angus M. Duthie, Partner

Sears Investment Management Co.
Xerox Center
55 West Monroe Street, 32nd Floor
Chicago, IL 60603
312-875-0415
Contact: Manager

Sucsy, Fischer & Company
135 South LaSalle, #616
Chicago, IL 60603
312-346-4545
Contact: Lawrence G. Sucsy
           President
           Paul Fischer
           Vice President

Technology Partners
1910 Surrey Lane
Lake Forest, IL 60045
312-234-8440
Contact: Peter J. Gillespie
           Managing Partner

INDIANA

Biddinger Investment
  Capital Corporation
9102 N. Meridian Street, Suite 500
Indianapolis, Indiana 46260
317-844-7390
Contact: William Muirhead, III

Circle Ventures, Inc.
20 North Meridian Street
Indianapolis, IN 46204
317-636-7242
Contact: Manager

Corporation for
  Innovation Development
One North Capitol Avenue, #520
Indianapolis, IN 46204
317-635-7325
Contact: Manager

Equity Resource Company, Inc.
One Plaza Place
Post Office Box 6
South Bend, IN 46624
219-237-5255
Contact: Michael J. Hammes

1st Source Capital Corporation
100 North Michigan
Post Office Box 1602
South Bend, IN 46634
219-236-2180
Contact: Manager

Heritage Venture Group, Inc.
One Indiana Square, #2400
Indianapolis, IN 46204
317-635-5696
Contact: Arthur A. Angotti

Mount Vernon Venture Capital Co.
Post Office Box 40177
Indianapolis, IN 46240
317-259-8720
Contact: Thomas J. Grande

White River Capital Corporation
500 Washington Street
Post Office Box 929
Columbus, IN 47202
812-376-1759
Contact: Manager

IOWA

R. W. Allsop & Associates
Corporate Center East, #210
2750 First Avenue NE
Cedar Rapids, IA 52402
319-363-8971
Contact: Paul D. Rhines

Iowa Venture Capital Fund, L.P.
800 American Building
Cedar Rapids, IA 52401
319-363-8249
Contact: Donald Flynn,
President
David Schroder,
Executive Vice President

Pappajohn Capital Resources
2116 Financial Center
Des Moines, IA 50309
515-244-5746
Contact: John Pappajohn

KANSAS

R. W. Allsop & Associates
8700 Monrovia Street
Lenexa, KS 66215
913-492-9542
Contact: Manager

KENTUCKY

**Kentucky Highlands
Investment Corporation**
911 North Main Street
Post Office Box 628
London, KY 40741
606-864-5175
Contact: Manager

LOUISIANA

Louisiana Equity Capital Corporation
451 Florida Street
Post Office Box 1511
Baton Rouge, LA 70821
504-389-4421
Contact: Tom Adamek

Walnut Street Capital Company
2330 Canal Street
New Orleans, LA 70119
504-821-4952
Contact: William D. Humphries

MAINE

Maine Capital Corporation
70 Center Street
Portland, Maine 04101
207-772-1001
Contact: David M. Coit

MARYLAND

ABS Ventures Limited Partnership
135 East Baltimore Street
Baltimore, MD 21202
301-727-1700
Contact: Bruns H. Grayson,
Managing Partner

Arete Ventures, Inc.
6110 Executive Blvd., Suite 1040
Rockville, MD 20852
301-881-2555
Contact: Manager

Broventure Capital Management
16 West Madison Street
Baltimore, MD 21201
301-727-4520
Contact: William M. Gust,
General Partner
Harvey C. Branch,
General Partner

Emerging Growth Partners
400 East Pratt Street, #610
Baltimore, MD 21202
301-332-1021
Contact: Howard P. Colhoun,
General Partner
Peter S. Welles, General Partner

First Maryland Capital, Inc.
107 West Jefferson Street
Rockville, MD 20850
301-251-6630
Contact: Manager

Greater Washington Investors, Inc.
5454 Wisconsin Avenue, #1315
Chevy Chase, MD 20815
301-656-0626
Contact: Cyril W. Draffin, Jr.

New Enterprise Associates
1119 Saint Paul Street
Baltimore, MD 21202
301-244-0115
Contact: Frank A. Bonsal, Jr.

T. Rowe Price Threshold Fund, L.P.
100 East Pratt Street
Baltimore, MD 21202
301-547-2179
Contact: Manager

Suburban Capital Corporation
6610 Rockledge Drive
Bethesda, MD 20817
301-493-7025
Contact: Pete Linsert
Steve Dubin

MASSACHUSETTS

Acquivest Group, Inc.
10 Speen Street
Framingham, MA 01701
617-875-3242
Contact: S. John Loscocco, President

Advanced Technology Ventures
Ten Post Office Square
Boston, MA 02109
617-423-4050
Contact: Albert E. Paladino

Aegis Fund Limited Partnership
1 Cranberry Hill
Lexington, MA 02173
617-862-0200
Contact: Manager

American Research & Development
45 Milk Street
Boston, MA 02109
617-423-7500
Contact: Marie Norton
Administrative Manager

Analog Devices Enterprises
2 Technology Way
Norwood, MA 02062
617-329-4700
Contact: Laurence Sullivan

Applied Technology Partners, L.P.
55 Wheeler Street
Cambridge, MA 02138
617-354-4107
Contact: Frederick B. Bamber

Bain Capital Fund
Two Copley Place
Boston, MA 02116
617-572-3000
Contact: Robert F. White
Joshua Bekenstein

BancBoston Ventures, Inc.
100 Federal Street
Boston, MA 02110
617-434-2442
Contact: Paul F. Hogan, President

Battery Ventures
200 Portland Street
Boston, MA 02114
617-367-1011
Contact: Richard D. Frisbie
    Robert G. Barrett
    Howard Anderson

Bessemer Venture Partners
83 Walnut Street
Wellesley Hills, MA 02181
617-237-6050
Contact: William T. Burgin

Boston Capital
   Ventures Limited Partnership
One Devonshire Place
Suite 2913
Boston, MA 02109
617-227-6550
Contact: A. Dana Callow, Jr.
    Donald J. Steiner
    H. J. von der Goltz

Boston Ventures Management, Inc.
   Boston Ventures, L.P.
45 Milk Street, Fifth Floor
Boston, MA 02109
617-292-8125
Contact: Manager

Burr, Egan, Deleage & Co.
One Post Office Square, #3800
Boston, MA 02109
617-482-8020
Contact: Jonathan Flint
    Frank Kenny
    Esther Sharp

Charles River Ventures
67 Batterymarch Street
Boston, MA 02110
617-439-0477
Contact: Richard M. Burns
    John T. Neises
    Robert F. Higgins

Chatham Venture Corporation
450 Bedford Street
Lexington, MA 02173
617-863-0970
Contact: Euan C. Malcolmson,
    President
    Stephen J. Gaal,
    Principal

Churchill International
125 Technology Drive, #7
Waltham, MA 02154
617-893-6555
Contact: Julie Dunbar

Clafin Capital Management, Inc.
185 Devonshire Street
Boston, MA 02110
617-426-6505
Contact: Thomas M. Claflin, II
    Lloyd C. Dahmen
    John O. Flender

Copley Venture Partners
Federal Reserve Plaza
Boston, MA 02210
617-722-6030
Contact: Manager

Eastech Management Company, Inc.
One Liberty Square, 9th Floor
Boston, MA 02109
617-338-0200
Contact: Michael H. Shanahan

EG & G Ventures, Inc.
45 William Street
Wellesley, MA 02181
617-237-5100
Contact: T. P. Theodores,
    Vice President

Faneuil Hall Associates
One Boston Place
Boston, MA 02108
617-723-1955
Contact: David Riddiford

Fidelity Venture Associates, Inc.
82 Devonshire Street
Boston, MA 02109
617-570-6450
Contact: Donald R. Young

First Chicago Venture Capital
1 Financial Center
Boston, MA 02111
617-542-9185
Contact: Kevin M. McCafferty
 Vice President

Fleet Venture Partners
60 State Street, #1730
Boston, MA 02109
617-367-6701
Contact: James A. Saalfield

Fowler, Anthony & Co.
20 Walnut Street
Wellesley, MA 02181
617-237-4201
Contact: John A. Quagliaroli, President

Greylock Management Corporation
One Federal Street
Boston, MA 02110
617-423-5525
Contact: Daniel S. Gregory

Hambrecht & Quist
One Hollis Street, #102
Wellesley, MA 02181
617-237-2099
Contact: Manager

Hambro International Venture Fund
One Boston Place, Suite 810
Boston, MA 02108
617-722-7055
Contact: Manager

**John Hancock
Venture Capital Fund, L.P.**
1 Financial Center, 39th Floor
Boston, MA 02111
617-350-4002
Contact: Lois Kasten

Harbour Financial Company
357 Fox Hill Street
Westwood, MA 02090
617-461-0460
Contact: John R. Schwanbeck

HLM Partners
10 Liberty Square
Boston, MA 02109
617-423-3530
Contact: Manager

Investors in Industry
(see 3i- under T)

Massachusetts Capital Resource Co.
545 Boylston Street
Boston, MA 02116
617-536-3900
Contact: Manager

**Massachusetts Community
 Development Finance
 Corporation (CDFC)**
131 State Street, #600
Boston, MA 02109
617-742-0366
Contact: Judith Cranna

Massachusetts Venture Capital Corp.
59 Temple Place
Boston, MA 02111
617-426-0208
Contact: Manager

Matrix Partners
One Post Office Square
Boston, MA 02109
617-482-7735
Contact: Tim Barrows

McGowan, Leckinger, Berg
10 Forbes Road
Braintree, MA 02184
617-849-0020
Contact: Manager

Memorial Drive Trust
20 Acorn Park
Cambridge, MA 02140
617-864-5770
Contact: Jay Senerchia

Morgan Holland Ventures Corp.
1 Liberty Square
Boston, MA 02109
617-423-1712
Contact: Robert L. Rosbe, Jr.

New England Capital Corporation
One Washington Mall
Boston, MA 02108
617-722-6400
Contact: Z. David Patterson
            Executive Vice President

New England MESBIC, Inc.
50 Kearney Road, #3
Needham, MA 02194
617-449-2066
Contact: Dr. E. Chen

Orange Nassau
260 Franklin Street
Boston, MA 02110
617-439-6160
Contact: Richard D. Tadler
            Linda S. Linsalata

PaineWebber Venture
   Management Company
265 Franklin Street, #1501
Boston, MA 02110
617-439-8300
Contact: Amy Haley

Palmer Partners
300 Unicorn Park Drive
Woburn, MA 01801
617-933-5445
Contact: William H. Congleton
            Stephen J. Ricci
            John A. Shane

Regent Financial Corp.
10 Commercial Wharf West, #502
Boston, MA 02110
617-723-4820
Contact: Manager

Security Pacific Capital Corporation
50 Milk Street, 15th Floor
Boston, MA 02109
617-542-7601
Contact: Michael Cronin

The Sprout Group
1 Center Plaza, 6th Floor
Boston, MA 02108
617-570-8700
Contact: L. E. Reeder

Summit Ventures
One Boston Place, #3420
Boston, MA 02108
617-742-5500
Contact: Manager

TA Associates
45 Milk Street
Boston, MA 02109
617-338-0800
Contact: Manager

3i Capital
3i Ventures
99 High Street, #1530
Boston, MA 02110
617-542-8560
Contact: Ivan Momtchiloff, Chairman
            William Holm, VP, 3i Capital
            Allan Ferguson, VP, 3i Ventures

Transatlantic Capital Corporation
185 Devonshire Street
Boston, MA 02110
617-482-0015
Contact: John O. Flender, President

Turner Revis Associates
14 Union Wharf
Boston, MA 02109
617-227-9734
Contact: Manager

Ulin, Morton, Bradley & Welling
75 Federal Street
Boston, MA 02110
617-423-0003
Contact: Peter A. Ulin

UNC Ventures
195 State Street, #700
Boston, MA 02109
617-723-8300
Contact: Manager

UST Capital Corp.
40 Court Street
Boston, MA 02108
617-726-7171
Contact: Walter Dick, Vice President

**The Venture Capital
Fund of New England**
160 Federal Street, 23rd Floor
Boston, MA 02110
617-439-4646
Contact: Manager

Venture Founders
One Cranberry Hill
Lexington, MA 02173
617-863-0900
Contact: Alexander L. M. Dingee, Jr.
         Ross Yeiter

Zero Stage Capital Equity Fund, L.P.
1 Broadway, Kendall Square
Cambridge, MA 02142
617-876-5355
Contact: Manager

MICHIGAN

ACCEL Telecom
2020 Hogback Road
Ann Arbor, MI 48104
313-971-4451
Contact: Dixon R. Doll

Great Lakes Funding & Leasing
Post Office Box 371
Mt. Morris, MI 48458
313-687-4400
Contact: Daniel P. Allen, General Partner

MBW Management, Inc.
2000 Hogback Road, #2
Ann Arbor, MI 48105
313-971-3100
Contact: Ian Bund, Managing Director
         Dick Goff,
             Vice President and CFO

NBD Venture Capital Group
800 First National Building
201 South Main Street
Ann Arbor, MI 48104
313-663-0702
Contact: Carlene D. Dettleff,
             Secretary/Associate Treasurer
         Philip Waldrop,
             Investment Associate

Regional Financial Enterprises
325 East Eisenhower Parkway, #103
Ann Arbor, MI 48104
313-769-0941
Contact: Jim Parsons, General Partner

Taurus Financial Group, Inc.
601 South Norton Road, #A-8
Corunna, MI 48817-1244
517-743-5729
Contact: Robert G. Machala, Chairman

MINNESOTA

Cherry Tree Ventures
3800 West 80th Street, #1400
Minneapolis, MN 55431
612-893-9012
Contact: Gordon F. Stofer,
　　　　　Managing General Partner

FBS Venture Capital Co./
　FBS Small Business Investment Co.
Braemar Office Park
8000 W. 78th Street, Suite 300
Edina, MN 55435
612-829-1122
Contact: Ray Allen,
　　　　　Executive Vice President

IAI Venture Capital Group
1100 Dain Tower
Post Office Box 357
Minneapolis, MN 55440
612-371-7780
Contact: Mitchell Dann, General Partner
　　　　　Steve Weisbrod, General Partner

Minnesota Seed Capital, Inc.
1660 South Highway 100
Parkdale Plaza, #330
Minneapolis, MN 55416-1519
612-545-5684
Contact: Thomas M. Neitge,
　　　　　Special Limited Partner
　　　　　Thomas K. Rice,
　　　　　Special Limited Partner

North Star Ventures, Inc.
100 South 5th Street, #2200
Minneapolis, MN 55402
612-333-1133
Contact: Terrence Glarner, President

Northland Capital Corporation
Missabe Building, #613
227 West First Street
Duluth, MN 55802
218-722-0545
Contact: George G. Barnum, Jr.
　　　　　President

Norwest Growth Fund, Inc.
2800 Piper Jaffray Tower
Minneapolis, MN 55402
612-372-8770
Contact: Douglas E. Johnson,
　　　　　Vice President
　　　　　Leonard J. Brandt,
　　　　　Vice President
　　　　　John P. Whaley,
　　　　　Vice President

Norwest Equity Capital
2800 Piper Jaffray Tower
Minneapolis, MN 55402
612-372-8770
Contact: John E. Lindahl, Vice President
　　　　　John L. Thomson, Vice President

Pathfinder Venture Capital Funds
7300 Metro Boulevard, #585
Minneapolis, MN 55435
612-835-1121
Contact: A. J. Greenshields,
　　　　　Investments Officer

Piper Jaffray Ventures Incorporated
222 South Ninth Street
Minneapolis, MN 55402
612-342-6310
Contact: David P. Crosby,
　　　　　Managing Director
　　　　　Peter Gillette, Jr.,
　　　　　Managing Director

Threshold Ventures, Inc.
430 Oak Grove Street, #303
Minneapolis, MN 55403
612-874-7199
Contact: John L. Shannon, Jr., President

MISSOURI

R. W. Allsop & Associates
111 West Port Plaza, #600
St. Louis, MO 63146
314-434-1688
Contact: Robert Kuk, General Partner

Capital for Business, Inc.
1000 Walnut Street, 18th Floor
Kansas City, MO 64106
816-234-2357
Contact: Bart Bergman, Vice President

Capital for Business, Inc.
11 South Meramec, #800
St. Louis, MO 63105
314-854-7427
Contact: James B. Hebenstreit, President
William O. Cannon, Vice President

Harbour Group Investments
7701 Forsyth Boulevard, #550
St. Louis, MO 63105
314-727-5550
Contact: Manager

Intech Group, Inc.
130 South Bemiston, #703
St. Louis, MO 63105
314-863-3888
Contact: William W. Canfield, President

Intercapco West, Inc.
7800 Bonhomme
St. Louis, MO 63105
314-863-0600
Contact: Mark J. Lincoln, President

**MorAmerica Capital Corporation and
InvestAmerica Venture Group, Inc.**
Commerce Tower Building, #2724
911 Main Street
Kansas City, MO 64105
816-842-0114
Contact: Kevin F. Mullane, Vice President

MONTANA

Rocky Mountain Capital, Inc.
505 Securities Building
Billings, MT 59101
406-256-1984
Contact: E. E. Kuhns,
President and Chairman

NEVADA

United Venture Capital, Inc.
2001 Foothill Road
Post Office Box 109
Genoa, NV 89411
702-883-6395
Contact: Manager

Wallner & Co.
Post Office Box 4563
Incline Village, NV 89450
702-832-7771
Contact: Gary Acquavella, C.P.A.

NEW HAMPSHIRE

Hampshire Capital Corporation
75 Concord Street, #204
Post Office Box 468
Portsmouth, NH 03801
603-431-7755
Contact: Philip G. Baker

NEW JERSEY

ACCEL Partners
One Palmer Square
Princeton, NJ 08542
609-683-4500
Contact: James R. Swartz
Arthur C. Patterson
Dixon R. Doll

Bradford Associates
22 Chambers Street
Princeton, New Jersey 08540
609-921-3880
Contact: Bradford Mills
         Winston J. Churchill

Bridge Capital Investors
Glenpoint Center West
Teaneck, NJ 07666
201-836-3900
Contact: Donald Remey,
         Managing Director

DSV Partners
221 Nassau Street
Princeton, NJ 08542
609-924-6420
Contact: Morton Collins
         James Bergman
         Robert Hillas

Edelson Technology Partners
Park 80 West, Plaza Two
Saddle Brook, NJ 07662
201-843-4474
Contact: Harry Edelson, General Partner
         Anthony Bussa, Partner
         Ray Bosso, Partner

Edison Venture Fund
90 Nassau Street
Princeton, NJ 08540
609-683-1900
Contact: John H. Martinson
         James F. Mrazek

GeoCapital Ventures
2115 Linwood Avenue
Fort Lee, NJ 07024
201-461-9292
Contact: Steve Clearman

InnoVen Group
Park 80 West, Plaza One
Saddle Brook, NJ 07662
201-845-4900
Contact: G. A. Lodge, CEO
         R. J. Rasmussen, President
         H. D. Lambert, Vice President

Johnson & Johnson
  Development Corporation
One Johnson & Johnson Plaza
New Brunswick, NJ 08933
201-524-6407
Contact: C. M. Anderson, President

Johnston Associates, Inc.
181 Cherry Valley Road
Princeton, NJ 08540
609-924-3131
Contact: Robert F. Johnston,
         President

KBA Partners, L.P.
Parker Plaza
400 Kelby Street
Fort Lee, NJ 07024
201-461-8585
Contact: Richard King, General Partner
         Richard Black, General Partner

MBW Management, Inc.
365 South Street
Morristown, NJ 07960
201-285-5533
Contact: Phil McCarthy, Managing Director
         Wayne Clevenger

Med-Tech Ventures, Inc.
201 Tabor Road
Morris Plains, NJ 07950
201-540-3457
Contact: Manager

Monmouth Capital Corporation
125 Wyckoff Road, P. O. Box 335
Eatontown, NJ 07724
201-542-4927
Contact: Ralph B. Patterson
Executive Vice President

Princeton/Montrose Partners
101 Poor Farm Road
Princeton, NJ 08540
609-921-1590
Contact: Ronald R. Hahn
Managing General Partner
Donald R. Stroben
Managing General Partner
Richard J. Defieux,
General Partner

Tappan Zee Capital Corp.
201 Lower Notch Road
Little Falls, New Jersey 07424
201-256-8280
Contact: Jack Birnberg,
Chairman of the Board

**Unicorn Ventures Ltd./
Unicorn Ventures II, L.P.**
6 Commerce Drive
Cranford, NJ 07016
201-276-7880
Contact: Frank P. Diassi, General Partner

NEW MEXICO

Associated Southwest Investors, Inc.
2400 Louisiana, N.E., #4-225
Albuquerque, NM 87110
505-881-0066
Contact: John R. Rice

Equity Capital Corporation
119 East Marcy Street, #101
Santa Fe, NM 87501
505-988-4273
Contact: Jerry A. Henson, President

Meadows Resources, Inc.
1650 University N.E., #500
Albuquerque, NM 87102
505-768-6200
Contact: Charlie Mollo

NEW YORK

Ackley Capital Corporation
1 Paper Mill Place
Honeoye Falls, NY 14472
716-624-2024
Contact: Edward J. Ackley, President

Adler & Company
375 Park Avenue, #3303
New York, NY 10152
212-759-2800
Contact: Frederick R. Adler,
General Partner
Dr. Yuval Binur
Gill Cogan

Adler & Shaykin
375 Park Avenue, #1401
New York, NY 10152
212-319-2800
Contact: Leonard Shaykin

Alimansky Venture Group
605 Madison Avenue, #300
New York, NY 10022
212-832-7300
Contact: Linda D. Sabia,
Managing Director

American Corporate Services
515 Madison Avenue
New York, NY 10022
212-688-9691
Contact: Michael Simon,
Vice President

AMEV Capital Corporation
One World Trade Center, #5001
New York, NY 10048-0495
212-775-9100
Contact: Martin S. Orland, President
Bruce Bromberg, Vice President
Emmett P. Bonner III,
Vice President

AXA Capital Corp.
Nine West 57 Street
New York, NY 10019
212-421-7870
Contact: Manager

Bessemer Venture Partners
630 Fifth Avenue
New York, NY 10111
212-708-9304
Contact: Robert Buescher, Partner

Biotech Capital Corporation
600 Madison Avenue, 21st Floor
New York, NY 10022
212-758-7722
Contact: Constance Harrison,
Vice President

BT Capital Corporation
280 Park Avenue, #10W
New York, NY 10017
212-850-1920
Contact: James G. Hellmuth, Chairman
Noel E. Urben, President

Buffalo Capital Corporation
Mount Morris Road
Geneseo, NY 14454
716-243-4310
Contact: John H. Hickman, Chairman
Linda A. McLaughlin, Secretary

Butler Capital
767 Fifth Avenue
New York, NY 10153
212-980-0606
Contact: Charles Sukenik,
Managing Director
Bill Walton, Principal

Chemical Venture Partners
277 Park Avenue
New York, NY 10172
212-310-4949
Contact: Steven J. Gilbert

Citicorp Venture Capital, Ltd.
Citicorp Center
153 East 53rd Street, 28th Floor
New York, NY 10043
212-559-1127
Contact: Peter Gerry, President
William Comfort, Chairman

Clinton Capital Corporation
419 Park Avenue South
New York, NY 10016
212-696-4334
Contact: Mitchell Rothken
Terry Jacobs

CMNY Capital Company, L.P.
77 Water Street
New York, NY 10005
212-437-7078
Contact: Robert Davidoff, General Partner
Howard Davidoff, Vice President

Coleman Ventures, Inc.
5909 Northern Boulevard
East Norwich, NY 11732
516-626-3642
Contact: Gregory S. Coleman, President

Concord Partners
535 Madison Avenue, 8th Floor
New York, NY 10022
212-906-7000
Contact: Peter Leidel
            Vice President

Crown Advisors, Ltd.
225 Broadway, #612
New York, NY 10007
212-619-1840
Contact: Chester Siuda,
            President

Croyden Capital Corporation
45 Rockefeller Plaza, #2168
New York, NY 10111
212-974-0184
Contact: Lawrence Gorfinkle, President

CW Group, Inc.
1041 Third Avenue
New York, NY 10021
212-308-5266
Contact: Walter Channing, Jr.
            Barry Weinberg
            Charles Hartman

Davis Group
Post Office Box 6491
FDR Station
New York, NY 10022
212-977-8482
Contact: Roger David, Managing Partner

DeMuth, Folger & Terhune
One Exchange Plaza
at 55 Broadway
New York, NY 10006
212-509-5580
Contact: Donald F. DeMuth

Drexel Burnham Lambert Inc.
55 Broad Street
New York, NY 10004
212-480-3965
Contact: Alexa Mahnken

Eberstadt Fleming Inc.
1270 Avenue of the Americas, 11th Floor
New York, NY 10020
212-713-7701
Contact: Jack W. Lasersohn, Director,
            Venture Capital Division

Equity Growth Fund Corp.
112 E. 61 Street
New York, NY 10021
212-601-3123
Contact: William Ashwood

Euclid Partners Corporation
50 Rockefeller Plaza
New York, NY 10020
212-489-1770
Contact: Milton J. Pappas
            A. Bliss McCrum, Jr.
            Jeffrey T. Hamilton

Fairfield Equity Corporation
200 E. 42nd Street
New York, NY 10017
212-867-0150
Contact: Matthew A. Berdon

Ferranti High Technology, Inc.
515 Madison Avenue
New York, NY 10022
212-688-9828
Contact: Michael Simon,
            Vice President

First Century Partners
1345 Avenue of the Americas
New York, NY 10105
212-698-6108
Contact: David S. Lobel,
            General Partner

Fleet Venture Partners
666 Third Avenue
New York, NY 10017
212-972-8127
Contact: Habib Y. Gorgi,
            Vice President

Foster Management Company
437 Madison Avenue
New York, NY 10022
212-753-4810
Contact: Carolyn H. Flemming

Founders Equity
200 Madison Avenue
New York, NY 10016
212-953-0100
Contact: John Teeger, President
        Warren Haber, Chairman

The Franklin Corporation
767 5th Avenue
New York, NY 10153
212-486-2323
Contact: Alan Farkas, President
        James Eisberg, Secretary
        and House Counsel
        David J. Friedman
        Executive Vice President

Fundex Capital Corporation
525 Northern Boulevard
Great Neck, NY 11021
516-466-8550
Contact: Howard Sommer, President

GeoCapital Ventures
655 Madison Avenue
New York, NY 10021
212-752-0771
Contact: Irwin Lieber

Gibbons, Green Van Amerongen
600 Madison Avenue
New York, NY 10022
212-832-2400
Contact: Edward W. Gibbon, Partner

Globus Growth Group
44 West 24th Street
New York, NY 10010
212-243-1000
Contact: Stephen E. Globus, Chairman

Hambro International Venture Fund
17 East 71st Street
New York, NY 10021
212-288-7778
Contact: Fran Janis, Associate

The Hanover Capital Corporation
150 East 58th Street, #2710
New York, NY 10155
212-980-9670
Contact: John A. Selzer

Harvest Ventures, Inc.
767 Third Avenue
New York, NY 10017
212-838-7776
Contact: Harvey Wertheir,
        Managing Director
        Harvey Mallmeth,
        Managing Director

Holding Capital Management Corp.
685 Fifth Avenue, 14th Floor
New York, NY 10022
212-486-6670
Contact: S. A. Spencer, President
        James W. Donaghy,
        Vice President

Hutton Venture Investment Partners
1 Battery Park Plaza, #1802
New York, NY 10004
212-742-3722
Contact: James E. McGrath, President
        James F. Wilson, Vice President
        Timothy Noll, Vice President

Ibero-American Investors Corporation
38 Scio Street
Rochester, NY 14604
716-262-3440
Contact: Emilio L. Serrano
        President & CEO

Inco Venture Capital Management
One New York Plaza
New York, NY 10004
212-612-5620
Contact: Stuart F. Feiner, President
A. Douglas Peabody, Sr.
Vice President
George M. Middlemas,
Sr. Vice President

**International Technology
Ventures, Inc.**
200 Park Avenue, #5506
New York, NY 10166
212-972-5233
Contact: John Soden, President

Investech, L.P.
515 Madison Avenue, #2400
New York, NY 10022
212-308-5811
Contact: Carl S. Hutman

Irving Capital Corporation
1290 Avenue of the Americas
Third Floor
New York, NY 10019
212-408-4800
Contact: Kathleen Snyder

The Jordan Company
315 Park Avenue South
20th Floor
New York, NY 10010
212-460-1910
Contact: Manager

Josephberg Grosz & Co., Inc.
344 East 49th Street
New York, NY 10017
212-935-1050
Contact: Richard A. Josephberg
Ivan A. Grosz

Lawrence Venture Associates
515 Madison Avenue
New York, NY 10022
212-826-9080
Contact: Brian T. Horey, Associate

M & T Capital Corporation
One M & T Plaza
Buffalo, NY 14240
716-842-5881
Contact: Joseph V. Parlato, President
Norma E. Gracia, Treasurer

**Manufacturers Hanover
Venture Capital Corporation**
140 East 45th Street, 30th Floor
New York, NY 10017
212-808-0109
Contact: Edward L. Koch, III,
Vice President
Kevin P. Falvey, Vice President
Bryan J. Carey, Assist. V.P.

Medallion Funding Corp.
205 E. 42nd Street, #2020
New York, NY 10017
212-682-3300
Contact: Alvin Murstein

**Minority Equity
Capital Company, Inc.**
275 Madison Avenue
New York, NY 10016
212-686-9710
Contact: Donald F. Greene
Clarence W. Arrington

ML Venture Partners II, L.P.
717 Fifth Avenue, 22nd Floor
New York, NY 10022
212-980-0410
Contact: Manager

Morgan Stanley
  Venture Partners, L.P.
1251 Avenue of the Americas
New York, NY 10020
212-703-8485
Contact: William F. Murdy,
             General Partner
         Guy L. de Chazal,
             General Partner

Nazem & Company
600 Madison Avenue
New York, NY 10022
212-644-6433
Contact: Fred Nazem

New Enterprise Associates
119 East 55th Street
New York, NY 10022
212-371-8210
Contact: Howard D. Wolfe, Jr.

North American Capital Corp.
510 Broad Hollow Road
Melville, NY 11747
516-752-9600
Contact: Manager

North Street Capital Corporation
250 North Street RA-6S
White Plains, NY 10625
914-335-2500
Contact: Ralph L. McNeal, President

Northwood Ventures
56 School Street
Glen Cove, NY 11542
516-759-4633
Contact: Peter G. Schiff,
             General Partner

Novatech Resource Corporation
103 East 37th Street
New York, NY 10016
212-725-2555
Contact: Manager

Alan Patricof Associates, Inc.
545 Madison Avenue, 15th Floor
New York, NY 10022
212-753-6300
Contact: Alan Patricof, Chairman

Pennwood Capital Corporation
9 West 57th Street, #3980
New York, NY 10019
212-753-1600
Contact: Manager

Pioneer Ventures Co.
113 East 55th Street
New York, NY 10022
212-980-9094
Contact: Manager

The Pittsford Group, Inc.
8 Lodge Pole Road
Pittsford, NY 14534-3814
716-223-3523
Contact: Logan M. Cheek, III,
             Managing Principal

The Prospect Group, Inc.
645 Madison Avenue
New York, NY 10022
212-758-8500
Contact: Manager

Prudential Venture Capital
717 Fifth Avenue, #1600
New York, NY 10022
212-753-0901
Contact: Manager

Questec Enterprises, Inc.
328 Main Street
Huntington, NY 11743
516-351-1222
Contact: Manager

Rain Hill Group, Inc.
90 Broad Street
New York, NY 10004
212-483-9162
Contact: Manager

Rand Capital Corporation
1300 Rand Building
Buffalo, NY 14203
716-853-0802
Contact: Keith B. Wiley, Vice President
        Thomas J. Bernard,
          Vice President

Reprise Capital Corporation
585 Stewart Avenue
Garden City, New York 11530
516-222-2555
Contact: Irwin B. Nelson, President
        Stanley Tulchin, Chairman

Revere AE Capital Fund
745 Fifth Avenue, 19th Floor
New York, NY 10151
212-888-6800
Contact: Dora Chin

Rothschild Ventures Inc.
One Rockefeller Plaza
New York, NY 10020
212-757-6000
Contact: Jess L. Belser, President, CEO

Schroder Venture Managers
1 State Street
New York, NY 10004
212-269-6500
Contact: Jeffrey Collinson

**Sevin Rosen Management
Company**
200 Park Avenue, #4503
New York, NY 10166
212-687-5115
Contact: Manager

Shearson Lehman Brothers, Inc.
American Express Tower
World Financial Center
New York, NY 10285
212-298-2808
Contact: Sidney Berman,
        Vice President Investment
        Banking

S/L Health Care Ventures
1250 Broadway
New York, NY 10001
212-714-1470
Contact: Harold R. Werner
        Richard P. Lyman
        James S. Burns
        Wallace H. Steinberg

Southgate Venture Partners
Lincoln Building
60 East 42nd Street
Suite 3906
New York, NY 10165
212-744-2044
Contact: Rodney Pitts

The Sprout Group
140 Broadway
New York, New York 10005
212-504-3600
Contact: R. E. Kroon

SRK Management Company
126 East 56th Street, 33rd Floor
New York, NY 10022
212-371-0900
Contact: Victoria Hamilton

TA Associates
919 Third Avenue
New York, NY 10022
212-838-9660
Contact: Jacqueline C. Morby

Tessler & Cloherty, Inc.
420 Madison Avenue
New York, NY 10017
212-752-8010
Contact: Manager

Transportation Capital Corp.
60 East 42nd Street
New York, NY 10165
212-697-4885
Contact: Robert Silver

Vega Capital Corp.
720 White Plains Road
Scarsdale, NY 10583
914-472-8550
Contact: Ronald A. Linden, Vice President

Vencon Management, Inc.
301 West 53rd Street
New York, NY 10019
212-581-8787
Contact: Manager

Venrock Associates
30 Rockefeller Plaza, #5508
New York, NY 10112
212-649-5600
Contact: Ted McCortney

Venture Funding Group
49 West 12th Street, Executive Suite
New York, NY 10011
212-691-9895
Contact: Allan E. Skora, President

Venture Lending Associates
767 Fifth Avenue
New York, NY 10153
212-980-0606
Contact: Manager

Warburg, Pincus Ventures, Inc.
466 Lexington Avenue, 10th Floor
New York, NY 10017
212-878-0600
Contact: Christopher W. Brody
        Stephen W. Fillo
        Sidney Lapidus

Weiss, Peck & Greer CDA II
One New York Plaza, 30th Floor
New York, NY 10004
212-908-9500
Contact: E. Theodore Stolberg, Partner

Welsh, Carson, Anderson & Stowe
1 World Financial Center, #3601
New York, NY 10281
212-945-2000
Contact: Patrick J. Welsh

Wertheim & Co.
200 Park Avenue
New York, NY 10166
212-578-0200
Contact: Corporate Financial Department

J. H. Whitney & Co.
630 Fifth Avenue, #3200
New York, NY 10111
212-757-0500
Contact: Edward Ryan, General Partner

Winfield Capital Corp.
237 Mamaroneck Avenue
White Plains, NY 10605
914-949-2600
Contact: Stanley Pechman, President

Winthrop Ventures
74 Trinity Place
New York, NY 10006
212-422-0100
Contact: C. Brown

Wood River Capital Corporation
645 Madison Avenue
New York, NY 10022
212-750-9420
Contact: Elizabeth W. Smith
        Peter Wendell

NORTH CAROLINA

Delta Capital, Inc.
227 N. Tryon Street, Suite 201
Charlotte, NC 28202
704-372-1410
Contact: A. B. Wilkins, Jr., President

Falcon Capital Corporation
400 W. 5th Street
Greenville, NC 27834
919-752-5918
Contact: Manager

Heritage Capital Corporation
2290 First Union Plaza
Charlotte, NC 28282
704-334-2867
Contact: Herman McManway

Kitty Hawk Capital, Ltd.
1640 Independence Center
Charlotte, NC 28246
704-333-3777
Contact: Walter H. Wilkinson, Jr.
W. Chris Hegele

NCNB Venture Co., L.P.
One NCNB Plaza, T-39
Charlotte, NC 28255
704-374-5723
Contact: S. Epes Robinson, General Partner

Southgate Venture Partners
Delta Capitaling
227 N. Tryon Street
Suite 201
Charlotte, NC
Contact: Alex Wilkins

Venture First, Ltd.
2422 Reynolda Road
Winston-Salem, NC 27106
919-722-9600
Contact: M. Campbell Cawood,
General Partner

OHIO

A.T. Venture Capital Group
900 Euclid Avenue, T-18
Cleveland, OH 44101
216-687-4970
Contact: Robert C. Salipante

Basic Search
Park Place, 10 West Streetsboro
Hudson, OH 44236
216-656-2442
Contact: Burton D. Morgan, President

Cardinal Development Capital Fund
40 South Third Street, Suite 460
Columbus, OH 43215
614-464-5557
Contact: Richard F. Bannon
J. Thomas Walker
John N. Holscher

Clarion Capital Corporation
35555 Curtis Boulevard
Eastlake, OH 44094
216-953-0555
Contact: Morton A. Cohen

First City Venture Fund
35555 Curtis Boulevard
Eastlake, OH 44094
216-953-0555
Contact: Morton A. Cohen

First Ohio Capital Corporation
P. O. Box 1868
606 Madison Avenue
Toledo, OH 43603
419-259-7150
Contact: David J. McMacken

Lubrizol Enterprises, Inc.
29400 Lakeland Boulevard
Wickliffe, OH 44092
216-943-4200
Contact: Donald L. Murfin, President
Bruce H. Grasser, Vice President

Miami Valley Capital, Inc.
315 Talbott Tower
Dayton, OH 45402
513-222-7222
Contact: Everett Telljohn,
Chairman and President

Morgenthaler Ventures
700 National City Bank Building
Cleveland, OH 44114
216-621-3070
Contact: Paul Brentlinger,
General Partner

National City Capital Corporation
629 Euclid Avenue
Post Office Box 5756
Cleveland, OH 44114
216-575-2491
Contact: John B. Naylor, President
    Martha A. Barry, Vice President

Primus Capital Fund
1375 East 9th Street, #2140
Cleveland, OH 44114
216-621-2185
Contact: Jim Bartlett, II
    Loyal Wilson

Scientific Advances, Inc.
601 West Fifth Avenue
Columbus, OH 43201-3195
614-294-5541
Contact: Thomas W. Harvey,
        Vice President
    Paul F. Purcell, Vice President
    Daniel J. Shea, Vice President

Seed One
Park Place
10 West Streetsboro Street
Hudson, OH 44236
216-656-2442
Contact: Burton D. Morgan

The Small Business Advocacy, Inc.
Town Square Professional Center
526 Nilles Road, #5
Fairfield, OH 45014
513-829-0880
Contact: Marc E. Brown, President

OKLAHOMA

**Alliance Business
  Investment Company**
One Williams Center, Suite 2000
Tulsa, OK 74172
918-584-3581
Contact: Mark R. Blankenship
    Investment Officer

Davis Venture Partners
One Williams Center, Suite 2000
Tulsa, OK 74172
918-584-7272
Contact: Michael Stone, Partner
    Barry Davis, Partner
    Gary Smith, Partner
    Mark R. Blankenship, Partner

Signal Capital Corp.
1 Leadership Square, #400
Oklahoma City, OK 73102
405-235-4440
Contact: Arthur J. Miller

OREGON

Cable, Howse & Ventures, Inc.
1800 One Main Place
101 Southwest Main
Portland, OR 97204
503-248-9646
Contact: Bart Alexander, Manager

InterVen Partners
227 S. W. Pine Street, #200
Portland, OR 97204
503-223-4334
Contact: Wayne Kingsley, General Partner
    Keith Larson, General Partner

Northern Pacific Capital Corporation
1201 S.W. 12th Avenue, #608
Portland, OR 97205
503-241-1255
Contact: Joseph P. Tennant, President

**Norwest Venture
  Capital Management, Inc.**
3018 1st National Tower
1300 S. W. 5th Avenue
Portland, OR 97201
503-223-6622
Contact: Tony Miadich,
        Vice President and Partner
    Dale Vogel,
        Vice President and Partner
    Michael Cohen, Investment Partner

Rainier Venture Partners
One Lincoln Center, #440
10300 Southwest Greenburgh Rd.
Portland, OR 97223
503-245-5900
Contact: Richard Drew, Partner

Rosenfeld & Co.
1211 Southwest Sixth Avenue
Portland, OR 97204
503-228-3255
Contact: William W. Rosenfeld, Jr.,
        Managing Partner

Shaw Venture Partners
851 S. W. Sixth Avenue #800
Portland, OR 97204
503-228-4884
Contact: Alan Dishlip, Partner

PENNSYLVANIA

Alliance Enterprise Corporation
1801 Market Street, 3rd Floor
Philadelphia, PA 19103
215-977-3925
Contact: Terrence Hicks, Vice President

Century IV Partners
1760 Market Street
Philadelphia, PA 19103
215-751-9444
Contact: Thomas R. Morse,
        Senior Associate

CoreStates Enterprise Fund
One Penn Center of
  Suburban Station, Suite 1360
1617 JFK Boulevard
Philadelphia, PA 19103
215-568-4677
Contact: Paul A. Mitchell, President

First Valley Capital Corporation
640 Hamilton Mall, 8th Floor
Allentown, PA 18101
215-776-6760
Contact: Matthew W. Thomas, President

Fostin Capital Corp.
681 Andersen Drive
Pittsburgh, PA 15220
or
Post Office Box 67
Pittsburgh, PA 15230
412-928-8900
Contact: William F. Woods, President

**Greater Philadelphia Venture
  Capital Corporation**
225 South 15th Street, # 920
Philadelphia, PA 19102
215-732-1666
Contact: Martin M. Newman,
        General Manager

Hillman Ventures, Inc.
2000 Grant Building
Pittsburgh, PA 15219
412-281-2620
Contact: Stephen J. Banks,
        Vice President

Howard, Lawson & Co.
Two Penn Center Plaza, #410
Philadelphia, PA 19102
215-988-0010
Contact: Michael A. Cuneo, Partner

Innovest Group, Inc.
1700 Market #1228
Philadelphia, PA 19103
215-564-3960
Contact: Richard E. Woosnam, President
        Nila K. Sendzik, Vice President

Keystone Venture
  Capital Management Co.
211 South Broad Street, 9th Floor
Philadelphia, PA 19107
215-985-5519
Contact: Timothy W. Cunningham
          Vice President

Kopvenco, Inc.
3100 Koppers Building
Pittsburgh, PA 15219
412-227-2222
Contact: Lester L. Murray, President

Meridian Capital Corp.
Blue Bell West, #222
Blue Bell, PA 19422
215-278-8907
Contact: K. C. Albrecht, President

NEPA Venture Fund, L.P.
125 Goodman Drive
Bethlehem, PA 18015
215-865-6550
Contact: Frederick J. Beste, III,
          General Partner
          Glen R. Bressner,
          General Partner

Philadelphia Citywide
  Development Corporation
714 Market Street, #433
Sovereign Building
Philadelphia, PA 19106
215-238-7676
Contact: Dean Rosencranz, President

Philadelphia Industries
1401 Walnut Street
Second Floor
Philadelphia, PA 19102
215-569-9900
Contact: John J. Murray,
          Vice President
          Corporate Development

PNC Venture Capital Group
Pittsburgh National Building, 19th Floor
Fifth Avenue and Wood Street
Pittsburgh, PA 15222
412-355-2245
Contact: David McL. Hillman,
          Executive Vice President

Robinson Venture Partners
6507 Wilkens Avenue
Pittsburgh, PA 15217
412-661-1200
Contact: Stephen Robinson, General Partner

Security Pacific Capital Corporation
P. O. Box 512
Washington, PA 15301
412-223-0707
Contact: Daniel A. Dye

TDH II
259 Radnor-Chester Road, Suite 200
Radnor, PA 19087
215-964-0112
Contact: J. B. Doherty, Partner
          Stephen W. Harris, Associate
          Ellen J. Wiggins, Associate

Trivest Venture Fund
Post Office Box 36
Ligonier, PA 15658
412-471-0151
Contact: James H. Knowles, Jr.,
          General Partner

Venture Associates
Two Penn Center Plaze, #410
Philadelphia, PA 19102
215-988-0010
Contact: Michael A. Cuneo, Partner

VenWest, Inc.
Westinghouse Building
Gateway Center
Pittsburgh, PA 15222
412-642-5858
Contact: John W. Brock, Jr., President

RHODE ISLAND

The Earl Kinship Capital Corporation
2401 Hospital Trust Tower
Providence, RI 02903
401-831-4800
Contact: Richard J. Ramsden,
        President and CEO

Fleet Venture Partners I
111 Westminster Street
Providence, RI 02903
401-278-6770
Contact: Robert M. Van Degna
        Managing General Partner

Moneta Capital Corporation
Governor Financial Center
285 Governor Street
Providence, RI 02906
401-861-4600
Contact: Arnold Kilberg

Narragansett Capital Corporation
40 Westminster Street
Providence, RI 02903
401-751-1000
Contact: Arthur D. Little
      Robert D. Manchester
      Gregory P. Barber

Old Stone Capital Corporation
1 Old Stone Square
Providence, RI 02903
401-278-2559
Contact: Arthur Barton

River Capital Corporation
One Hospital Trust Plaza, Suite 930W
Providence, RI 02903
401-861-7470
Contact: Robert A. Comey

SOUTH CAROLINA

Carolina Venture Capital Corp.
14 Archer Road
Hilton Head Island, SC 29928
803-842-3101
Contact: Manager

Reedy River Ventures
Post Office Box 17526
Greenville, SC 29606
803-297-9196
Contact: Jack Sterling

TENNESSEE

Capital Services & Resources, Inc.
5159 Wheelis Drive, #104
Memphis, TN 38117
901-761-2156
Contact: Charles Y. Bancroft

DeSoto Capital Corporation
290 Walnut Bend Road South, #1
Cordova, TN 38108
901-757-8383
Contact: Rudolph Holmes, President

Financial Resources, Inc.
2800 Sterick Building
Memphis, TN 38103
901-527-9411
Contact: Milton C. Picard, Chairman
      A. Arthur Halley, Jr., President

Lawrence Venture Associates
3401 West End Avenue, Suite 680
Nashville, TN 37203
615-383-0982
Contact: Tom Gallagher

Massey Burch Investment Group, Inc.
310 25th Avenue North, #103
Nashville, TN 37203
615-329-9449
Contact: Manager

Valley Capital Corporation
100 W. MLK Boulevard
Krystal Building, Suite 806
Chattanooga, TN 37402
615-265-1557
Contact: Faye Munger

**West Tennesee Venture
Capital Corporation**
152 Beale Street
Post Office Box 300
Memphis, TN 38103
901-527-6091
Contact: Manager

TEXAS

Acorn Ventures, Inc.
2401 Fountainview, Suite 950
Houston, TX 77057
713-977-7421
Contact: Stuart Schube
           Martin O'Malley

**Alliance Business
   Investment Company**
One Shell Plaza, #3990
Houston, TX 77002
713-224-8224
Contact: Leon Davis

Allied Bancshares Capital Corporation
Post Office Box 3326
Houston, TX 77253
713-226-1625
Contact: Manager

BancTexas Capital Inc.
1601 Elm Street
Post Office Box 2249
Dallas, TX 75221
214-969-6231
Contact: Manager

**Capital Southwest Corp./
   Capital Southwest Venture Corp.**
12900 Preston Road, #700
Dallas, TX 75230
214-233-8242
Contact: William R. Thomas
           J. Bruce Duty
           Patrick F. Hamner

Berry Cash Southwest Partnership
One Galleria Tower
13355 Noel Road, #1375
Dallas, TX 75240
214-392-7279
Contact: Manager

Charter Venture Group, Inc.
2600 Citadel Plaza Drive
Sixth Floor
Houston, TX 77008
713-863-0704
Contact: Manager

Citicorp Venture Capital, Ltd.
717 North Harwood
Suite #2920, L.B. 87
Dallas, TX 75201
214-880-9670
Contact: Thomas F. McWilliams
           Newell V. Starke

Collins & Weinberg
1700 N. Market Street, #200
Dallas, TX 75202
214-748-9300
Contact: Richard Collins

Criterion Venture Partners
1000 Louisiana, Suite 6200
Houston, TX 77002
713-751-2408
Contact: David O. Wicks, Jr.
           Scott Albert

J. H. Crutchfield & Company
1000 Westlake High Drive, #4B
Austin, TX 78746
512-327-6810
Contact: Manager

Dougery, Jones & Wilder
5420 LBJ Freeway
Two Lincoln Centre, #1100
Dallas, TX 75240
214-960-0077
Contact: Manager

Enterprise Capital Corporation
3501 Allen Parkway
Houston, TX 77019
713-526-8070
Contact: Fred S. Zeidman

First Dallas Financial Company
3302 Southland Center, #LB 268
Dallas, TX 75201
214-922-0070
Contact: Manager

Idanta Partners
201 Main Street, #3200
Fort Worth, TX 76102
817-338-2020
Contact: Dev Purkayastha

InterFirst Venture Corporation
901 Main Street, 10th Floor
Dallas, TX 75202
214-977-3164
Contact: M. C. Masur
        J. A. O'Donnell

Mapleleaf Capital Corporation
55 Waugh Drive, Suite 710
Houston, TX 77007
713-880-4494
Contact: Edward M. Fink, President

**MESBIC Financial
   Corporation of Dallas**
12655 North Central Expressway, #814
Dallas, TX 75243
214-991-1597
Contact: Tom Gerron, Vice President
         & Controller

MSI Capital/Triad Ventures Ltd.
6510 Abrams Road, #650
Dallas, TX 75231
214-341-1553
Contact: Nick Stanfield

MVenture Corp.
1704 Main Street, #1901
Dallas, TX 75266
214-741-1469
Contact: Thomas Bartlett,
              Investment Officer
         Michael D. Brown, Vice President

Omega Capital Corporation
755 South 11th Street, #250
Beaumont, TX 77701
409-832-0221
Contact: Frank Ryan, Jr., CPA
              General Manager

Orange Nassau
13355 Noel Road, #635
Dallas, TX 75240
214-385-9685
Contact: F. Dan Blanchard
         Martin J. Silver

Porcari, Fearnow & Assoc., Inc.
1900 West Loop South
Houston, TX 77027
713-840-7500
Contact: Manager

Republic Venture Group, Inc.
2820 RepublicBank Tower
Post Office Box 655961
Dallas, TX 75265
214-922-5078
Contact: Robert H. Wellborn
              President

Retzloff Capital Corp.
Post Office Box 41250
Houston, TX 77240
713-466-4690
Contact: Steve Retzloff, President

H. Donald Rose, Incorporated
Post Office Box 741924
Dallas, TX 75374
214-349-8811
Contact: H. Donald Rose, President

R. Patrick Rowles & Co., Inc.
4299 San Felipe, #100
Houston, TX 77027
713-521-0388
Contact: R. Patrick Rowles

Rust Ventures, L.P.
114 West Seventh Street, #1300
Austin, TX 78701
512-479-0055
Contact: Ken DeAngelis
            Joe Aragona

**San Antonio Venture Group, Inc./
MESBIC of San Antonio, Inc.**
2300 W. Commerce Street, #300
San Antonio, TX 78207
512-223-3633
Contact: Tom Woodley
            Mike Parish

SBI Capital Corp.
Post Office Box 570368
Houston, TX 77257-0368
713-975-1188
Contact: William E. Wright, President

Sevin Rosen Management Company
13455 Noel Road, #1670
Dallas, TX 75240
214-960-1744
Contact: Manager

Southwest Enterprise Associates
5420 LBJ Freeway, #1266
Dallas, TX 75240
214-991-1620
Contact: Manager

The Southwest Venture Partnerships
300 Convent, #1400
San Antonio, TX 78205
512-227-1010
Contact: Michael Bell

**Taylor & Turner/Rotan Mosle
Technology Partners, Ltd.**
3800 RepublicBank Center
700 Louisiana
Houston, TX 77002
713-236-3180
Contact: Manager

Tenneco Ventures, Inc.
1010 Milam #T-2919
Houston, TX 77002
Office Box 2511, zip 77252
713-757-8776
Contact: Manager

Texas Capital Corporation
1341 West Mockingbird, #1250E
Dallas, TX 75247
214-638-0652
Contact: David G. Franklin
            Tom L. Beecroft

Triad Ventures Limited
301 West 6th Street
Post Office Box 1987
Austin, TX 78767
512-472-7171
Contact: Hobby Abshier
            Rex Gwinn

T.V.P. Associates, Limited
2777 Stemmons Freeway, #925
Dallas, TX 75205
214-631-0600
Contact: James Silcock

United Mercantile Capital Corporation
444 Executive Center Boulevard, #222
El Paso, TX 79902
915-533-6375
Contact: L. Joe Justice

West Central Capital Corporation
440 Northlake Center, #206
Dallas, TX 75238
214-348-3969
Contact: Manager

Woodland Capital Company
3007 Skyway Circle North
Irving, TX 75038
214-659-9500
Contact: Stewart D. Siebens, President

VIRGINIA

Atlantic Venture Partners
801 N. Fairfax Street, #404
Alexandria, VA 22314
703-548-6026
Contact: Wallace L. Bennett

Basic Investment Corp.
6723 Whittier Avenue, Office 201
McLean, VA 22101
703-356-4300
Contact: Ed Sandler

Hillcrest Group
Nine South 12th Street
Richmond, VA 23219
804-643-7358
Contact: A. Hugh Ewing
        John P. Funkhouser

Metropolitan Capital Corporation
2550 Huntington Avenue
Alexandria, VA 22303
703-960-4698
Contact: S. W. Austin, Vice President

Wheat, First Securities
707 East Main Street
Post Office Box 1357
Richmond, VA 23211
804-649-2311
Contact: Sheldon Ruben

WASHINGTON

Cable & Howse Venture
777 108th N.E., #2300
Bellevue, WA 98004
206-646-3030
Contact: Wayne C. Wager

Capital Resource Corporation
1001 Logan Building
Seattle, WA 98101
206-623-6550
Contact: T. Evan Wyckoff, President

Genesis Capital L.P.
Post Office Box 5065
Bellevue, WA 98009
206-454-7211
Contact: David Kratter, General Partner

Olympic Venture Partner
1 Bellevue Center, #1710
411 108th Avenue N.E.
Bellevue, WA 98004
206-455-1470
Contact: George Clute

Olympic Venture Partner
1 Lincoln Center, #440
10300 S. W. Greenburg Road
Portland, OR 97223
503-245-9500
Contact: Rich Drew

Palms & Company, Inc.
6702 139th Avenue, N.E.
Suite 760
Redmond, WA 98052
206-883-3580
206-885-4401
206-885-0291
Contact: Peter J. Palms IV
        Michael Mandeville

The Phoenix Partners
1000 2nd Avenue, #3600
Seattle, WA 98104
206-624-8968
Contact: Stuart C. Johnston,
        Managing General Partner

Piper Jaffray & Hopwood, Inc.
1700 IBM Building
Seattle, WA 98101
206-223-3800
Contact: Gary Takas, Managing Director

Rainier Venture Partners
9725 S.E. 36th Street, #300
Mercer Island, WA 98040
206-455-1470
Contact: John Moser
        George Clute

John H. Resing
Post Office Box 5697
Bellevue, WA 98006
206-827-3548
Contact: John H. Resing, Partner

Washington Trust Equity Corp.
W. 717 Sprague Avenue
Post Office Box 2127
Spokane, WA 99210
509-455-3821
Contact: John M. Snead, III, President

WISCONSIN

R. W. Allsop & Associates
815 East Mason Street
Post Office Box 1368
Milwaukee, WI 53201
414-271-6510
Contact: Gregory B. Bultman,
        General Partner

Capital Investments, Inc.
744 North Fourth Street, #400
Milwaukee, WI 53203
414-273-6560
Contact: Robert L. Banner

Impact Seven, Inc.
320 Industrial Road
Turtle Lake, WI 54889
715-986-4171
Contact: William Bay, President

Lubar & Co.
777 E. Wisconsin Avenue, #3380
Milwaukee, WI 53202
414-291-9000
Contact: David J. Lubar
        William T. Donovan

M & I Ventures Corporation
770 N. Water Street
Milwaukee, WI 53202
414-765-7910
Contact: John T. Byrnes, President
        Andrew E. Marein

Marine Venture Capital, Inc.
111 E. Wisconsin Avenue
Milwaukee, WI 53202
414-765-2274
Contact: Wayne Foreman
        Colleen Henderson

MorAmerica Capital Corporation
600 East Mason Street, #300
Milwaukee, WI 53202
414-276-3839
Contact: Steven J. Massey

Venture Investors of Wisconsin
100 State Street
Madison, WI 53703
608-256-8185
Contact: John Neis

Wind Point Partners
1525 Howe Street
Racine, WI 53403
414-631-4030
Contact: Arthur DelVesco

WYOMING

Capital Corporation of Wyoming, Inc.
Post Office Box 3599
Casper, WY 82602
307-234-5438
Contact: Scott Weaver

CANADIAN VENTURE
CAPITAL FIRMS

ALBERTA

Aeonian Capital Corporation
602 - 12th Avenue S. W.
Suite 400
Calgary, Alberta
T2R 1J3
403-264-4394
Contact: C. Alan Smith

Alta-Can Telecom Inc.
411 1st Street S. E.
Floor 26H
Calgary, Alberta
T2G 4Y5
403-231-8535
Contact: A. A. MacKinnon, President
Norman Clark, Vice President
David Campbell,
Director of Finance

AVF Investments Ltd.
Suite 300
1550 - 8th Street S. W.
Calgary, Alberta
T2R 1K1
403-228-9152
Contact: Cliff James

Gold Bar Developments Ltd.
P. O. Box 3160
Edmonton, Alberta
403-420-6666
Contact: Mr. Sandy A. Mactaggart

Manvest Ltd.
840 - 6th Avenue S. W.
Calgary, Alberta
403-294-5487
Contact: Cindy Winther

Vencap Equities Alberta Ltd.
10180 101st Street
Edmonton, Alberta
T5J 3S4
403-420-1171
Contact: Derek Mather, President
Richard Rutherford, Vice President
Sandy Slator,
Executive Vice President

ATLANTIC

Ochterloney Investments Limited
P. O. Box 634
Dartmouth, Nova Scotia
B2Y 3Y2
902-466-7471
Contact: Trenholme D. Lodge

BRITISH COLUMBIA

**Connor, Clark and Lunn Investment
Management Limited**
1040 West Georgia Street
Suite 2020
Vancouver, British Columbia
604-685-2020
Contact: Mr. G. H. MacDougall

Mac D. Campbell Associates Inc.
1285 West Pender Street
Suite 200
Vancouver, British Columbia
V6E 4B1
604-689-2621
Contact: Mac D. Campbell, President
Fred Kruberg, Associate

Ventures West Management Inc.
Suite 400
321 Water Street
Vancouver, British Columbia
V6B 1B8
604-688-9495
Contact: Michael J. Brown

ONTARIO

BG Acorn Capital Fund
141 Adelaide Street West
Suite 601
Toronto, Ontario
M5H 3L5
416-362-9009
Contact: Michael M. Boyd

Boyd, Stott & McDonald
Technologies Limited
55 York Street
Suite 1311
Toronto, Ontario
M5J 1R7
416-364-3767
Contact: Mr. W. H. McDonald, President

Capital Canada Limited
Sun Life Centre Tower
150 King Street West, #2308
Toronto, Ontario
M5H 1J9
416-598-7700
Contact: Robert J. Foster, President

Canada Overseas Investments Limited
P. O. Box 62
South Tower
Royal Bank Plaza
Toronto, Ontario
M5J 2J2
416-865-0266
Contact: Michael Koerner, President

Canadian Corporate Funding Ltd.
70 University Avenue, #1450
Toronto, Ontario
M5J 2M4
416-977-1450
Contact: Grant Brown, Sr. Vice President

Canadian Venture Capital Corp. Ltd.
120 Adelaide Street West
11th Floor
Toronto, Ontario
M5H 1V1
416-364-2271
Contact: Mr. J. Stewart

Citibank Canada
Capital Markets Group
Suite 1600
123 Front Street West
Toronto, Ontario
M5J 2M3
416-947-5500
Contact: John Puddington
            Vice President

Corporate Growth Assistance Ltd.
19 York Ridge Road
Willowdale, Ontario
M2P 1R8
416-222-7772
Contact: Millard S. Roth, President

Crown Life Insurance Company,
Special Investments
120 Bloor St. East
Toronto, Ontario
M4W 1B8
416-928-5761
416-928-5731
Contact: Carl J. MacCallam,
            Vice President of
            Special Investments

Gordon Capital Corporation
P. O. Box 67, Suite 5401
Toronto-Dominion Centre
Toronto, Ontario
M5K 1E7
416-364-9393
Contact: Richard Reid

Grayrock Capital Ltd. - Canada
2 International Blvd.
Rexdale, Ontario
M9W 1A2
416-675-4808
Contact: Wolf J. Gluck

Grenadier International Ltd.
1867 Young Street, #600
Toronto, Ontario
M4S 1Y5
416-482-7887
Contact: Ron Begg, President

Grieve Horner and Associates Inc.
20 Victoria Street
Suite 900
Toronto, Ontario
M5C 2N8
416-362-7668
Contact: Anthony Brown
         Ralph Horner

Helix Investments Limited
401 Bay Street, #2400
Toronto, Ontario
M5H 2Y4
416-367-1290
Contact: Ben Webster, Chairman
         Michael Needham, President

Hendron Financial Group Inc.
150 York Street, #800
Toronto, Ontario
M5H 3S5
416-362-7791
Contact: Mr. J. C. Hardy, President

Innovation Ontario Corporation
56 Wellesley Street West
7th Floor
North York, Ontario
M7A 2E7
416-963-5717
Contact: Jim Orgill

McConnell & Company Limited
390 Bay Street
Suite 1400
Toronto, Ontario
M5H 2Y2
416-364-1234
Contact: Frank McConnell, President

Middlefield Capital Fund
P. O. Box 192
1 First Canadian Place
58th Floor
Toronto, Ontario
M5X 1A6
416-362-8602
Contact: Garth Jestley, President

Noranda Enterprise Limited
90 Sparks Street, #1128
Ottawa, Ontario
K1P 5T8
613-230-6205
Contact: Mr. D. C. Cameron, President

Nortan Delta Ltd.
302 - 4019 Carling Avenue
Kanata, Ontario
K2K 2A3
613-592-3855
Contact: Mark M. Nortan, President

North American Ventures Fund
Suite 506
85 Bloor Street East
Toronto, Ontario
M4W 1A9
416-967-5774
Contact: George Fells, President

Northern Telecom Limited
Venture Capital Division
33 City Centre Drive
Mississauga, Ontario
L5B 3A2
416-275-0960
Contact: Raymond J. Herpers

**Ontario Centre for Resource
  Machinery Technology**
127 Cedar Street
4th Floor
Sudbury, Ontario
P3E 1B1
705-673-6606
Contact: John L. Dodge, President

Ontario Development Corporation
56 Wellesley Street West
Toronto, Ontario
M7A 2E7
416-965-4622
Contact: John Mitchell,
          Director of Loan Applicants
          Ernest R. Carter

Royal Bank Venture Capital Limited
13th Floor, South Tower
Royal Bank Plaza
Toronto, Ontario
M5J 2J5
416-974-6230
Contact: Brian D. Marshall, President
          Robert D. D. Forbes,
          Executive Vice President

RoyNat Inc.
1 First Canadian Place, #1040
P. O. Box 51
Toronto, Ontario
M5X 1B1
416-363-5404
Contact: Leo G. Legrove,
          Executive Vice President

SB Capital Corporation Ltd.
85 Bloor Street East, #506
Toronto, Ontario
M4W 1A9
416-967-5439
Contact: Mr. A. G. Fells, President
          Mitch Kostuch,
          Executive Vice President

Simmie & Simmie Incorporated
365 Bay Street
12th Floor
Toronto, Ontario
M5H 2V1
416-361-1938
Contact: A. Peter Simmie, President

Spar Aerospace Limited
Royal Bank Plaza, South Tower
P. O. Box 83
Toronto, Ontario
M5J 2J2
416-865-0480
Contact: John Neville,
          Sr. Vice President -
          Aviation & Ventures Sector

Varity Enterprises
595 Bay Street
Toronto, Ontario
M5G 2C3
416-593-3816
Contact: J. M. Felker, Sr. Vice President

VenGrowth Capital Funds
111 Richmond Street West, #805
Toronto, Ontario
M5H 2G4
416-947-9123
Contact: R. Earl Storie, Managing Partner

Venture Heights Capital Corporation
2161 Yonge Street, #802
Toronto, Ontario
M4S 3A6
416-488-8200
Contact: Andrew Wilkes, Vice President

Zarex Management
121 Bloor Street East
8th Floor
Toronto, Ontario
M4W 3M5
416-968-0339
Contact: Leslie I. Rupf, Chairman

QUEBEC

Alexis Nihon Corporation
6380 Cote de Liesse
Montreal, Quebec
H4T 1E3
514-737-3344
Contact: Donald Michelin

Altamira Capital Corp.
475 Michel Jasmin
Dorval, Quebec
H9P 1C2
514-631-2682
Contact: Mr. C. J. Winn,
          Vice President Finance

Federal Business Development Bank
800 Place Victoria
Suite 4600
Montreal, Quebec
H4Z 1L4
514-283-2252
Contact: Marc Vaillancourt,
          Sr. Vice President

Groupe Cantal, Inc.
835 boul. Des Recollets
Suite 300
Trois-Rivieres, Quebec
G8Z 3W5
819-375-6132
Contact: Claude Lampron, General Manager

Investissements NOVACAP Inc.
1981 McGill College
Suite 380
Montreal, Quebec
H3A 3A9
514-282-1383
Contact: M. Marc Beauchamp, President

LavalinTech Inc.
1100 Dorchester Boulevard W.
Montreal, Quebec
H3B 4P3
514-876-7812
Contact: Guy La Berge

LNS Systems, Inc.
7 Bovis Drive
Pointe Claire, Quebec
H9R 4W3
514-695-8130
Contact: Richard Prytula, President

Parcap Management Inc.
Suite 2310
1000 Sherbrooke Street West
Montreal, Quebec
H3A 3G4
514-281-0073
Contact: Mr. J. F. Morrissette,
          President

Societe D'Investissement Desjardins
Bureau 1717, C.P. 760
1 Complexe Desjardins
Montreal, Quebec
H5B 1B8
514-281-7131
Contact: Pierre Brunet,
          President

Glossary

Anti-dilution protection A device used to protect the investors' percentage ownership of the company upon conversion of their securities into common stock. The terms generally provide for a proportional adjustment in the number of shares of common stock issuable upon conversion in the event of stock splits, combinations, stock dividends, mergers or reclassifications, and in the conversion price in the event of issuances of common stock or securities convertible into common stock at a per share price lower than the conversion price of the preferred stock. Price anti-dilution provisions generally appear in one of two forms.

Conversion The transfer of preferred stock into common stock or other security initially issued to investors. Generally, such securities are convertible at any time at the option of the holder and automatically converted upon the initial public offering of the common stock of the company at a negotiated minimum per share price and an aggregate minimum offering price. Most often, shares of preferred stock are initially convertible one for one into shares of common stock at a conversion price equal to the original issue price of the preferred stock, subject to anti-dilution protection negotiated by the parties.

Demand registrations rights The rights entitling investors to force the company to register shares of common stock held by the investors, whether or not the company is registering its own securities. Demand registration rights are rarely used and are generally not exercisable for several years following the initial investment. In addition, the contract normally provides that for a demand to be effective, it both must be made by the holders of a negotiated minimum percentage of stock issued to investors and must cover the sale of a certain percentage of such shares outstanding.

Information rights Rights granted by the company to venture capital investors to receive on a regular and timely basis balance sheets, profit and loss statements, cash flow statements, budgets, projections, and comparisons of actual and projected results of the company. Generally, each investor receives quarterly and annual financial statements and annual budgets. Those investors owning a negotiated minimum percentage of the class of stock issued to investors will be entitled to the other aforementioned items. These rights generally terminate upon conversion into common stock of the security issued to investors upon the initial public offering of the company or if the company otherwise becomes a public reporting company.

Liquidation preference The right of holders of preferred stock to be repaid their investment prior to any payment to holders of common stock in the event of either the liquidation of the company or a merger or other transaction deemed to be a liquidation. Subsequent round investors paying a higher price than earlier round investors sometimes negotiate a senior liquidation preference, permitting them to be paid first. Alternatively, all holders of preferred stock are paid pro rata upon liquidation.

Mandatory redemption The right of investors, subject to restrictions imposed by law, to force the company to repurchase shares at a price equal to the per share purchase price plus a redemption premium. Mandatory redemption provisions often require the company to set aside a *sinking fund* for payment of the redemption price.

Optional redemption The right of the company to call all or some of the shares at specified intervals. The company's ability to call shares of preferred stock is intended to force conversion of the preferred stock into common stock if the redemption price is lower than the value of the common stock issuable upon conversion. By forcing conversion, the liquidation and dividend preferences and class voting rights of preferred stock can be eliminated. The *redemption premium*, the difference between the redemption price and the per share purchase price, may be scaled back over a period of years until the redemption price equals the original issue price plus accrued dividends, if any. Certain provisions of Federal income tax law limit the redemption premium by characterizing it as a distribution of additional stock on preferred stock if the premium is deemed unreasonable. Internal Revenue Service regulations provide a safe harbor for a redemption premium not in excess of 10 percent of the issue price on stock which is not redeemable for five years from the date of issue. Counsel will differ with respect to the advisability of a structure involving redemption premiums outside the safe harbor.

Participating preferred Preferred stock that participates pro rata with common stock in any assets of the company remaining after the preferred stock has already been paid upon liquidation.

Piggyback registration rights The rights of investors to include their shares of common stock in offerings of the company's securities, subject to certain negotiated limitations.

Preemptive right The privilege of a stockholder to maintain its proportionate ownership of the company by purchasing a pro rata share of any new issuance of quite or convertible debt securities. Stock issuances in connection with mergers, public offerings, employee incentive plans and business transactions of the company are generally excluded from the operation of a pre-emptive right. Venture capitalists differ with respect to insistence upon a pre-emptive right to future financings.

Ratchet-down A type of of anti-dilution reduces the conversion price to the lowest price per share at which the company issues common stock or securities convertible into common stock.

Redemption The repurchase by the company of shares of stock at a negotiated time and price.

Registration rights The rights granted to holders of shares of common stock issuable upon conversion of the preferred stock (or other security purchased by investors) to have the sale of those shares registered under federal and state securities laws at the expense of the company. The stock issued to venture capital investors is generally subject to restrictions on transfer imposed by law. Registration of investors' share is intended to provide liquidity for their investment by permitting sale to the public of investors' share.

Right of co-sale The agreement among the company, the venture capital investors, and the holders of large blocks of common stock (generally, the founders or management) that, in the event of a sale of common stock by any such holder, the investors may sell on the same terms a proportionate number of shares of stock held by them. The underlying idea is that management should not be able to get out or profit from a sale of its stock while the venture capitalists' investment remains in the company. Relatively few venture capitalist insist on take-along rights, and if granted, they normally terminate when the investors' stock becomes freely tradeable.

Right of First Refusal see *Preemptive right*.

Stock option plan A plan authorizing the board of directors of a company to grant to employees, consultants, officers and directors *options*, or the right to purchase shares of common stock of the company. Under current Federal income tax law, options are either *incentive stock options* (ISOs) or *nonqualified stock options* (NSOs or NQOs). Stock option plans can provide for both ISOs and NQOs. The determination of whether to grant an ISO or NQO in a particular instance should be made after consultation with the company's counsel and accountants as to the tax consequences for both optionees and the company and the accounting considerations affecting the company. Venture capitalists usually insist that the shares issuable upon exercise of options are generally subject to *vesting* or a *right of repurchase*. If the purchaser's employment by, or other association with, the company terminates, the company may repurchase at the exercise price a portion of the shares that decreases over time until no shares remain subject to repurchase (or all shares are fully vested). In addition, the company usually has a *right of* *first refusal* with respect to any sales or transfers of shares purchased upon option exercise. Vesting preserves the stock pool for future employees and, along with the right of first refusal, decreases the risk of minority ownership by outside stockholders.

Take along see *right of co-sale.*

Voting right The right granted to each share of stock to vote that share on matters on which shareholders are legally entitled to vote. Generally, each share of preferred stock purchased by an investor receives one vote for each share of common stock into which it is convertible on all matters on which it is entitled to vote, with the exception of the election of directors. Venture capitalists sometimes also demand that each series of preferred stock have the right to elect a negotiated number of directors to represent that series on the board of directors of the company.

Weighted average A type of anti-dilution that lowers the conversion price as a result of the new issue to the weighted average of the purchase price of the outstanding and newly issued stock. Generally, a pool of shares reserved for issuance to employees of the company under incentive plans is excepted from the operation of price anti-dilution provisions.

Bibliography

Allan, Lionel M., Esq., and Crandall, Nelson. D., Esq. *How To Structure The Classic Venture Capital Deal.* Englewood Cliffs, New Jersey: Prentice-Hall Corporation Service, 1983.

Anderson, James C.; Bruno, Albert V., and Tyebjee, Tyzoon, T. "Finding a Way Through the Venture Capital Maze," *Business Horizons* 28, No.1 (January-February 1985): 12-19.

Bekey, Michell. "Don't Call Just Any Lawyer," *Venture* 9, No. 1, (January 1987): 48-54.

Brandt, Steven C. *Strategic Planning In Emerging Companies.* Reading, Massachusetts: Addison-Wesley Publishing Company, 1981.

Burrill, G. Steven. "Using Business Plans to Finance Growth-Oriented Ventures," *The Business Lawyer* 39, No. 2, (February 1984).

Burrill, G. Steven, and Dittamore, Raymond. "Creative Financing for Biotechnology Companies," *Genetic Engineering News* (September 1985).

Business Week, 3 November, 1973: 96, 98.

Deloitte, Haskins & Sells. *Forming R & D Partnerships, An Entrepreneur's Guidebook.* New York, 1983.

Deloitte, Haskins & Sells. *Raising Venture Capital: An Entrepreneur's Guidebook.* New York, 1982.

Dominguez, John R. *Venture Capital.* Lexington, Massachusetts: Lexington Books, D.C. Heath and Company, 1974.

Gladstone, David J. *Venture Capital Handbook.* Reston, Virginia: Reston Publishing Company, Inc., Prentice-Hall, 1983.

Gupta, Udayan, "Venture Capitalists Face Tax and Accounting Hurdles," *Wall Street Journal*, 2 January, 1987, 8B.

Harroch, Richard D., Esq. *Start-Up Companies: Planning, Financing, and Operating the Successful Business.* New York: Law Journal Seminars-Press, 1985.

Kotkin, Joel. "Why Smart Companies Are Saying No to Venture Capital," *Inc.* 6, No. 8 (August 1984): 65-75.

Kozmetsky, George; Gill, Michael D., Jr.; and Smilor, Raymond W. *Financing and Managing Fast-Growth Companies: The Venture Capital Process.* Lexington, Massachusetts: Lexington Books, D.C. Heath and Company, 1985.

Morris, Jane K., ed. "Demand Consumes Supply: The Capital Pac Man," *Venture Capital Journal* 25, No. 8 (August 1985): 6-11, Wellesley Hills, Massachusetts: Venture Economics, Inc.

Morris, Jane K., ed. "NVCA Meeting Breaks Attendance Record Again," *Venture Capital Journal* 26, No. 5 (May 1986): 1, Wellesley Hills, Massachusetts: Venture Economics, Inc.

Morris, Jane K., ed. "Venture Funds—How Have They Changed?," *Venture Capital Journal* 26, No. 5 (May 1986): 8-16, Wellesley Hills, Massachusetts: Venture Economics, Inc.

Owen, Robert R.; Garner, Daniel R.; and Bunder, Dennis S. *The Arthur Young Guide to Financing for Growth.* New York: John Wiley & Sons, Inc., 1986.

Porter, Michael E. *Competitive Strategy: Techniques for Analyzing Industries and Competitors.* New York: The Free Press, Macmillan Publishing Co., Inc., 1980.

Pratt, Stanley, E.; Morris, Jane K., editors. *Pratt's Guide to Venture Capital Sources, ninth edition.* Wellesley Hills, Massachusetts: Venture Economics, Inc., 1985.

Silver, David A. *Up Front Financing: The Entrepreneur's Guide.* New York: John Wiley & Sons, Inc., 1982.

Silver, David A. *Venture Capital: The Complete Guide For Investors.* New York: John Wiley & Sons, Inc., 1985.

Silver, David A. *Who's Who In Venture Capital.* New York: John Wiley & Sons, Inc., 1984.

Taylor, Charlotte. *The Entrepreneurial Workbook: A Step-By-Step Guide To Starting And Operating Your Own Small Business.* New York: New American Library, 1985.

Tilling, T. and Toney, T. *High Tech: How to Find and Profit from Today's New Super Stocks.* New York: Simon and Schuster, 1983.

Timmons, Jeffrey A. "Careful Self-analysis and Team Assessment Can Aid Entrepreneurs," *Harvard Business Review* (November-December 1979): 198-206.

Venture Capital Where to Find It. National Association of Small Business Investment Companies, *1985 Membership Directory*, Washington, D.C.

Venture Magazine, Inc. *Venture's Guide to International Venture Capital.* New York: Simon and Schuster, 1985.

Wilson, John W. *The New Ventures, Inside the High-Stakes World of Venture Capital.* Reading, Massachusetts: Addison-Wesley Publishing Company, 1985.

Index